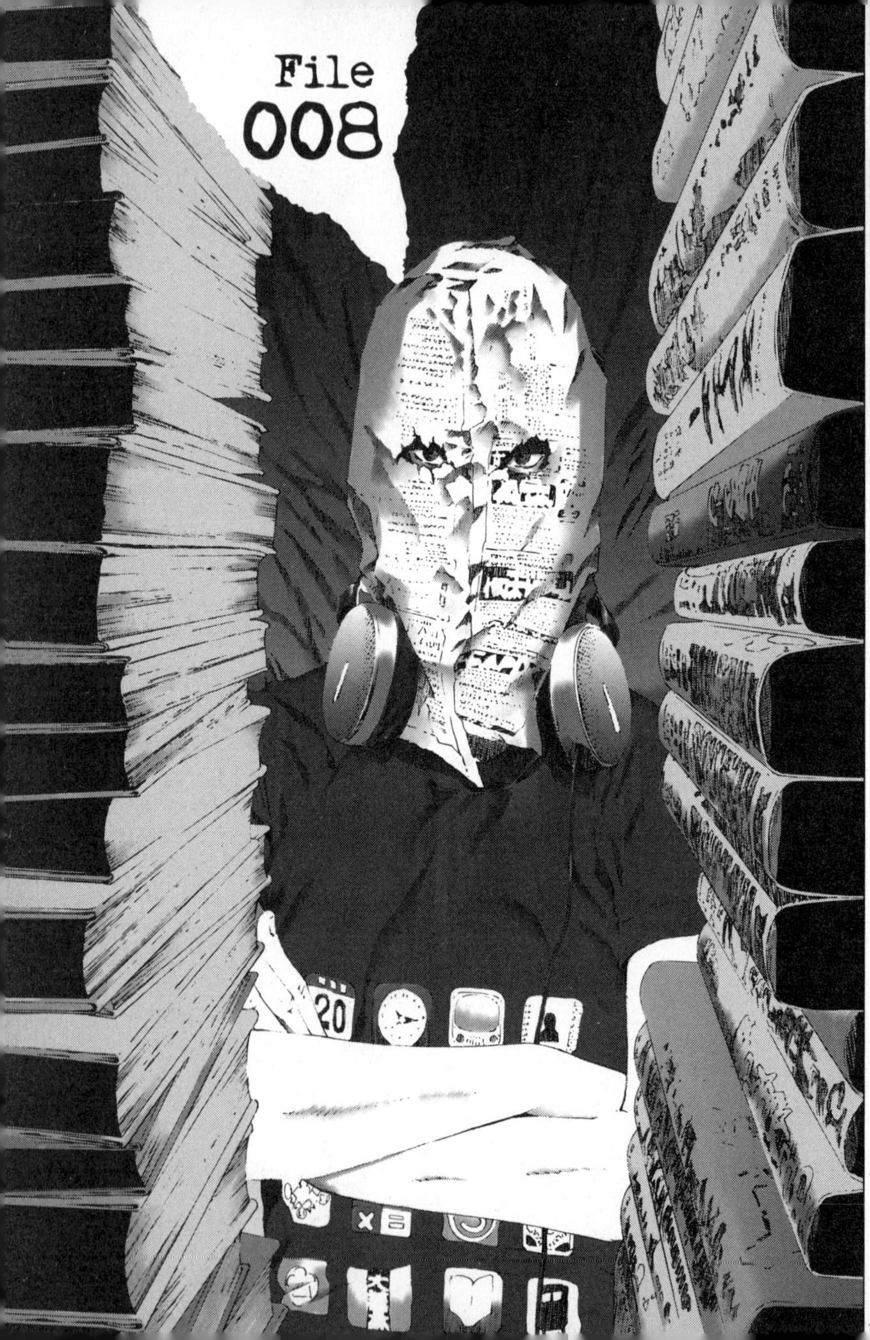
File
008

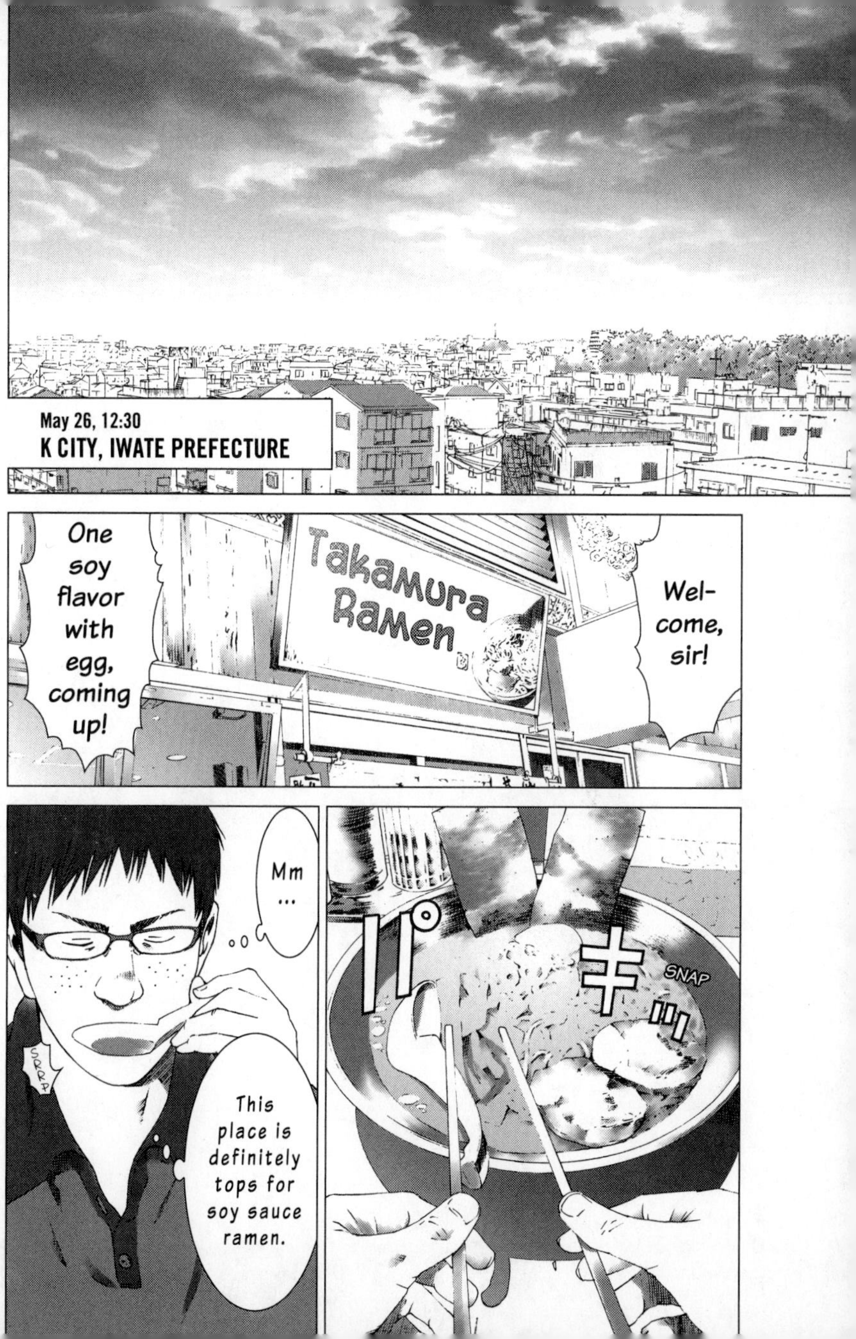
May 26, 12:30
K CITY, IWATE PREFECTURE
Wel-come, sir!
Takamura Ramen
One soy flavor with egg, coming up!
パキッ
SNAP
Mm ...
SRRP
This place is definitely tops for soy sauce ramen.

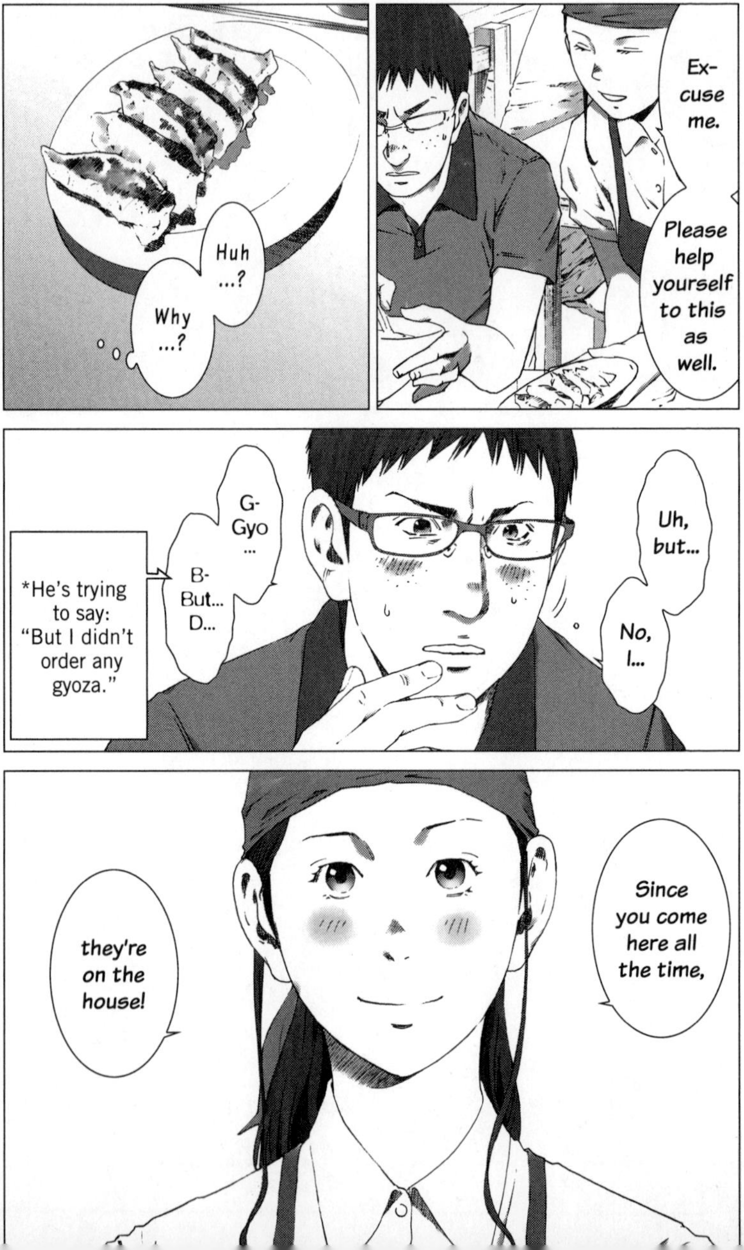
Ex-cuse me.
Please help yourself to this as well.
Huh ...?
Why ...?
Uh, but...
No, I...
G-Gyo ...
B-But... D...
*He's trying to say: "But I didn't order any gyoza."
Since you come here all the time,
they're on the house!

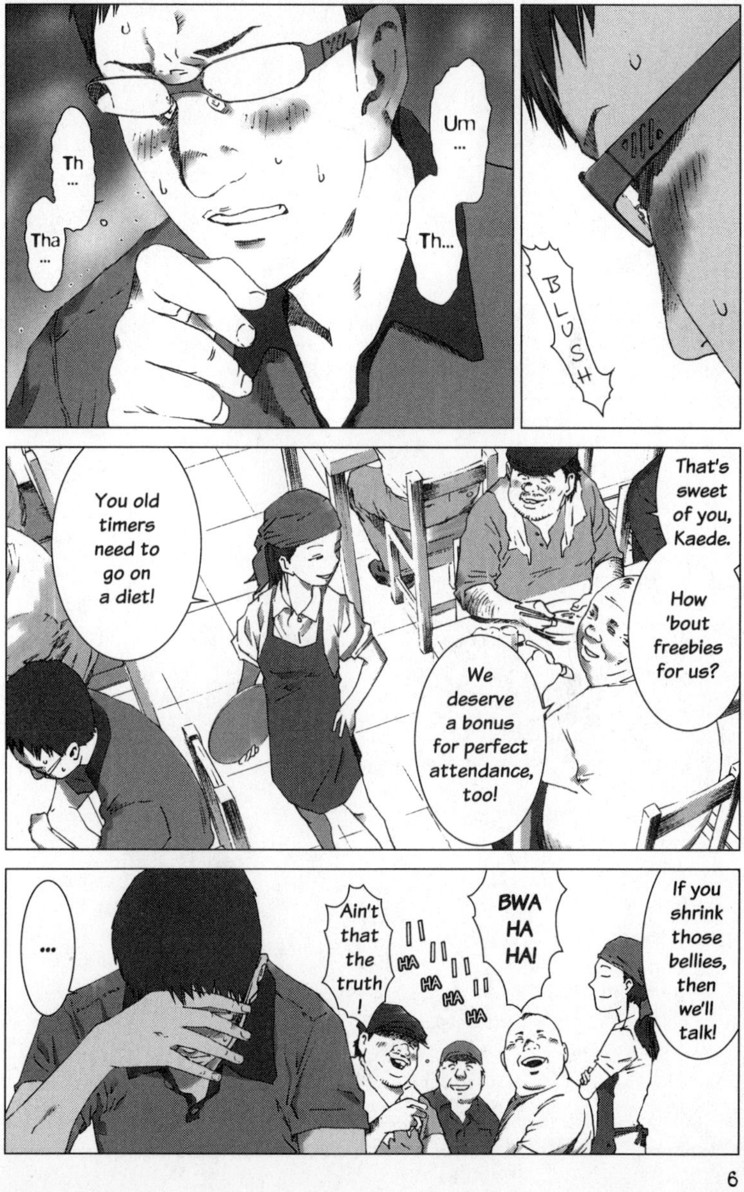
BLUSH
Um...
Th...
Th...
Tha...
That's sweet of you, Kaede.
How 'bout freebies for us?
We deserve a bonus for perfect attendance, too!
You old timers need to go on a diet!
If you shrink those bellies, then we'll talk!
BWA HA HA!
HA HA HA HA
Ain't that the truth!
...

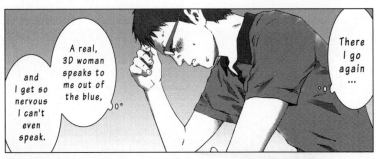

There
I go
again
...

A real,
3D woman
speaks to
me out of
the blue,

and
I get so
nervous
I can't
even
speak.

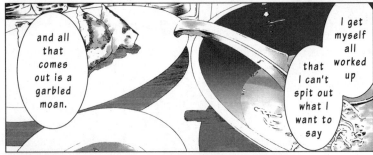

I get
myself
all
worked
up

that
I can't
spit out
what I
want to
say

and all
that
comes
out is a
garbled
moan.

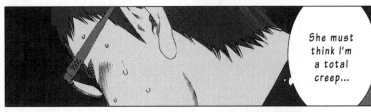

She must
think I'm
a total
creep...

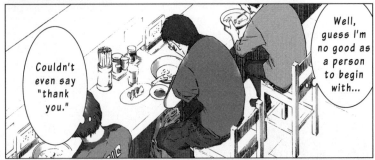

Well,
guess I'm
no good as
a person
to begin
with...

Couldn't
even say
"thank
you."

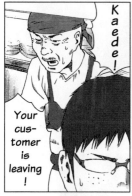

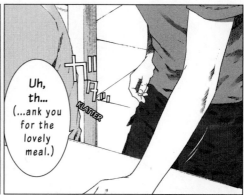

Uh, th... (...ank you for the lovely meal.)
KLATTER
Kaede!
Your customer is leaving!
THUP
THUP
SLIDE
Thank you very much, sir!
Please come again!

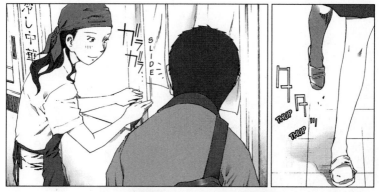

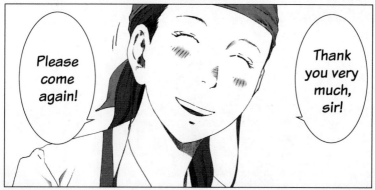

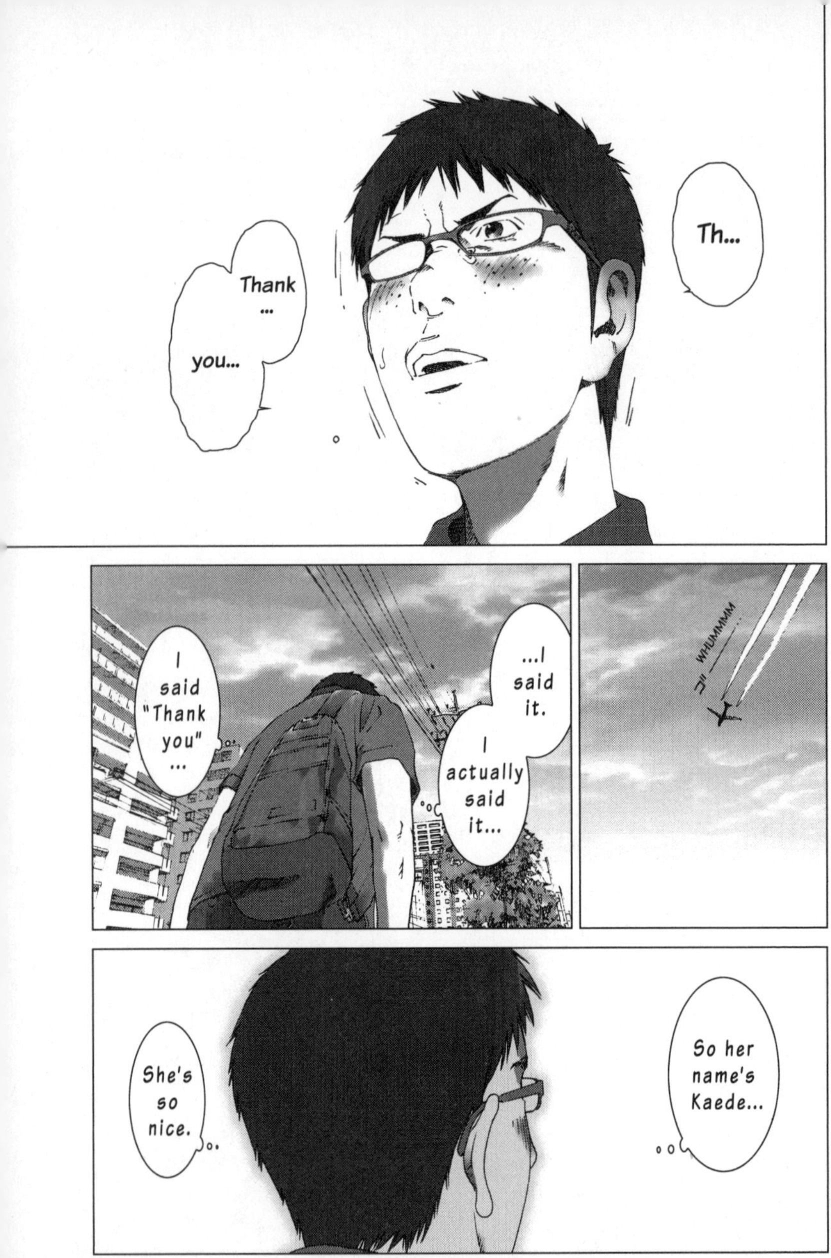
Th...
Thank ... you...
WHUMMMM
...I said it.
I actually said it...
I said "Thank you" ...
So her name's Kaede...
She's so nice.

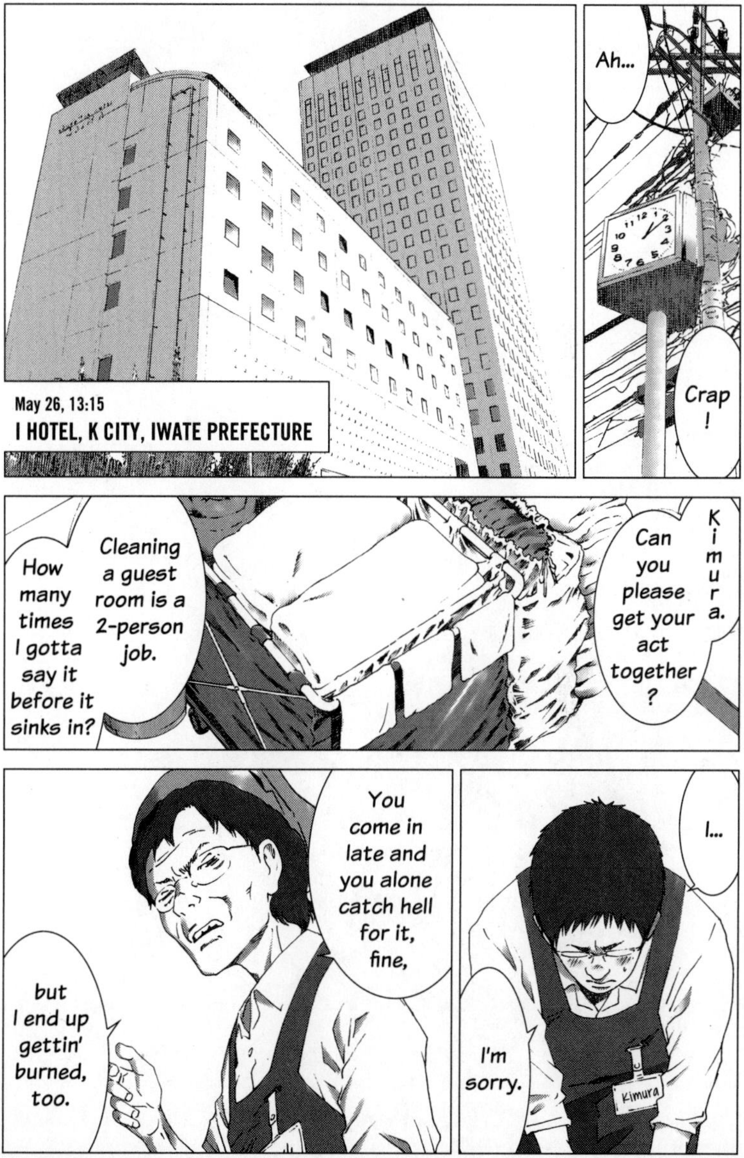
Ah...
Crap!
May 26, 13:15
I HOTEL, K CITY, IWATE PREFECTURE
Kimura.
Can you please get your act together?
Cleaning a guest room is a 2-person job.
How many times I gotta say it before it sinks in?
I...
I'm sorry.
Kimura
You come in late and you alone catch hell for it, fine,
but I end up gettin' burned, too.

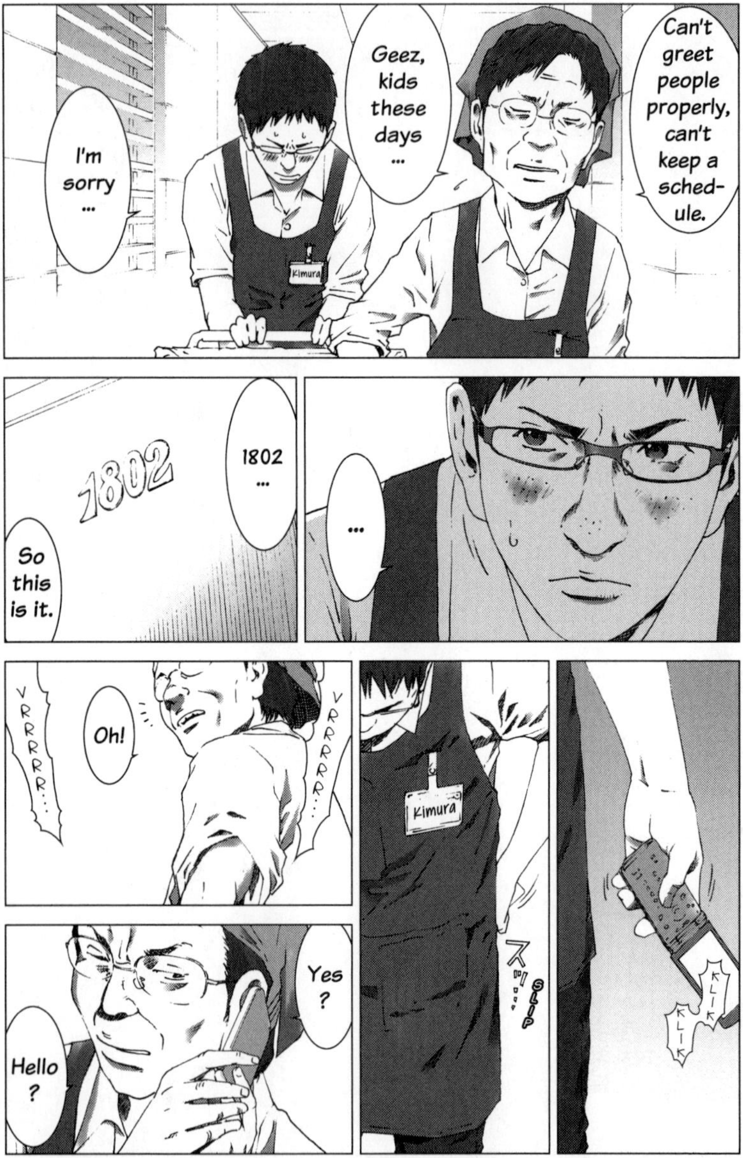
Can't greet people properly, can't keep a sched-ule.
Geez, kids these days ...
Kimura
I'm sorry ...
...
1802 ...
1802
So this is it.
KLIK
KLIK
Kimura
SLIP
VRRRRRR...
Oh!
VRRRRRR...
Yes?
Hello?

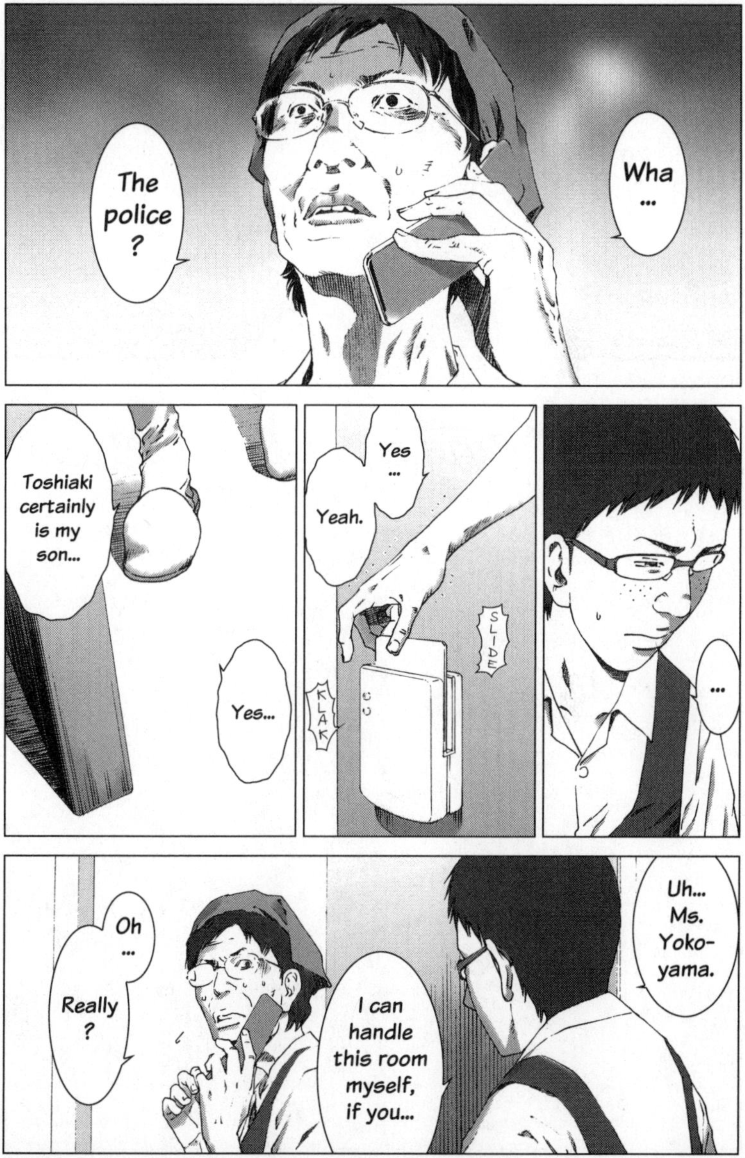
Wha ...
The police ?
...
Yes ...
Yeah.
SLIDE
KLAK
Toshiaki certainly is my son...
Yes...
Uh... Ms. Yoko-yama.
I can handle this room myself, if you...
Oh ... Really ?

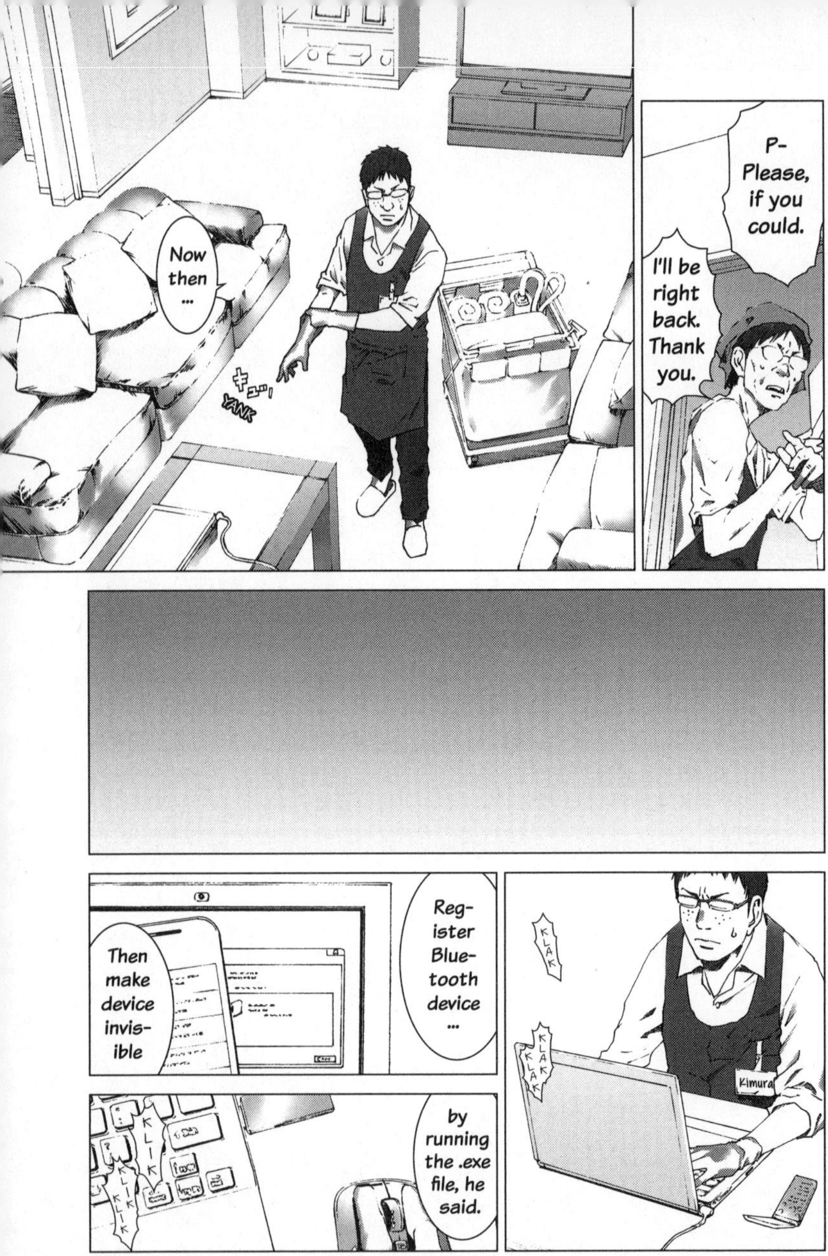
P- Please, if you could.
I'll be right back. Thank you.
Now then ...
キュッ
YANK
KLAK
KLAK KLAK
Register Bluetooth device ...
Then make device invisible
by running the .exe file, he said.
KLIK
KLIK
KLIK
Kimura

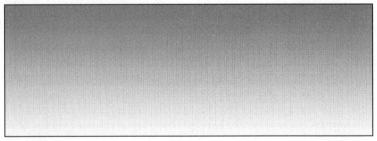

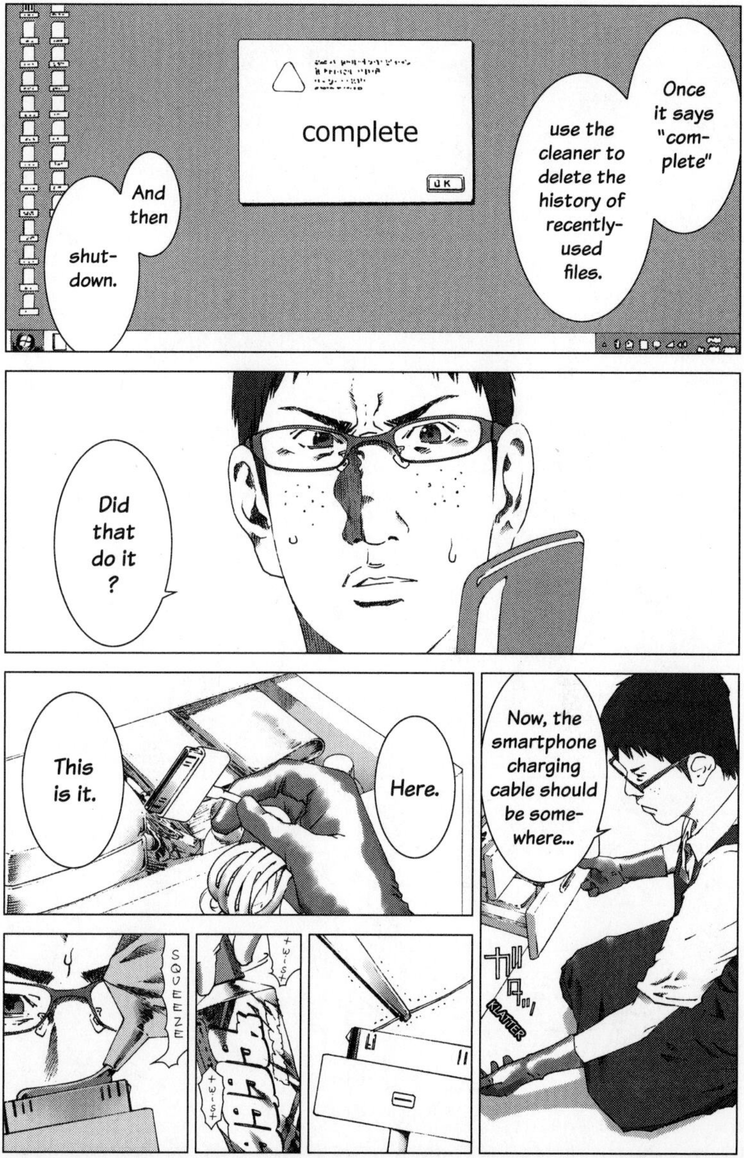
Once it says "complete"
use the cleaner to delete the history of recently-used files.
complete
And then shutdown.
Did that do it?
Now, the smartphone charging cable should be somewhere...
KLATTER
Here.
This is it.
twist
twist
SQUEEZE

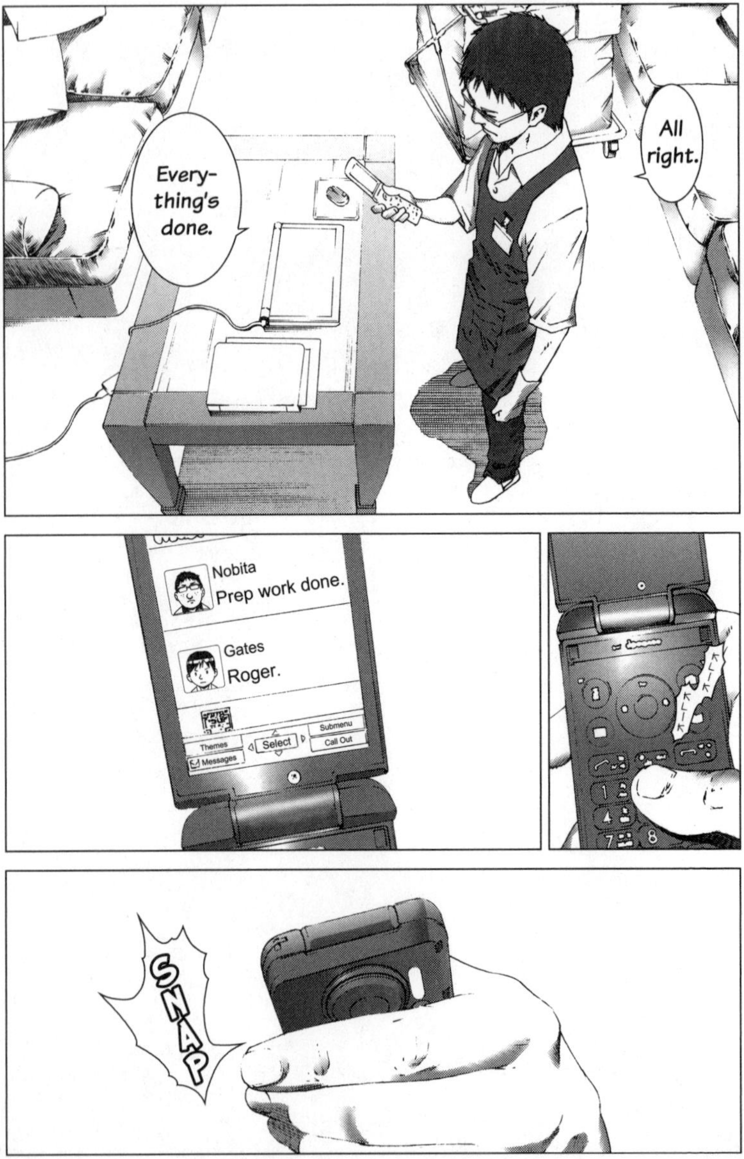
All right.
Every-thing's done.
Nobita
Prep work done.
Gates
Roger.
Themes
Messages
Select
Submenu
Call Out
SNAP

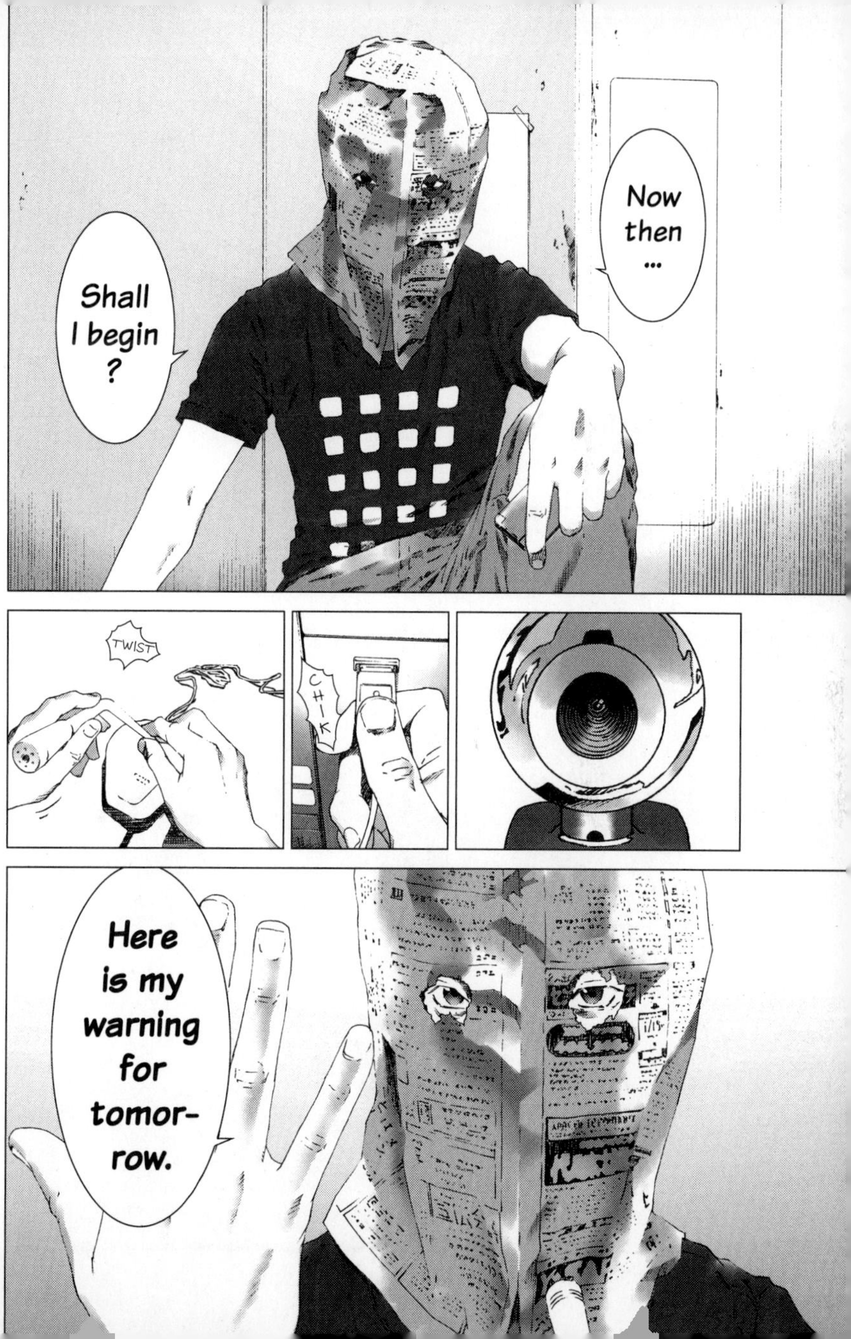
Now then ...
Shall I begin?
CHIK
TWIST
Here is my warning for tomorrow.

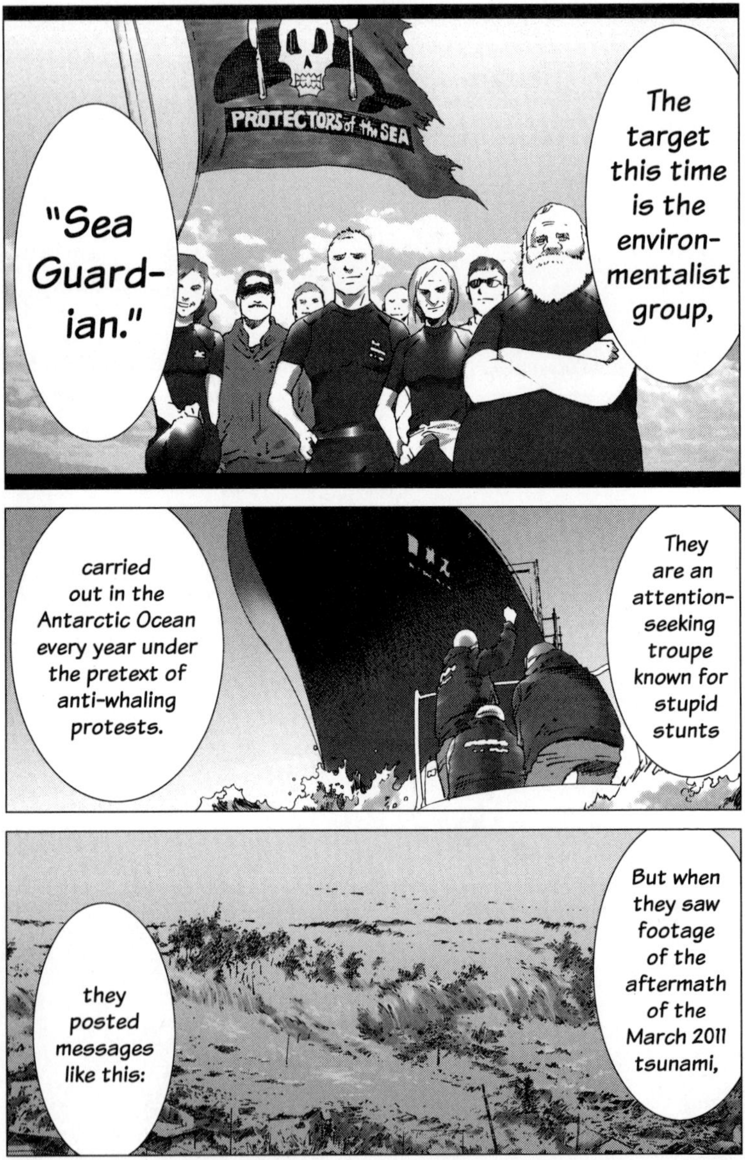

The target this time is the environmentalist group,
PROTECTORS of the SEA
"Sea Guardian."
They are an attention-seeking troupe known for stupid stunts
carried out in the Antarctic Ocean every year under the pretext of anti-whaling protests.
But when they saw footage of the aftermath of the March 2011 tsunami,
they posted messages like this:

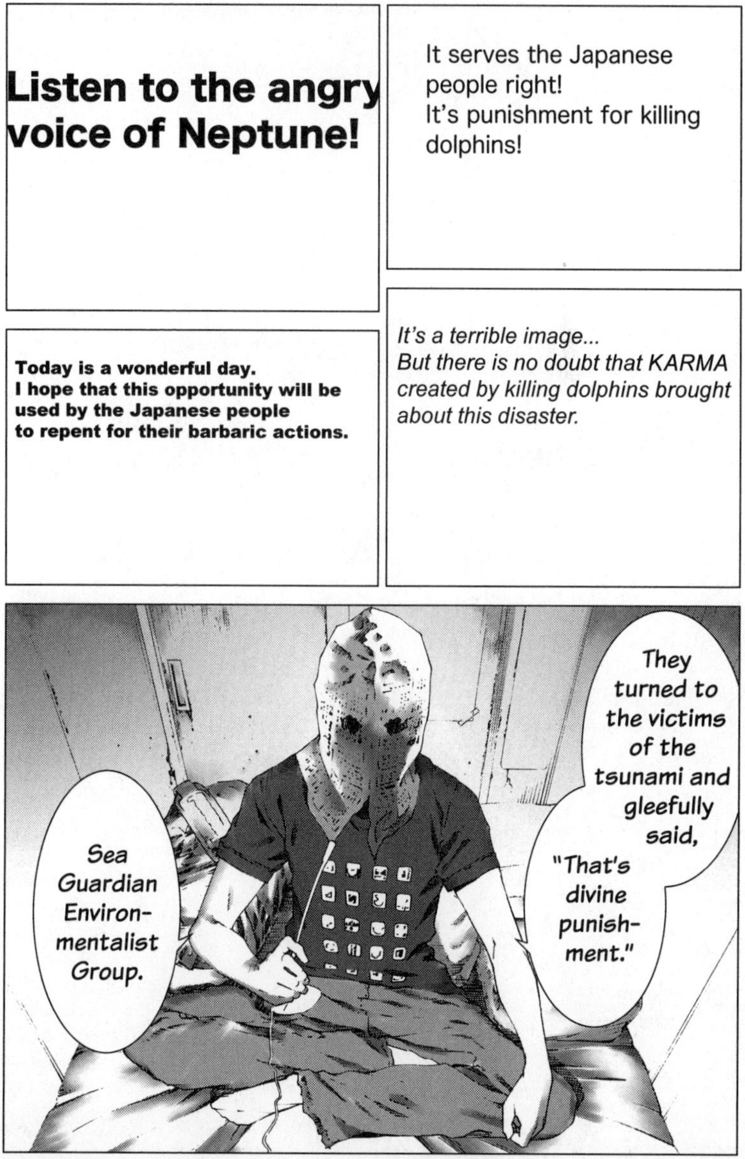
It serves the Japanese people right! It's punishment for killing dolphins!
Listen to the angry voice of Neptune!
It's a terrible image... But there is no doubt that KARMA created by killing dolphins brought about this disaster.
Today is a wonderful day. I hope that this opportunity will be used by the Japanese people to repent for their barbaric actions.
They turned to the victims of the tsunami and gleefully said, "That's divine punishment."
Sea Guardian Environmentalist Group.

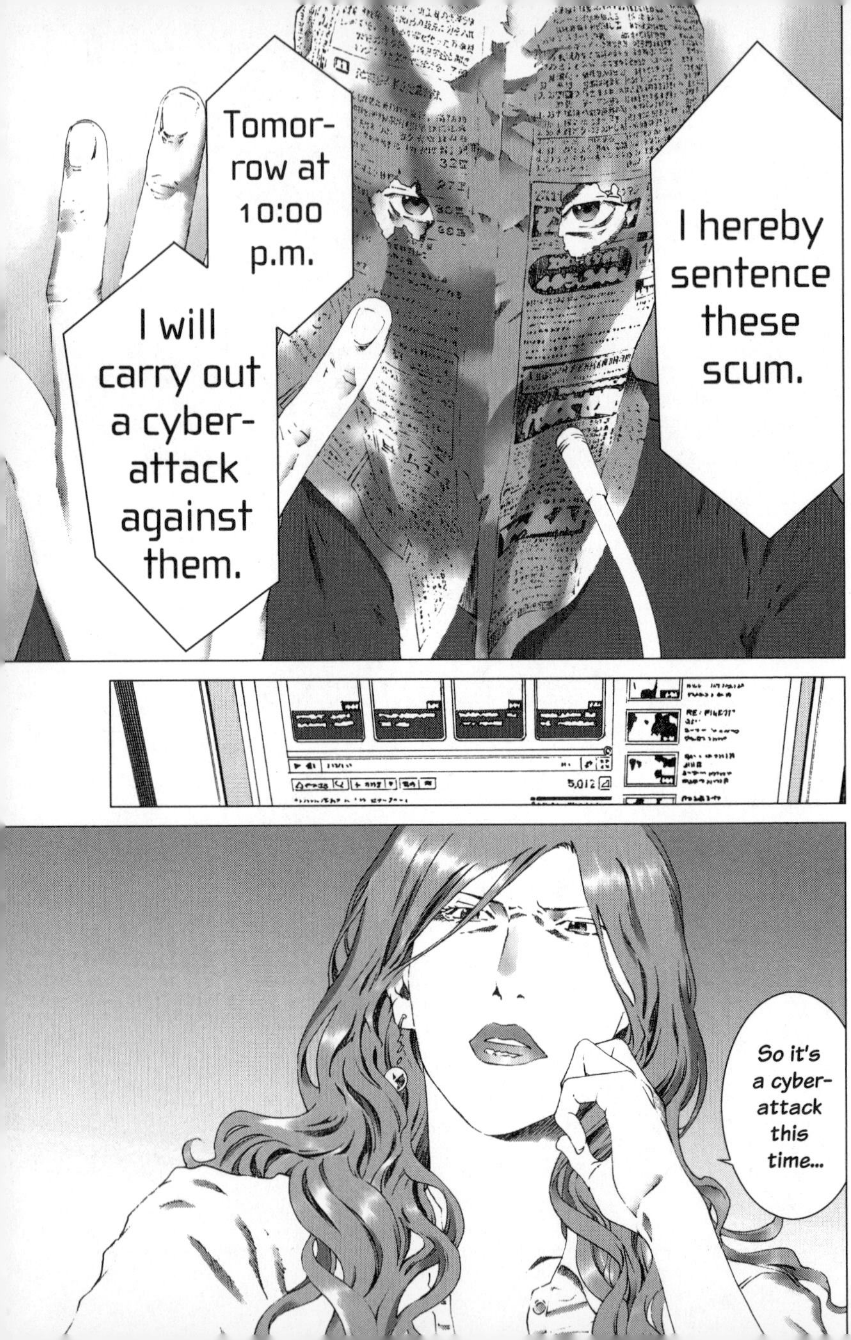
I hereby sentence these scum.
Tomorrow at 10:00 p.m.
I will carry out a cyber-attack against them.
5,012
So it's a cyber-attack this time...

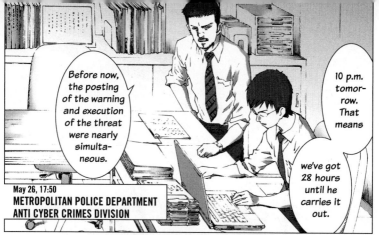

10 p.m. tomorrow. That means
we've got 28 hours until he carries it out.
Before now, the posting of the warning and execution of the threat were nearly simultaneous.
May 26, 17:50
METROPOLITAN POLICE DEPARTMENT
ANTI CYBER CRIMES DIVISION
Well, this time, we need to stop him.
But what's the specific target of this cyber-attack?
Will it be their official website?
The Sea Guardian-related site that's had a sudden surge in traffic
is the personal blog of their spokesman, Bob Parker.
He's started a campaign on it calling for Japan to refund disaster relief donations that it received.
Refund?

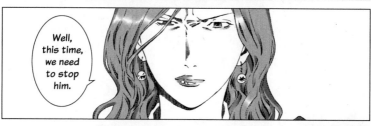

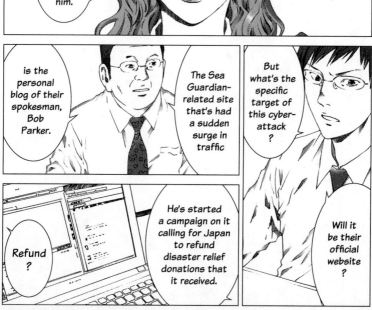

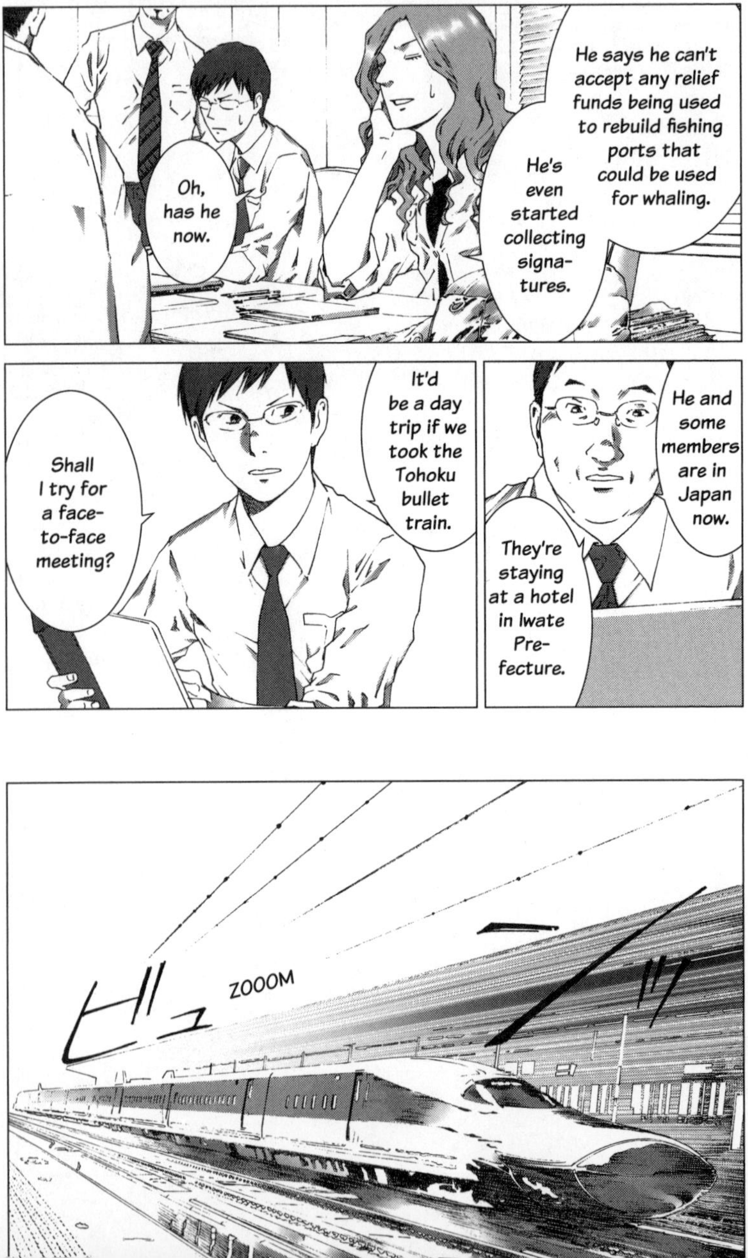
He says he can't accept any relief funds being used to rebuild fishing ports that could be used for whaling.
He's even started collecting signa-tures.
Oh, has he now.
He and some members are in Japan now.
They're staying at a hotel in Iwate Pre-fecture.
It'd be a day trip if we took the Tohoku bullet train.
Shall I try for a face-to-face meeting?
ZOOOM

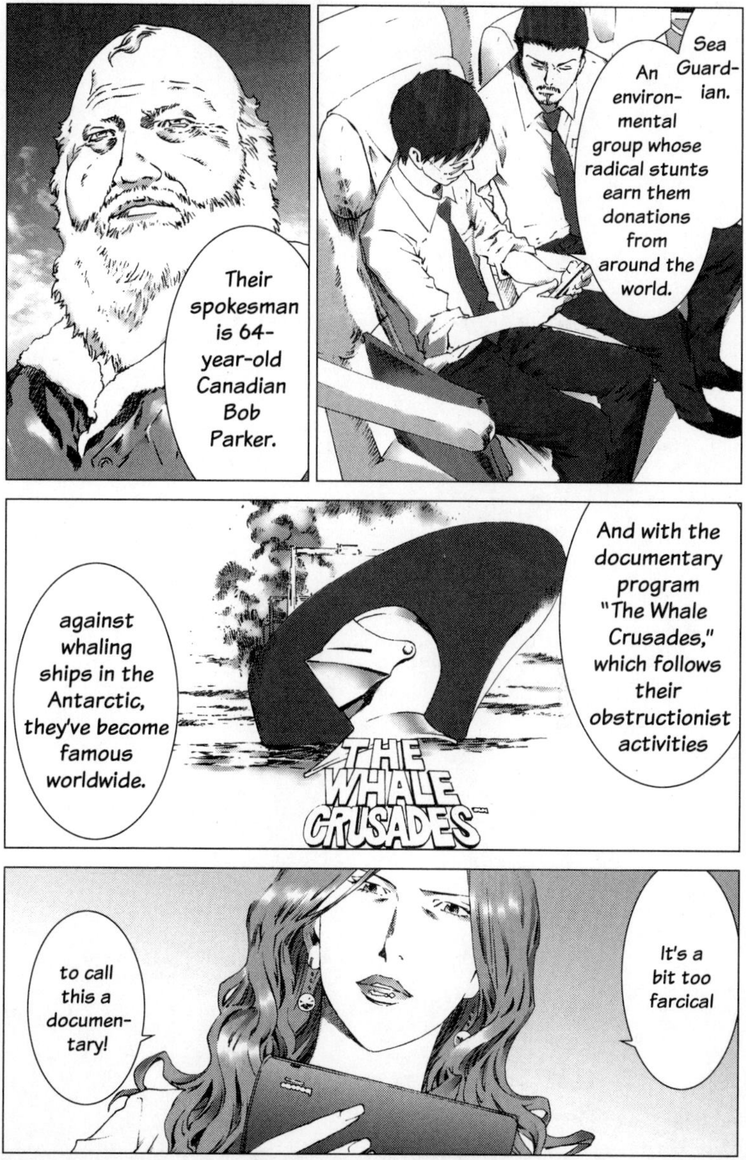

Sea Guardian.
An environmental group whose radical stunts earn them donations from around the world.
Their spokesman is 64-year-old Canadian Bob Parker.
And with the documentary program "The Whale Crusades," which follows their obstructionist activities
THE WHALE CRUSADES
against whaling ships in the Antarctic, they've become famous worldwide.
It's a bit too farcical
to call this a documentary!

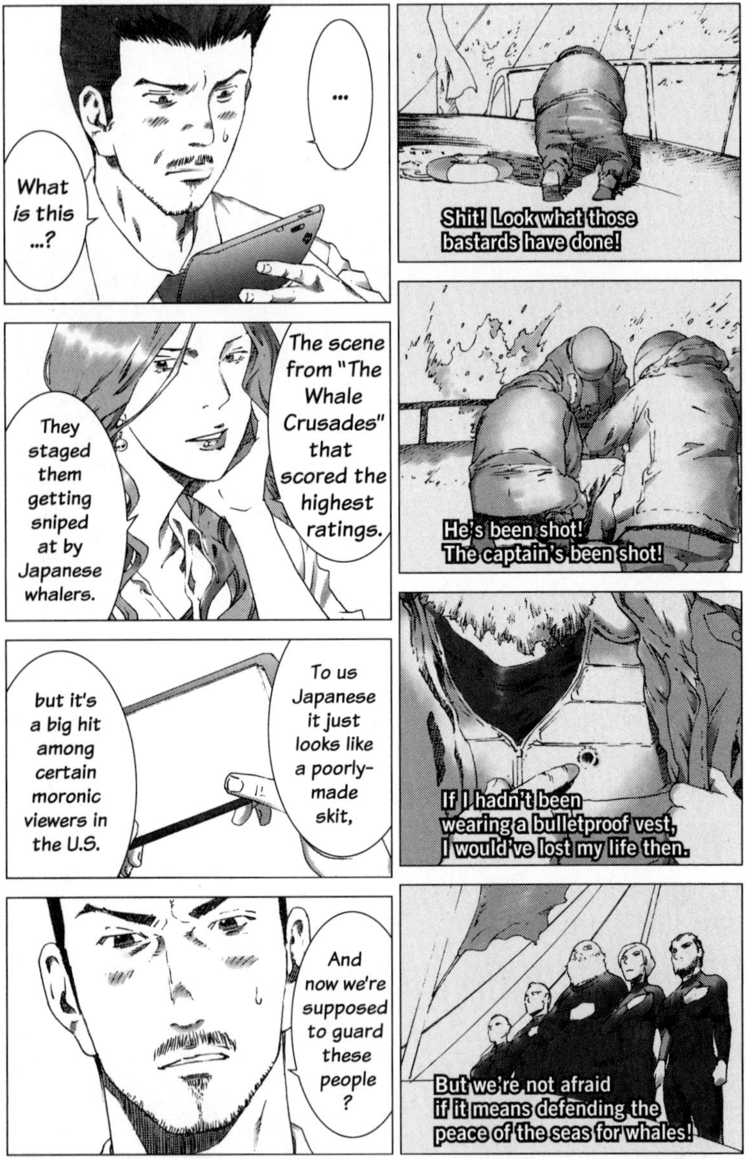
Shit! Look what those bastards have done!
...
What is this ...?
He's been shot! The captain's been shot!
The scene from "The Whale Crusades" that scored the highest ratings.
They staged them getting sniped at by Japanese whalers.
If I hadn't been wearing a bulletproof vest, I would've lost my life then.
To us Japanese it just looks like a poorly-made skit,
but it's a big hit among certain moronic viewers in the U.S.
But we're not afraid if it means defending the peace of the seas for whales!
And now we're supposed to guard these people ?

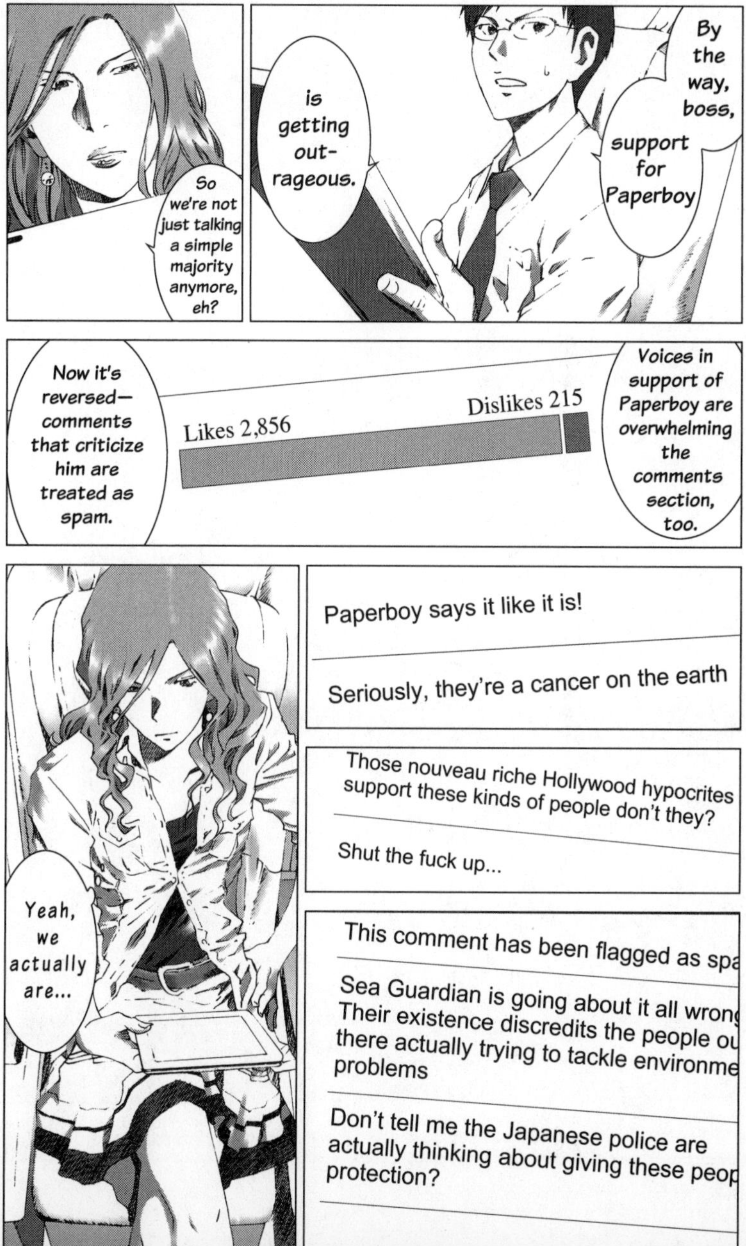

By the way, boss,
support for Paperboy
is getting out-rageous.
So we're not just talking a simple majority anymore, eh?
Voices in support of Paperboy are overwhelming the comments section, too.
Dislikes 215
Likes 2,856
Now it's reversed—comments that criticize him are treated as spam.
Paperboy says it like it is!
Seriously, they're a cancer on the earth
Those nouveau riche Hollywood hypocrites support these kinds of people don't they?
Shut the fuck up...
This comment has been flagged as spa
Sea Guardian is going about it all wrong Their existence discredits the people ou there actually trying to tackle environme problems
Don't tell me the Japanese police are actually thinking about giving these peop protection?
Yeah, we actually are...

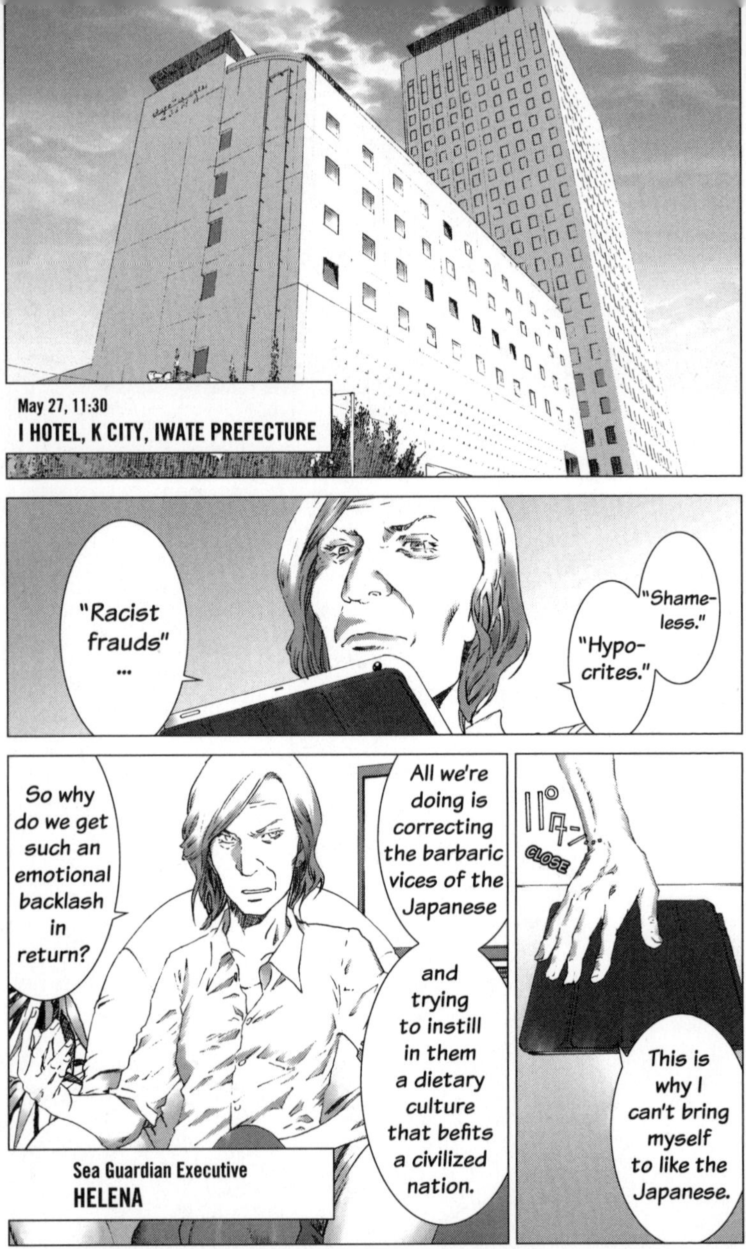
May 27, 11:30
I HOTEL, K CITY, IWATE PREFECTURE
"Shame-less."
"Hypo-crites."
"Racist frauds" ...
CLOSE
This is why I can't bring myself to like the Japanese.
All we're doing is correcting the barbaric vices of the Japanese
and trying to instill in them a dietary culture that befits a civilized nation.
So why do we get such an emotional backlash in return?
Sea Guardian Executive
HELENA

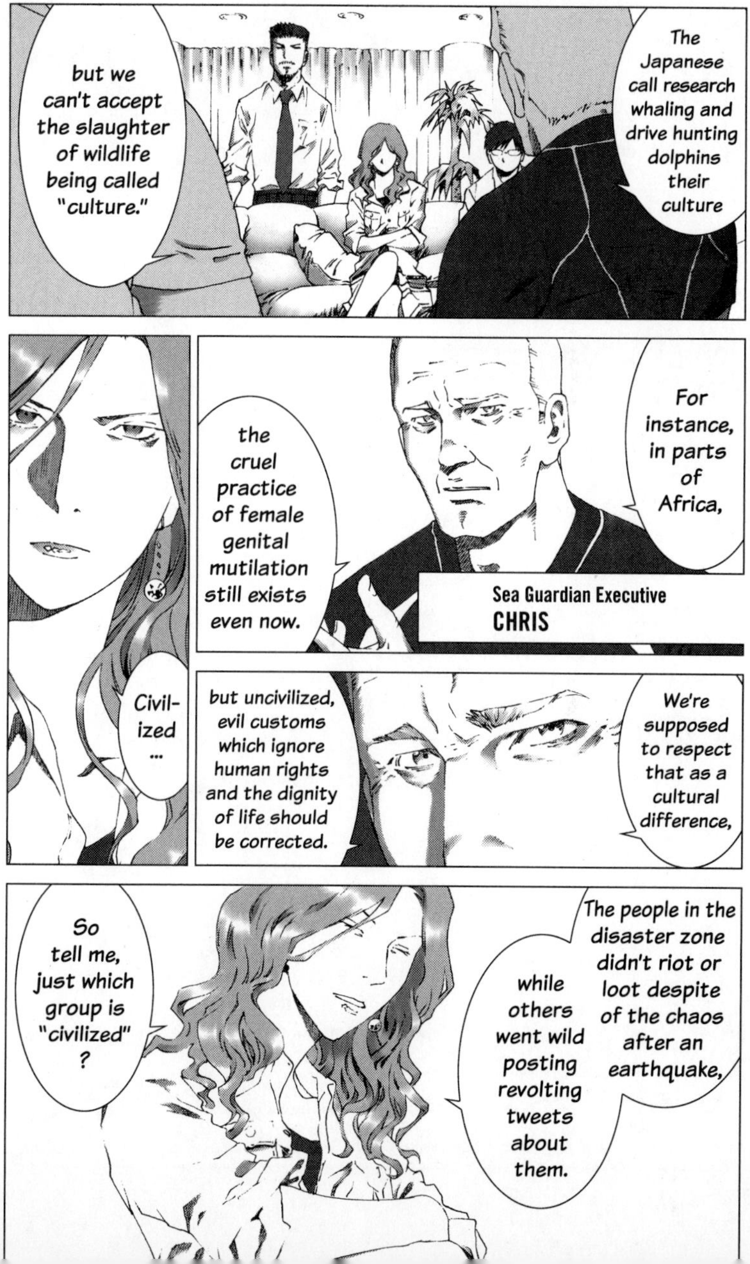
The Japanese call research whaling and drive hunting dolphins their culture
but we can't accept the slaughter of wildlife being called "culture."
For instance, in parts of Africa,
Sea Guardian Executive
CHRIS
the cruel practice of female genital mutilation still exists even now.
We're supposed to respect that as a cultural difference,
but uncivilized, evil customs which ignore human rights and the dignity of life should be corrected.
Civil-ized ...
The people in the disaster zone didn't riot or loot despite of the chaos after an earthquake,
while others went wild posting revolting tweets about them.
So tell me, just which group is "civilized" ?

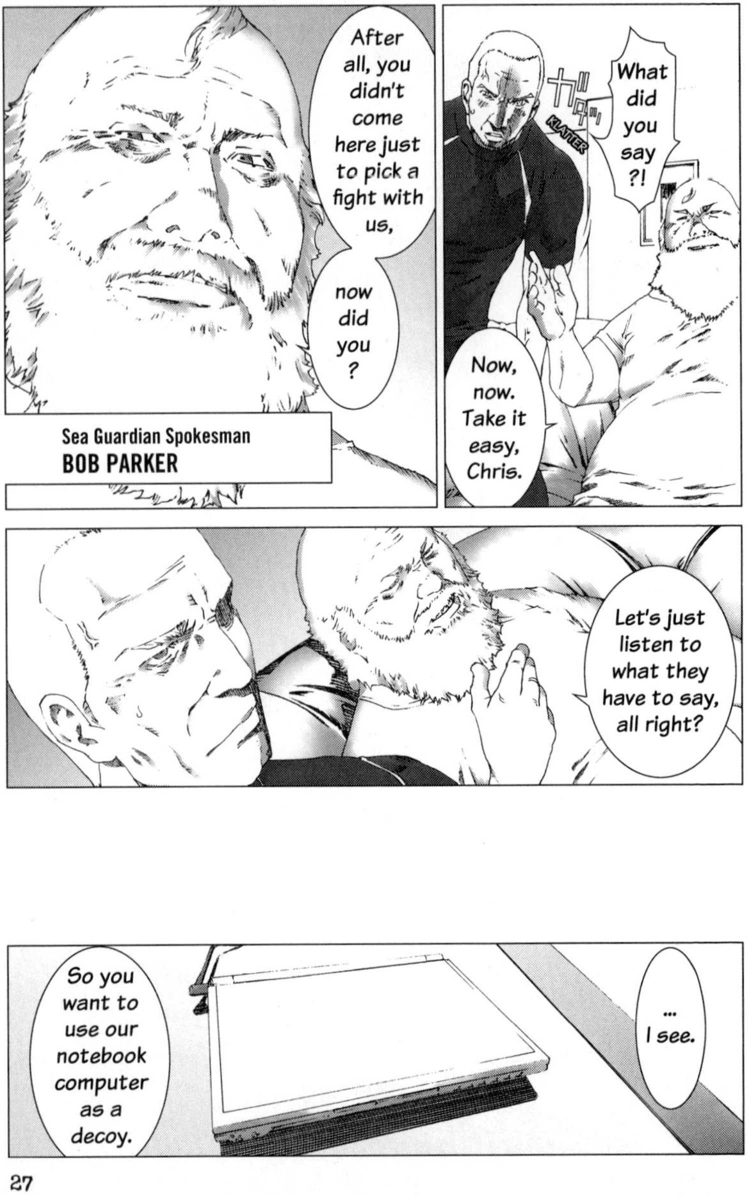
What did you say ?!
KLATTER
Now, now. Take it easy, Chris.
After all, you didn't come here just to pick a fight with us,
now did you ?
Sea Guardian Spokesman
BOB PARKER
Let's just listen to what they have to say, all right?
... I see.
So you want to use our notebook computer as a decoy.

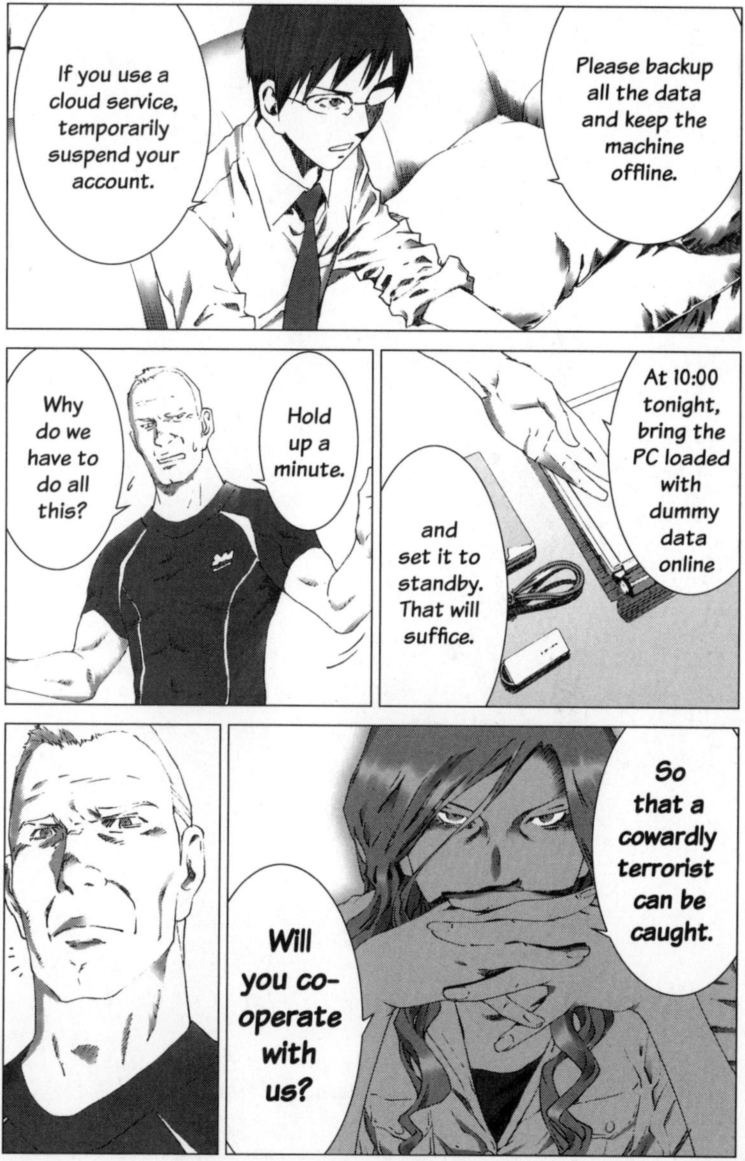
Please backup all the data and keep the machine offline.
If you use a cloud service, temporarily suspend your account.
At 10:00 tonight, bring the PC loaded with dummy data online
and set it to standby. That will suffice.
Hold up a minute.
Why do we have to do all this?
So that a cowardly terrorist can be caught.
Will you co-operate with us?

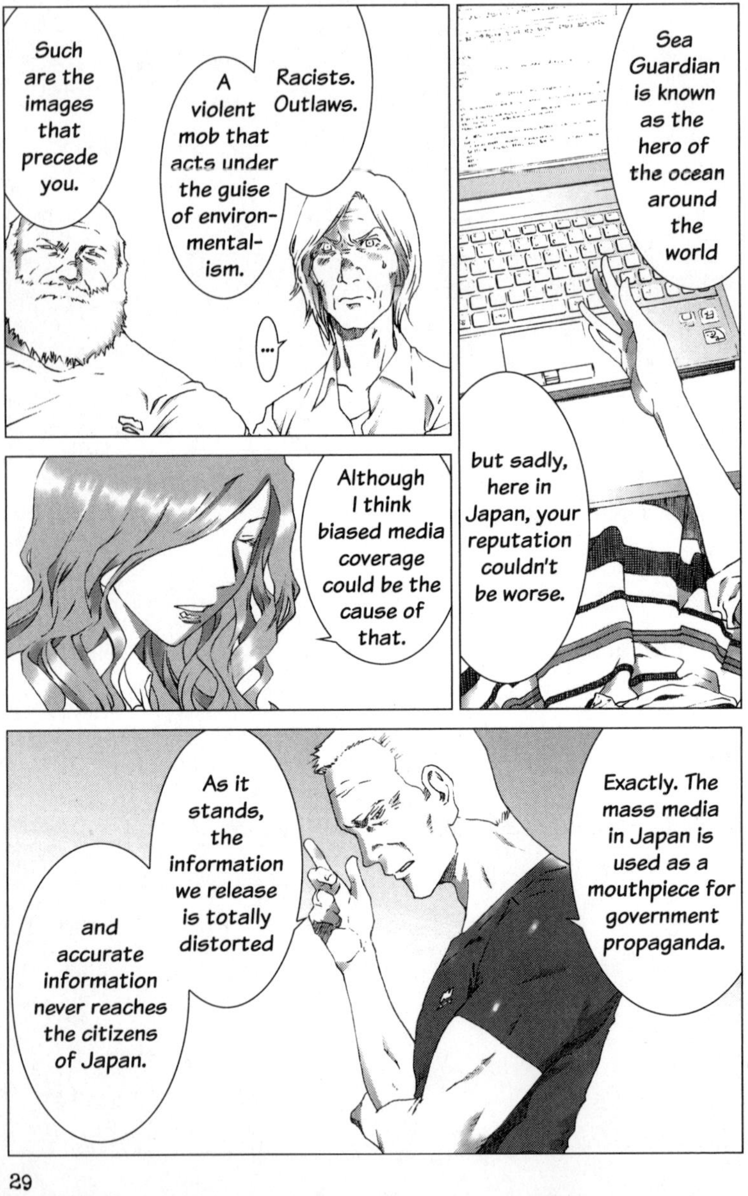
Sea Guardian is known as the hero of the ocean around the world
but sadly, here in Japan, your reputation couldn't be worse.
Racists. Outlaws.
A violent mob that acts under the guise of environmentalism.
Such are the images that precede you.
...
Although I think biased media coverage could be the cause of that.
Exactly. The mass media in Japan is used as a mouthpiece for government propaganda.
As it stands, the information we release is totally distorted
and accurate information never reaches the citizens of Japan.

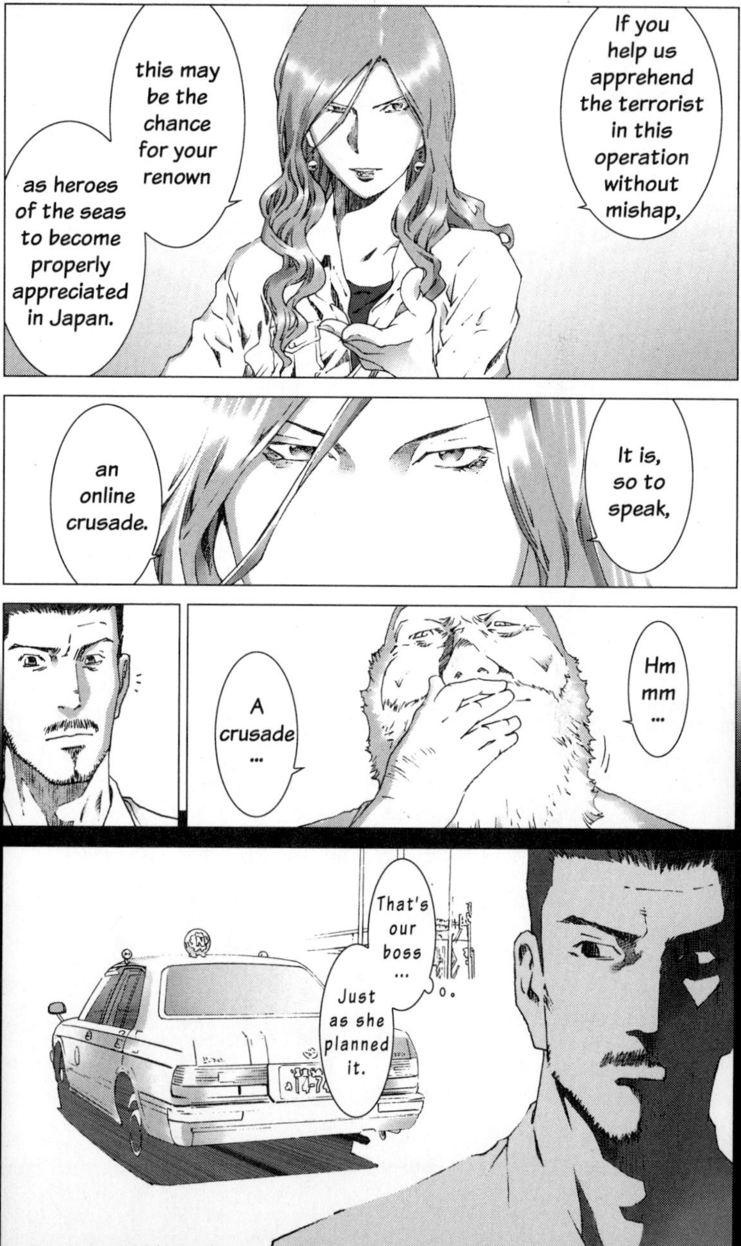
If you help us apprehend the terrorist in this operation without mishap,
this may be the chance for your renown
as heroes of the seas to become properly appreciated in Japan.
It is, so to speak,
an online crusade.
Hm mm ...
A crusade ...
That's our boss ...
Just as she planned it.

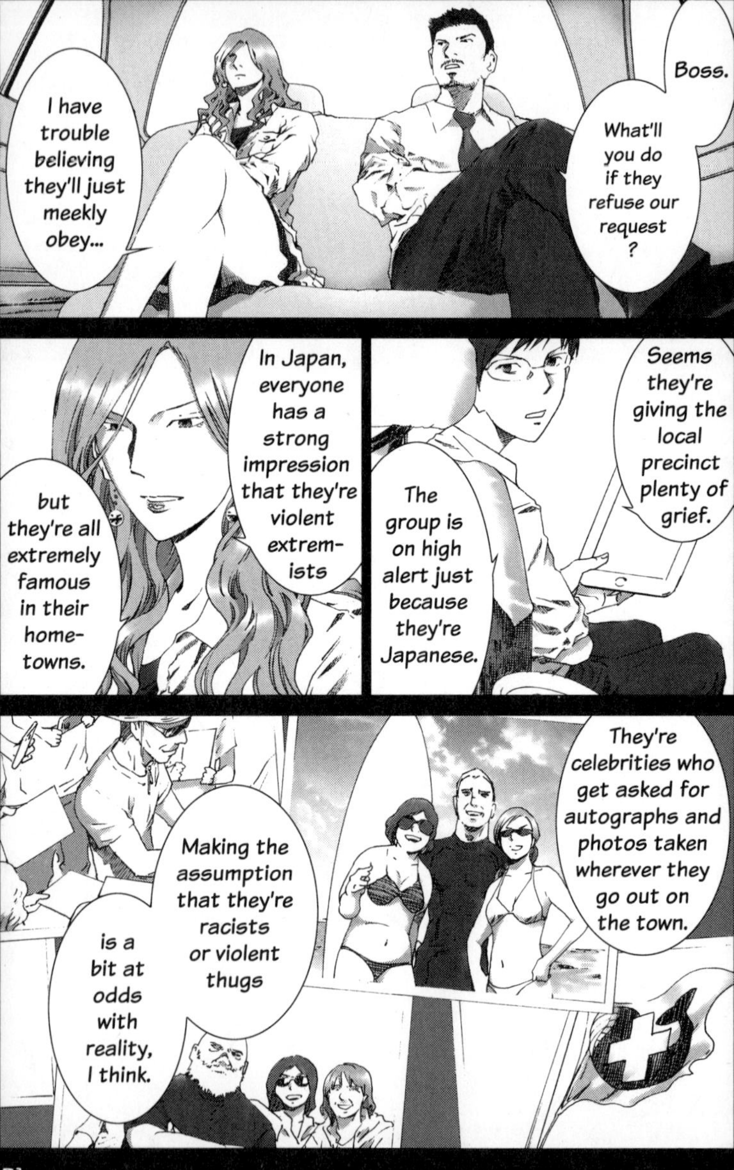
Boss.
What'll you do if they refuse our request?
I have trouble believing they'll just meekly obey...
Seems they're giving the local precinct plenty of grief.
The group is on high alert just because they're Japanese.
In Japan, everyone has a strong impression that they're violent extrem-ists
but they're all extremely famous in their home-towns.
They're celebrities who get asked for autographs and photos taken wherever they go out on the town.
Making the assumption that they're racists or violent thugs
is a bit at odds with reality, I think.

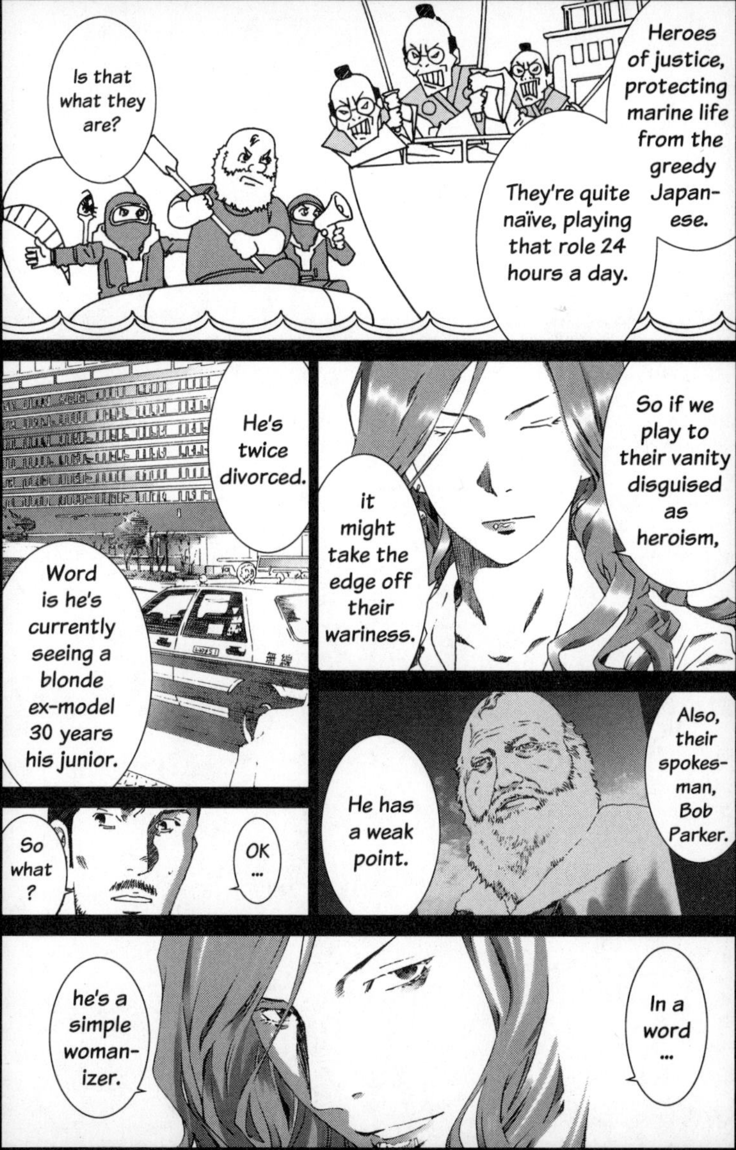
Heroes of justice, protecting marine life from the greedy Japanese.
They're quite naïve, playing that role 24 hours a day.
Is that what they are?
So if we play to their vanity disguised as heroism,
it might take the edge off their wariness.
Also, their spokesman, Bob Parker.
He has a weak point.
He's twice divorced.
Word is he's currently seeing a blonde ex-model 30 years his junior.
OK ...
So what ?
In a word ...
he's a simple womanizer.

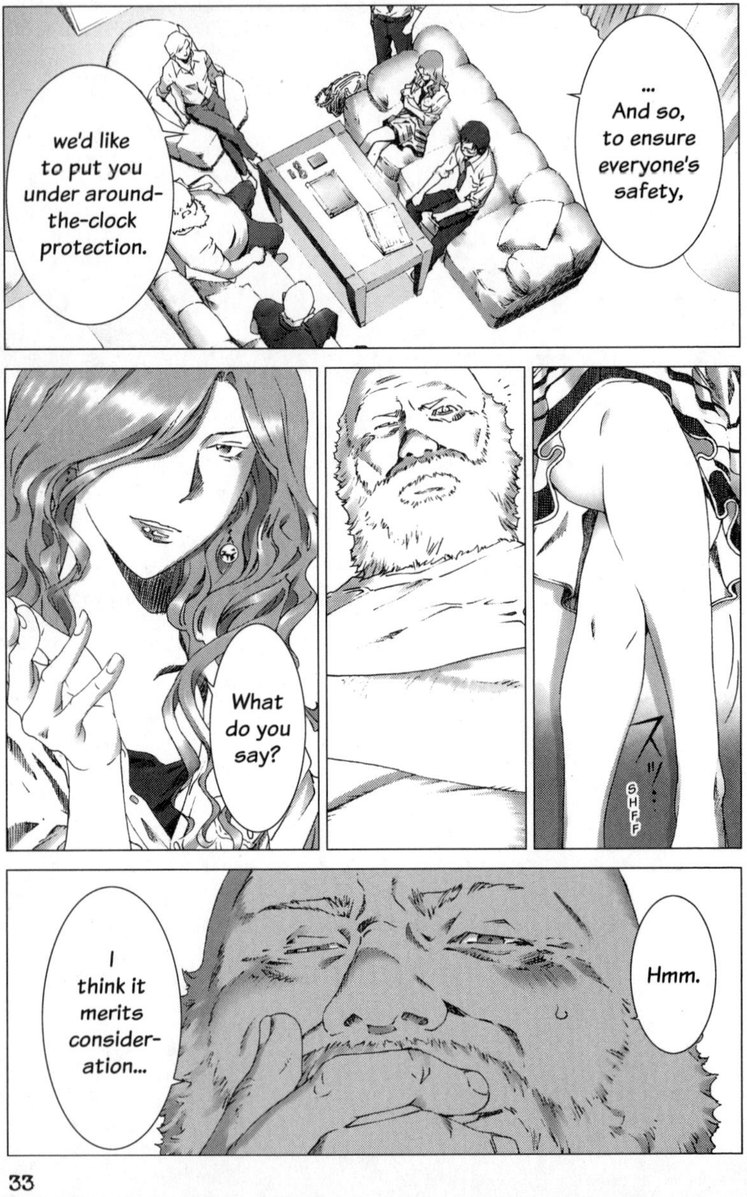
... And so, to ensure everyone's safety,
we'd like to put you under around-the-clock protection.
SHFF
What do you say?
Hmm.
I think it merits consider-ation...

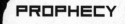
PROPHECY

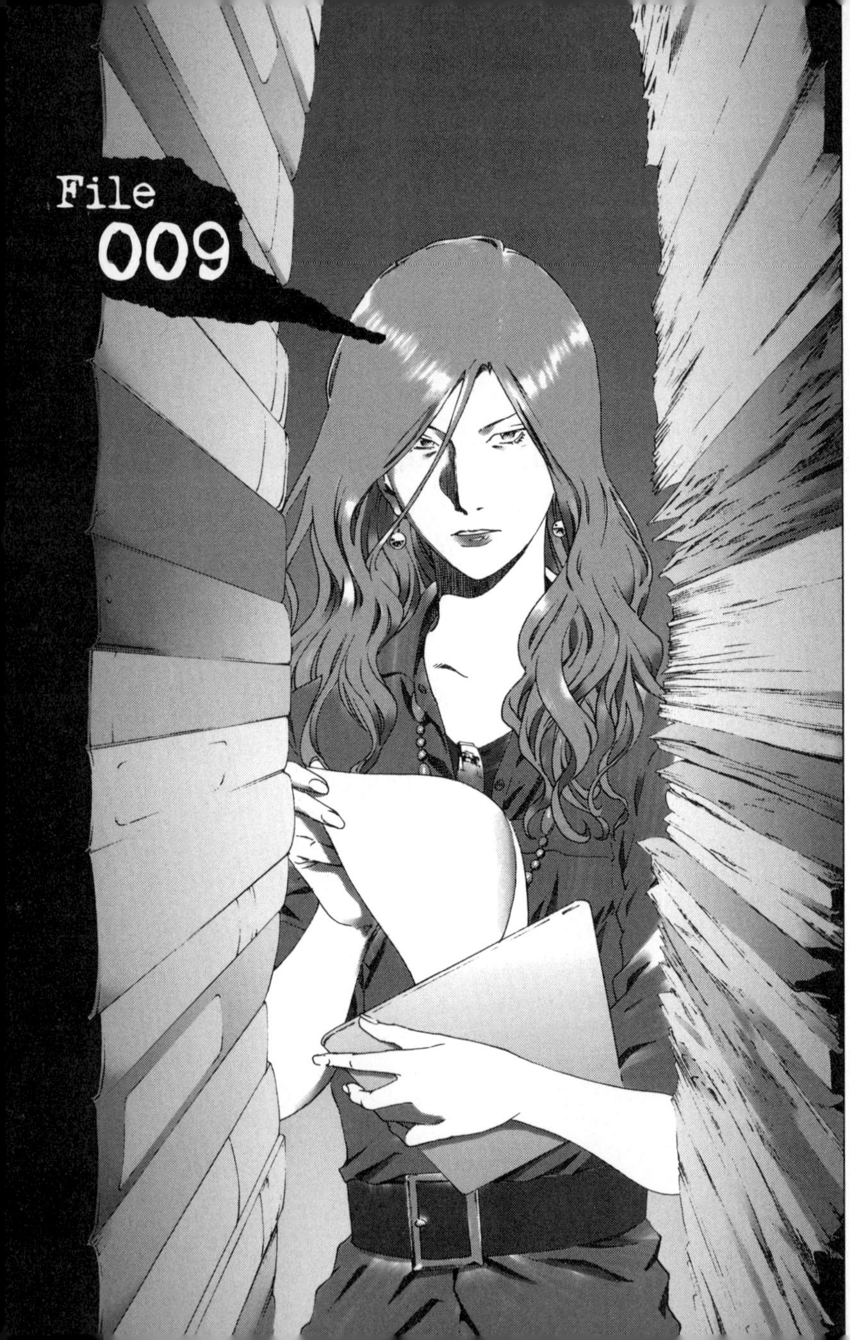
File
009

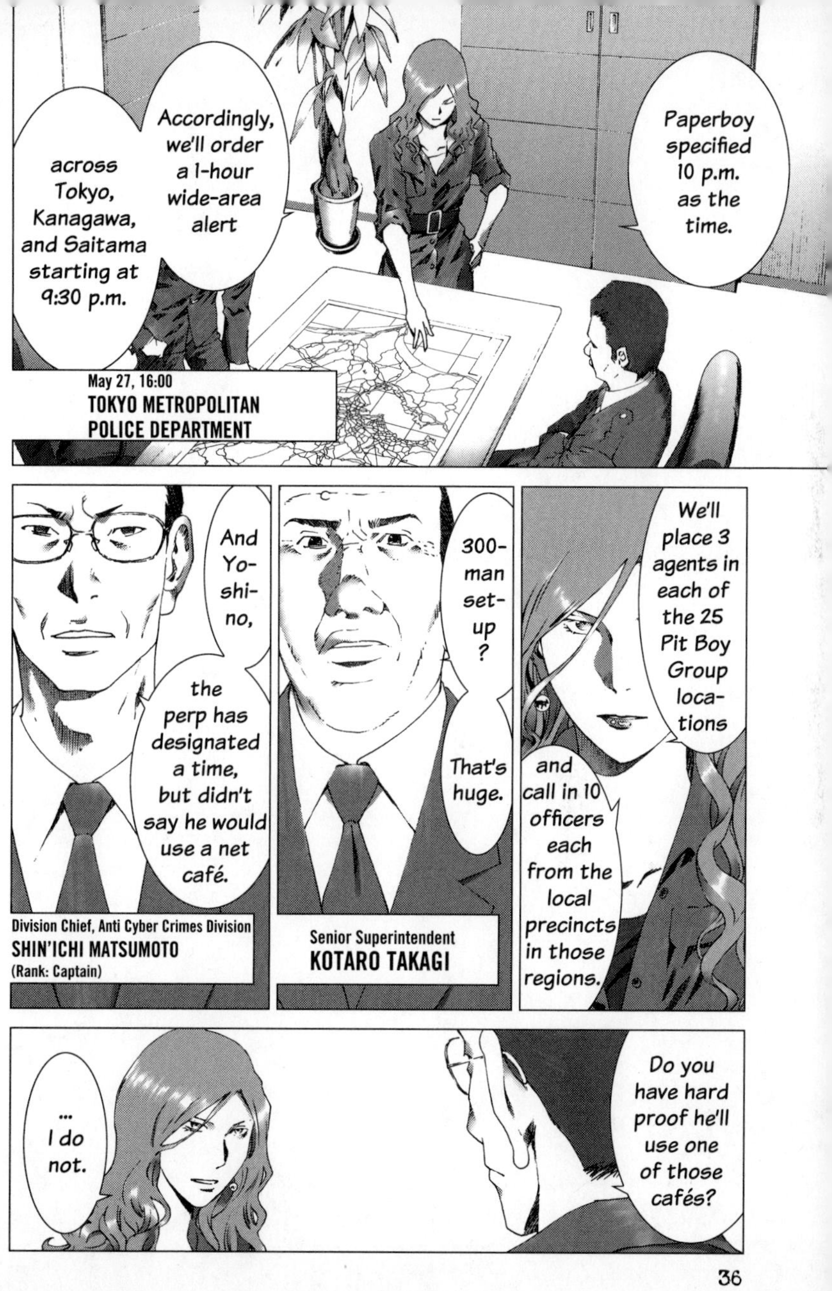
Paperboy specified 10 p.m. as the time.
Accordingly, we'll order a 1-hour wide-area alert
across Tokyo, Kanagawa, and Saitama starting at 9:30 p.m.
May 27, 16:00
TOKYO METROPOLITAN POLICE DEPARTMENT
We'll place 3 agents in each of the 25 Pit Boy Group locations
and call in 10 officers each from the local precincts in those regions.
300-man set-up?
That's huge.
Senior Superintendent
KOTARO TAKAGI
And Yoshino,
the perp has designated a time, but didn't say he would use a net café.
Division Chief, Anti Cyber Crimes Division
SHIN'ICHI MATSUMOTO
(Rank: Captain)
Do you have hard proof he'll use one of those cafés?
... I do not.

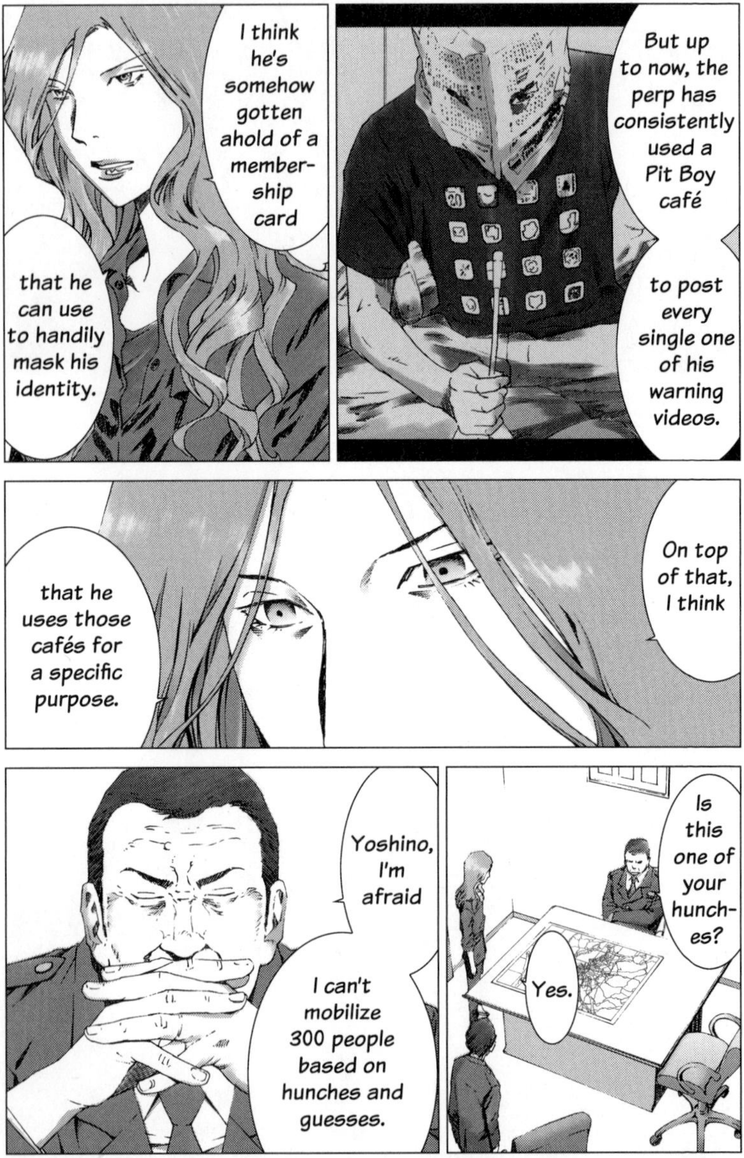
But up to now, the perp has consistently used a Pit Boy café
to post every single one of his warning videos.
I think he's somehow gotten ahold of a membership card
that he can use to handily mask his identity.
On top of that, I think
that he uses those cafés for a specific purpose.
Is this one of your hunches?
Yes.
Yoshino, I'm afraid
I can't mobilize 300 people based on hunches and guesses.

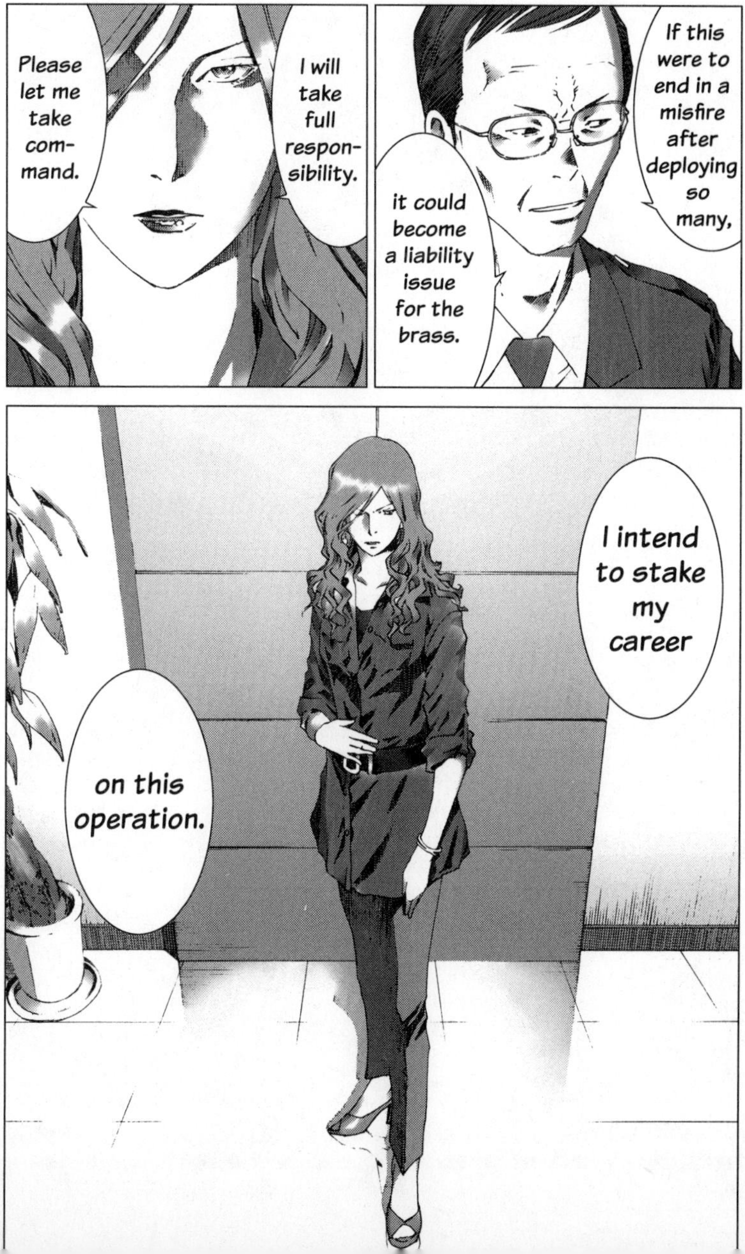
If this were to end in a misfire after deploying so many,
it could become a liability issue for the brass.
I will take full respon-sibility.
Please let me take com-mand.
I intend to stake my career
on this operation.

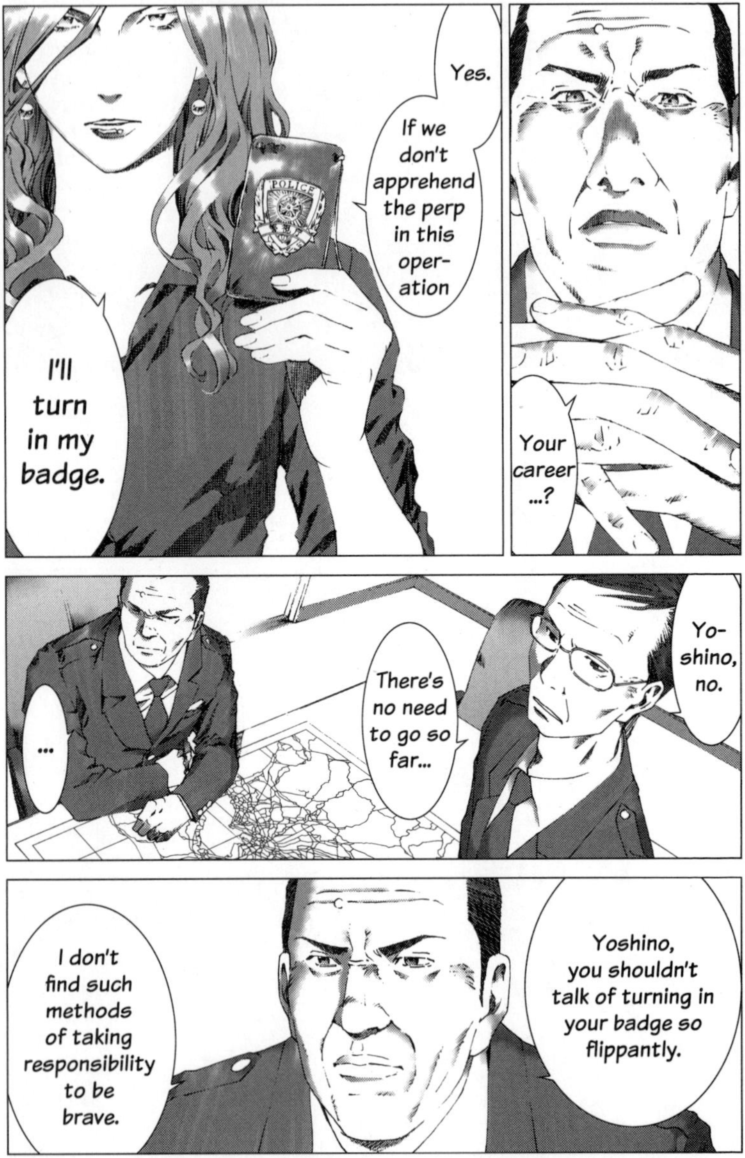
Your career ...?
Yes.
If we don't apprehend the perp in this oper- ation
I'll turn in my badge.
Yo- shino, no.
There's no need to go so far...
...
Yoshino, you shouldn't talk of turning in your badge so flippantly.
I don't find such methods of taking responsibility to be brave.

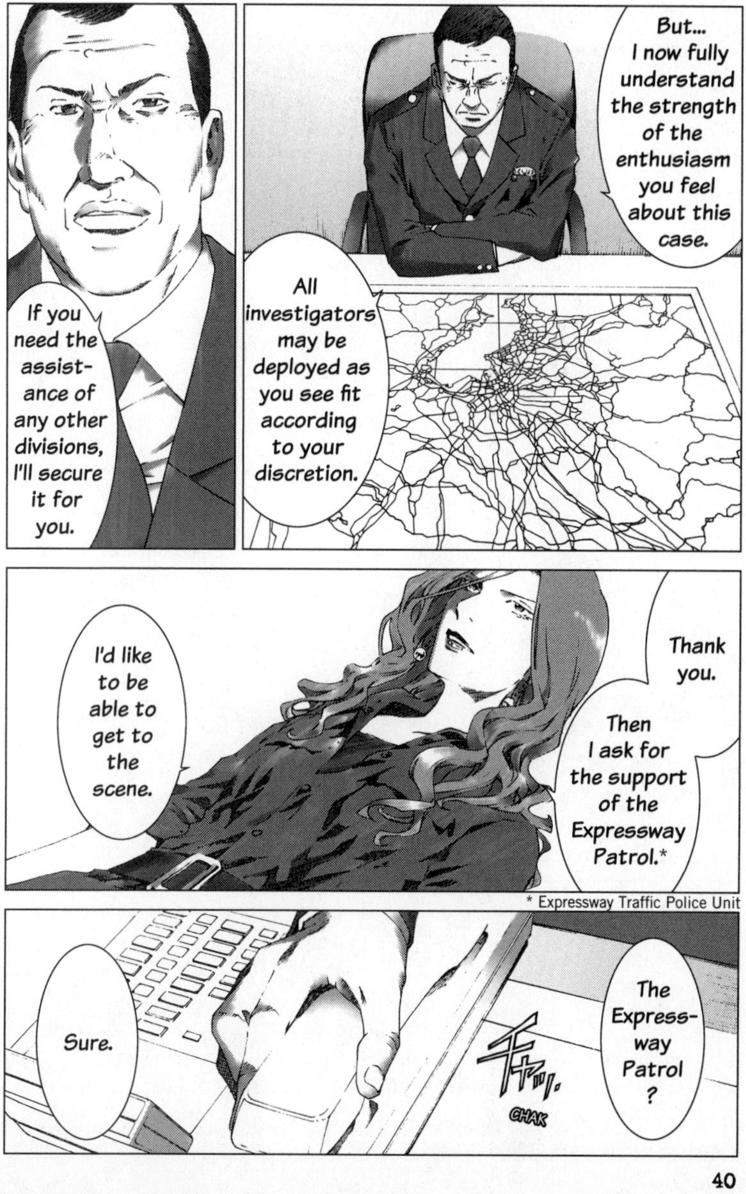
But... I now fully understand the strength of the enthusiasm you feel about this case.
All investigators may be deployed as you see fit according to your discretion.
If you need the assist-ance of any other divisions, I'll secure it for you.
Thank you.
Then I ask for the support of the Expressway Patrol.*
I'd like to be able to get to the scene.
The Express-way Patrol ?
CHAK
Sure.

* Expressway Traffic Police Unit

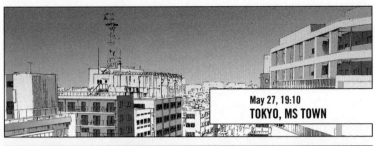

May 27, 19:10
TOKYO, MS TOWN

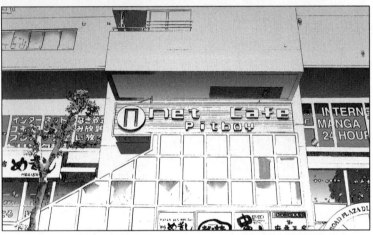

...

Pit Boy Employee
YUICHI AOYAMA

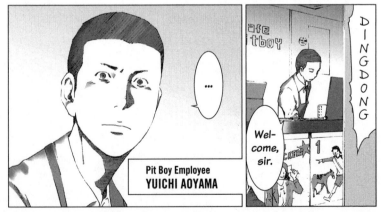

DINGDONG

Wel-
come,
sir.

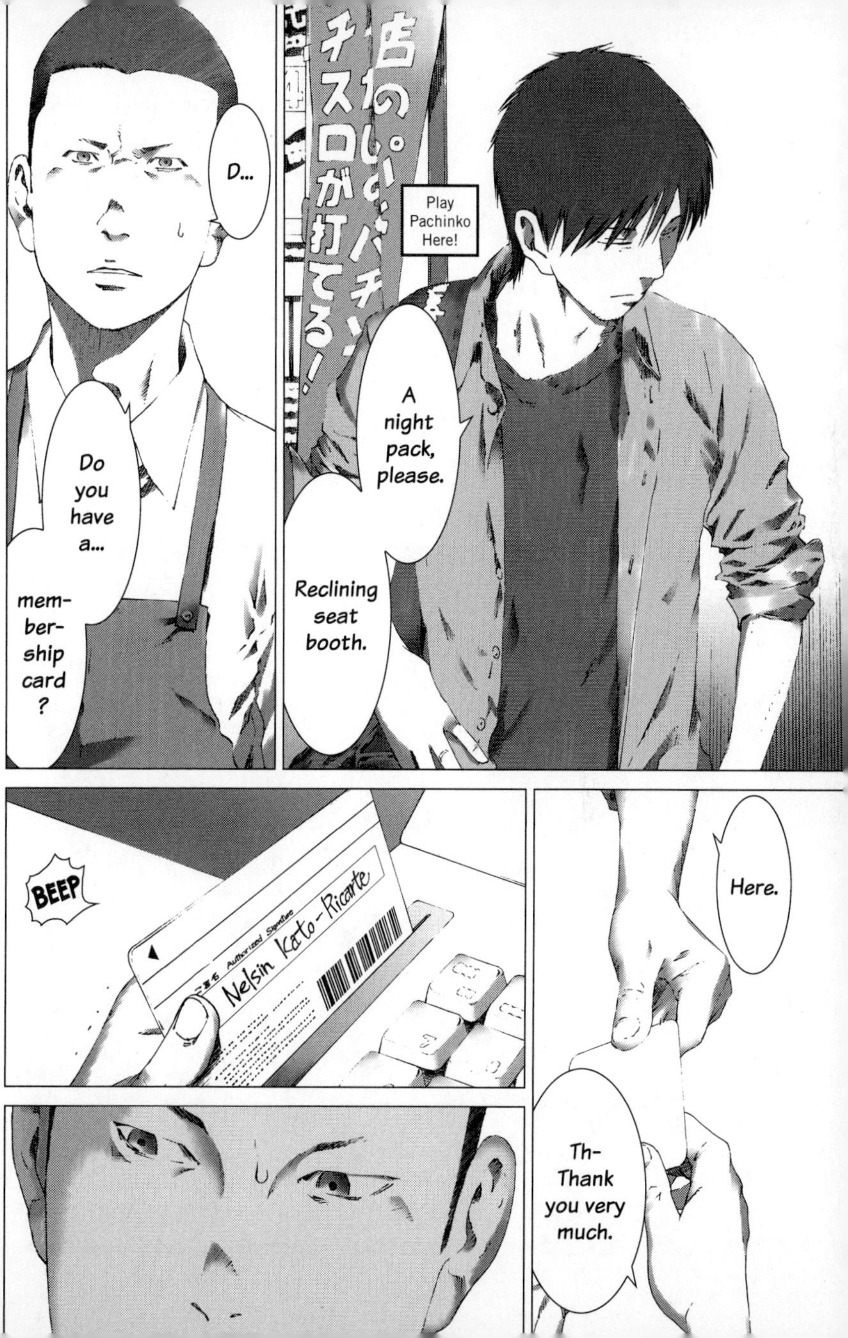
Play Pachinko Here!
A night pack, please.
Reclining seat booth.
D...
Do you have a...
mem-ber-ship card?
Here.
Th- Thank you very much.
BEEP
Authorized Signature
Nelsin Kato-Ricarte

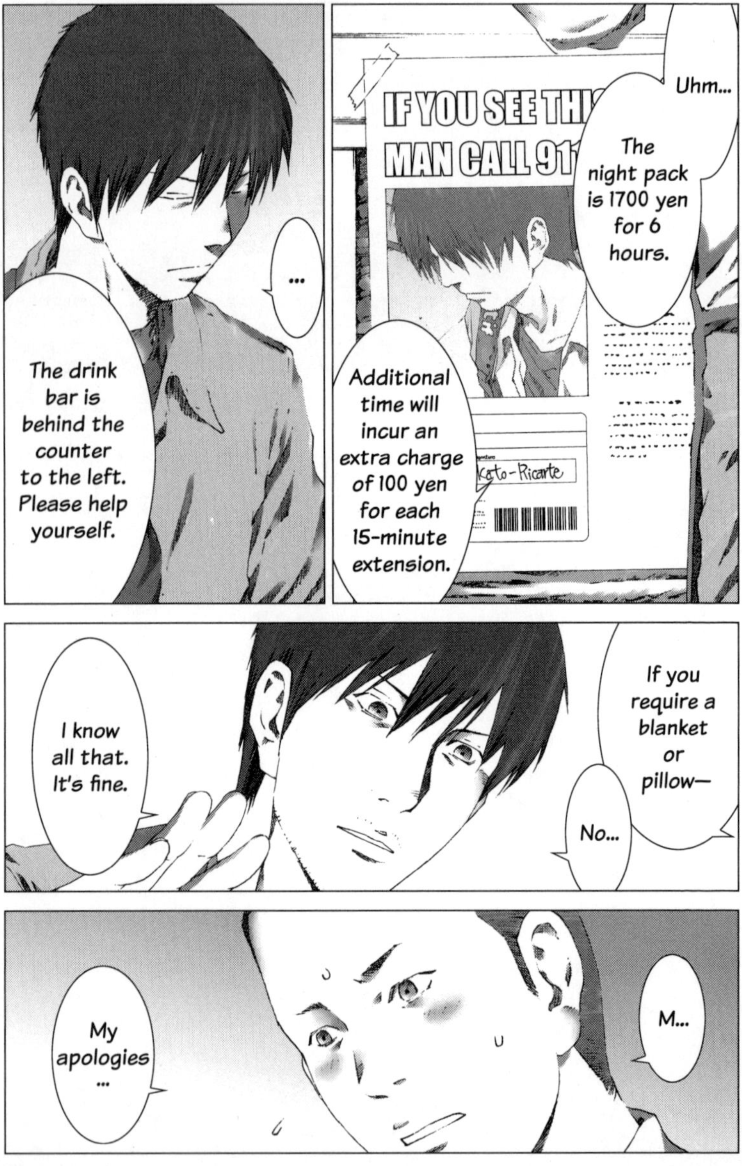
Uhm...
The night pack is 1700 yen for 6 hours.
IF YOU SEE THI
MAN CALL 91
Kato-Ricarte
Additional time will incur an extra charge of 100 yen for each 15-minute extension.
...
The drink bar is behind the counter to the left. Please help yourself.
If you require a blanket or pillow—
No...
I know all that. It's fine.
M...
My apologies ...

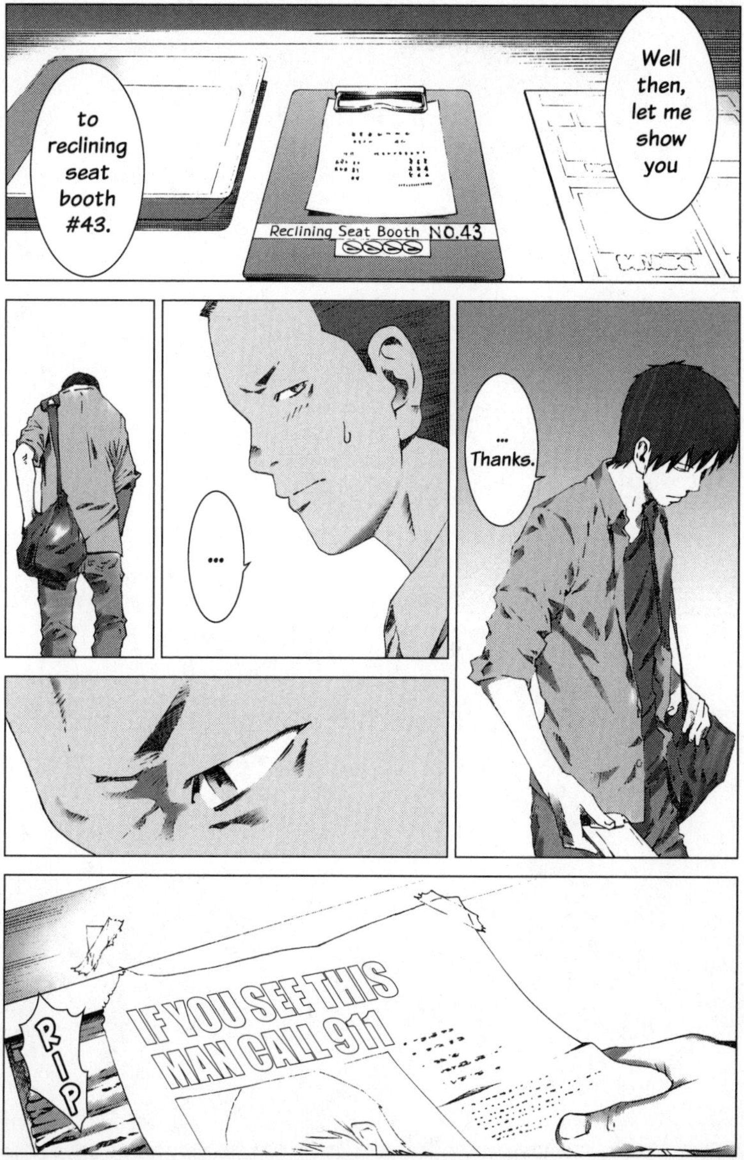
Well then, let me show you
to reclining seat booth #43.
Reclining Seat Booth NO.43
... Thanks.
...
RIP
IF YOU SEE THIS MAN CALL 911

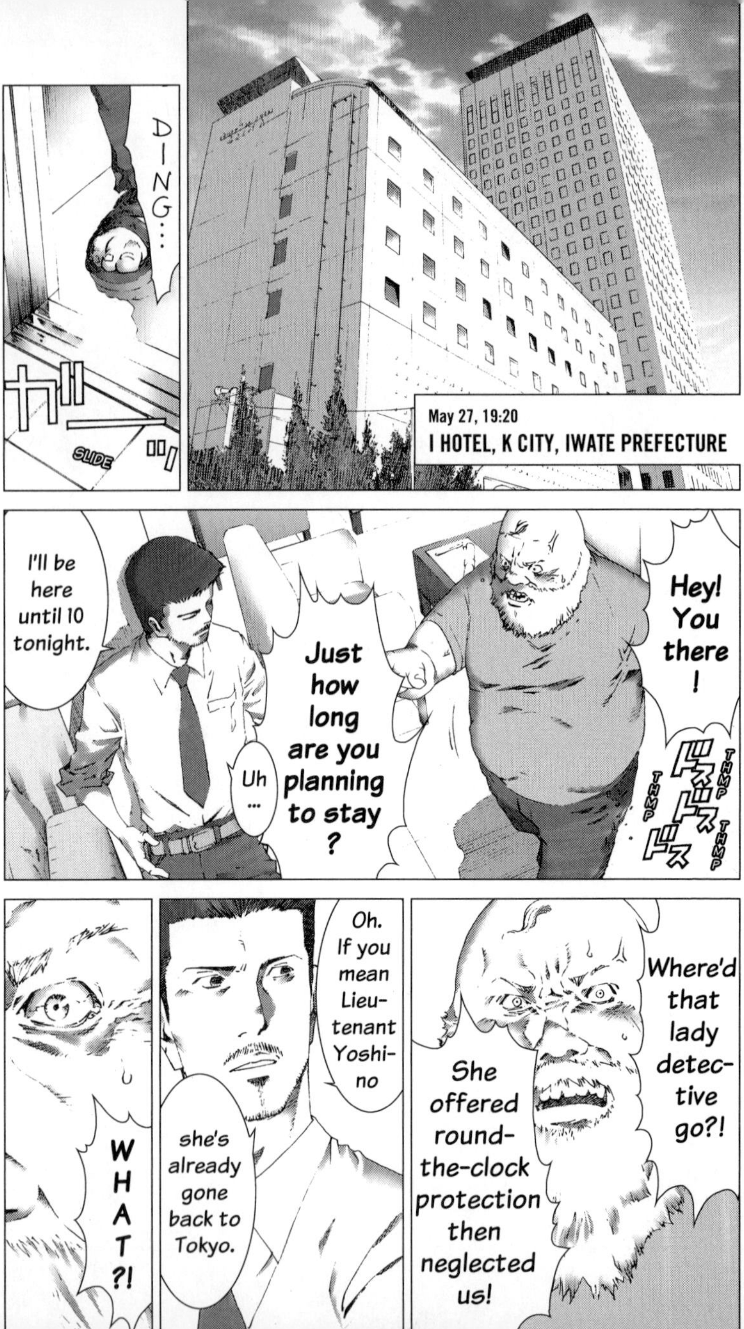
May 27, 19:20
I HOTEL, K CITY, IWATE PREFECTURE
DING...
SLIDE
Hey! You there!
THMP
THMP
THMP
Just how long are you planning to stay?
Uh...
I'll be here until 10 tonight.
Where'd that lady detective go?!
She offered round-the-clock protection then neglected us!
Oh. If you mean Lieutenant Yoshino
she's already gone back to Tokyo.
WHAT?!

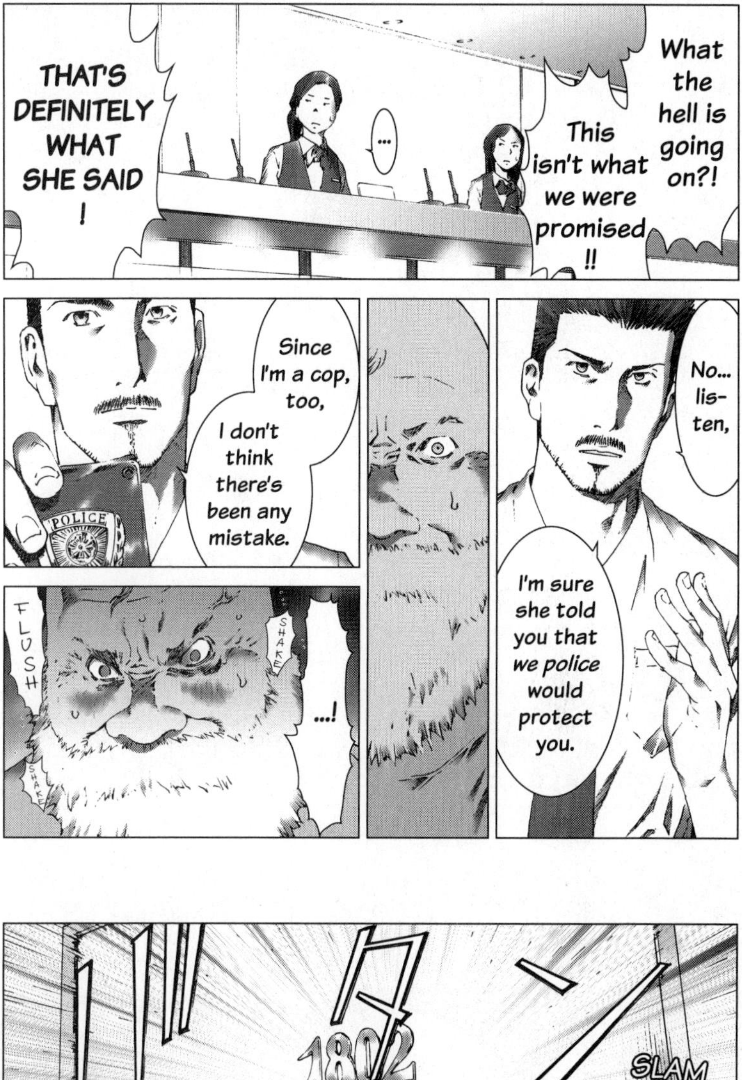
What the hell is going on?!
This isn't what we were promised!!
...
THAT'S DEFINITELY WHAT SHE SAID!
No... lis- ten,
I'm sure she told you that we police would protect you.
Since I'm a cop, too, I don't think there's been any mistake.
POLICE
SHAKE
...!
FLUSH
SHAKE
1802
SLAM

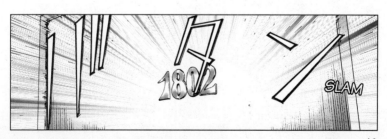

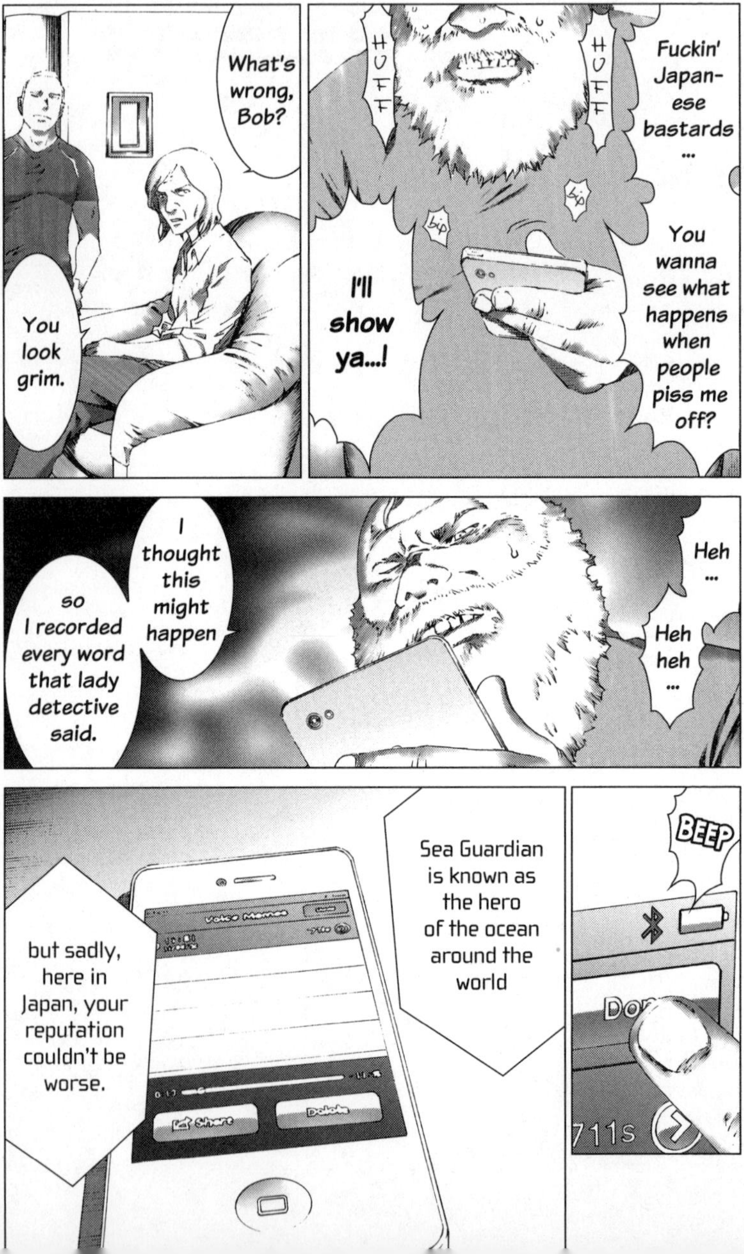

HUFF
HUFF
Fuckin' Japan-ese bastards...
bip
bip
You wanna see what happens when people piss me off?
I'll show ya...!
What's wrong, Bob?
You look grim.
Heh...
Heh heh...
I thought this might happen
so I recorded every word that lady detective said.
BEEP
711s
Sea Guardian is known as the hero of the ocean around the world
but sadly, here in Japan, your reputation couldn't be worse.

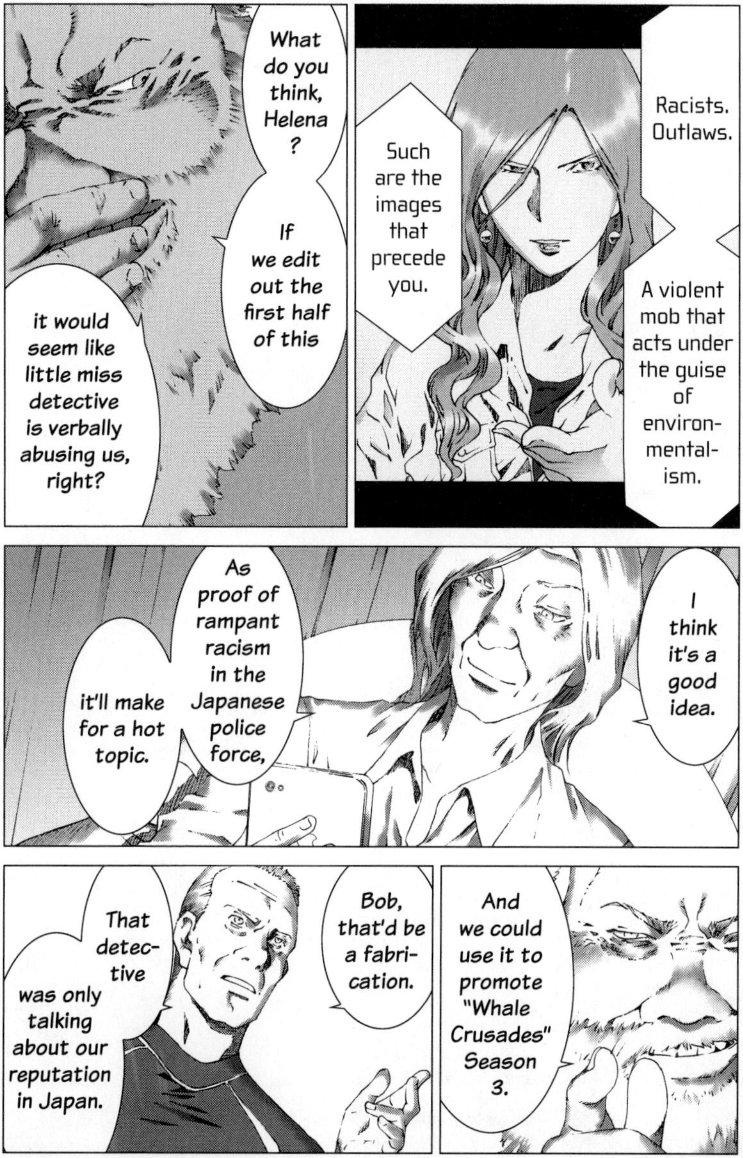

Racists. Outlaws.
A violent mob that acts under the guise of environmentalism.
Such are the images that precede you.
What do you think, Helena?
If we edit out the first half of this
it would seem like little miss detective is verbally abusing us, right?
I think it's a good idea.
As proof of rampant racism in the Japanese police force,
it'll make for a hot topic.
And we could use it to promote "Whale Crusades" Season 3.
Bob, that'd be a fabrication.
That detective was only talking about our reputation in Japan.

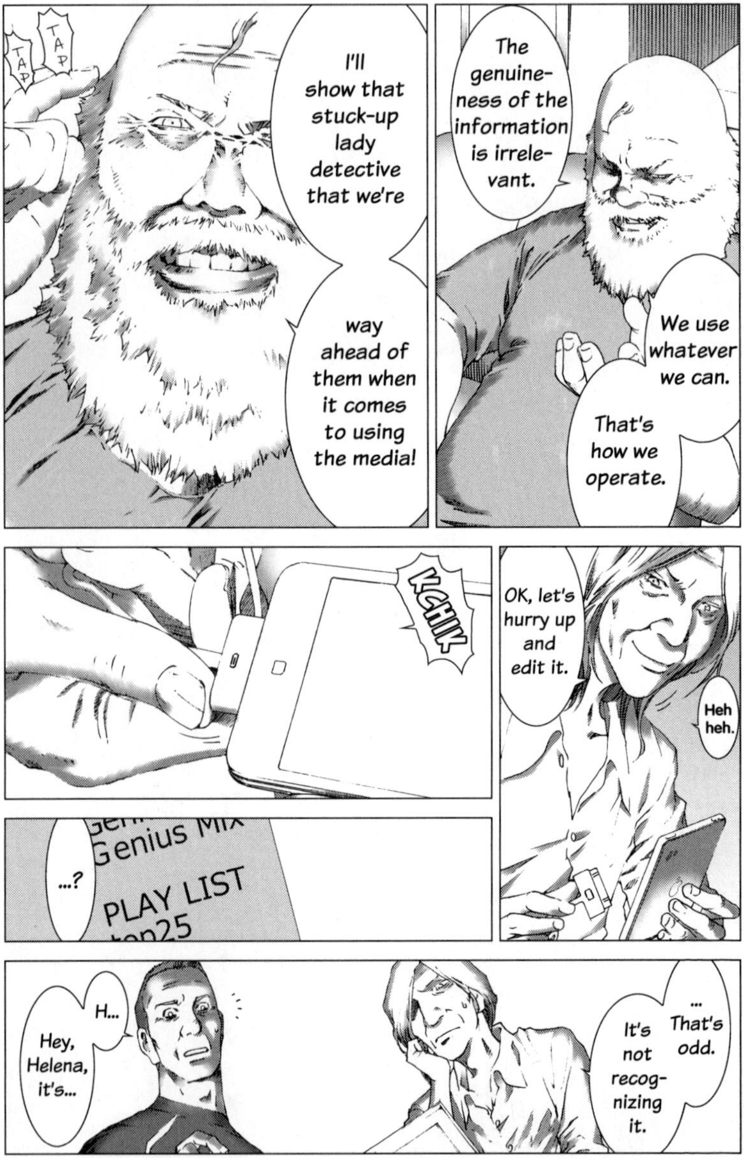
The genuineness of the information is irrelevant.
We use whatever we can.
That's how we operate.
TAP
TAP
I'll show that stuck-up lady detective that we're
way ahead of them when it comes to using the media!
OK, let's hurry up and edit it.
Heh heh.
KCHIK
Genius Mix
PLAY LIST
...?
... That's odd.
It's not recognizing it.
H...
Hey, Helena, it's...

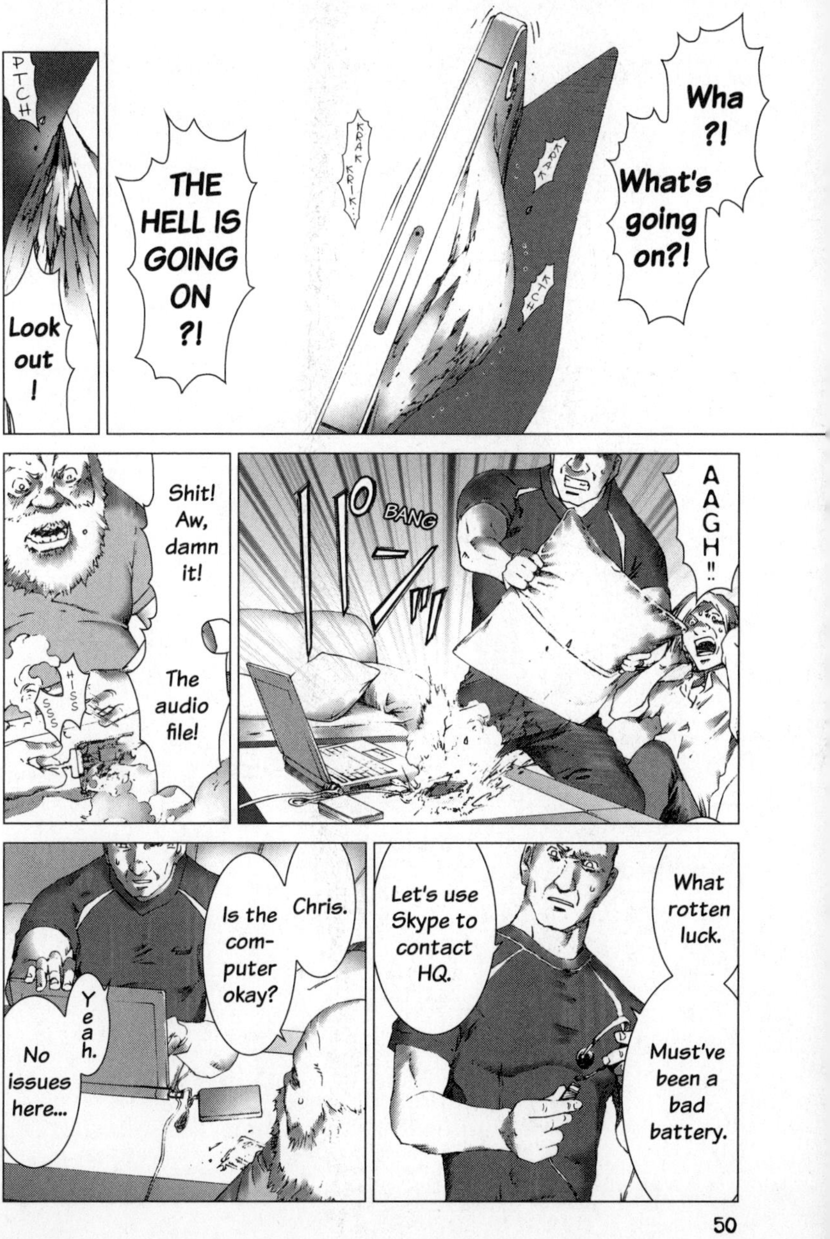

Wha ?!
What's going on?!
KRAK
KRAK KRIK...
KTCH
THE HELL IS GOING ON ?!
PTCH
Look out !
AAGH!!
BANG
Shit! Aw, damn it!
The audio file!
HISS SSS
What rotten luck.
Let's use Skype to contact HQ.
Must've been a bad battery.
Chris.
Is the computer okay?
Yeah.
No issues here...

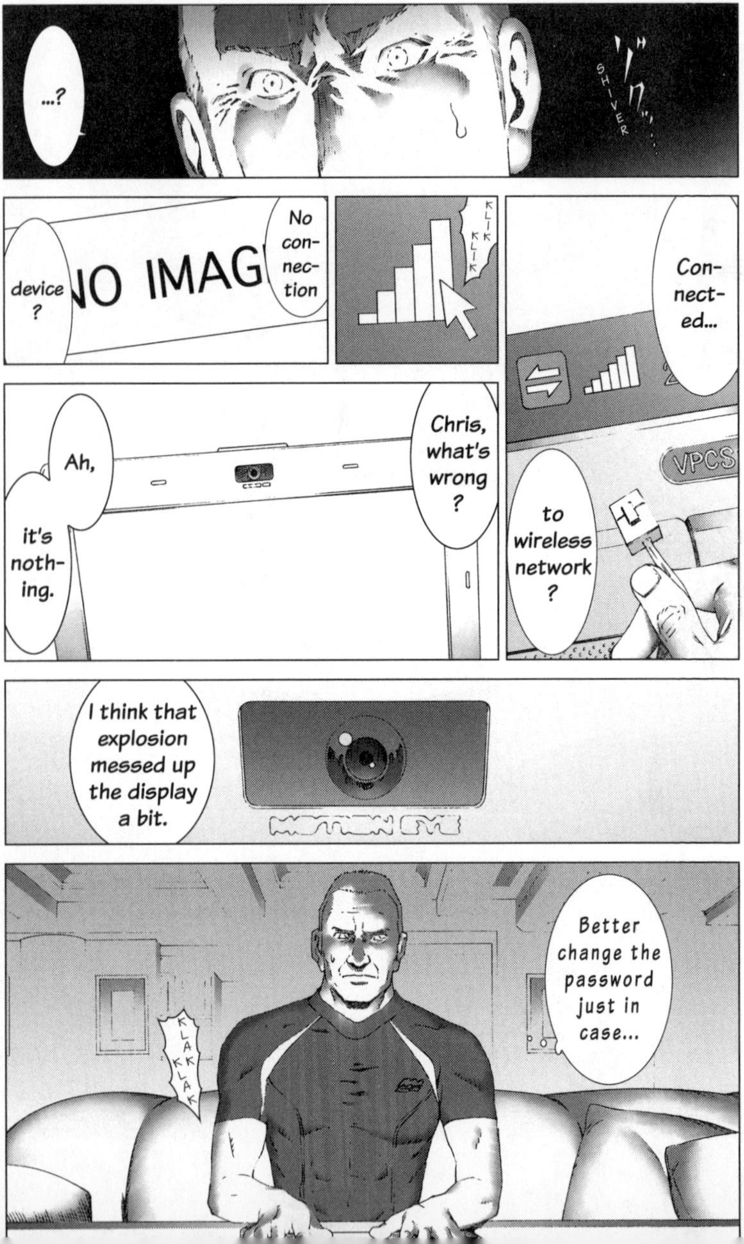
SHIVER
...?
Con-nect-ed...
to wireless network?
KLIK KLIK
No con-nec-tion
NO IMAG
device?
Chris, what's wrong?
Ah,
it's noth-ing.
I think that explosion messed up the display a bit.
Better change the password just in case...
KLAK KLAK

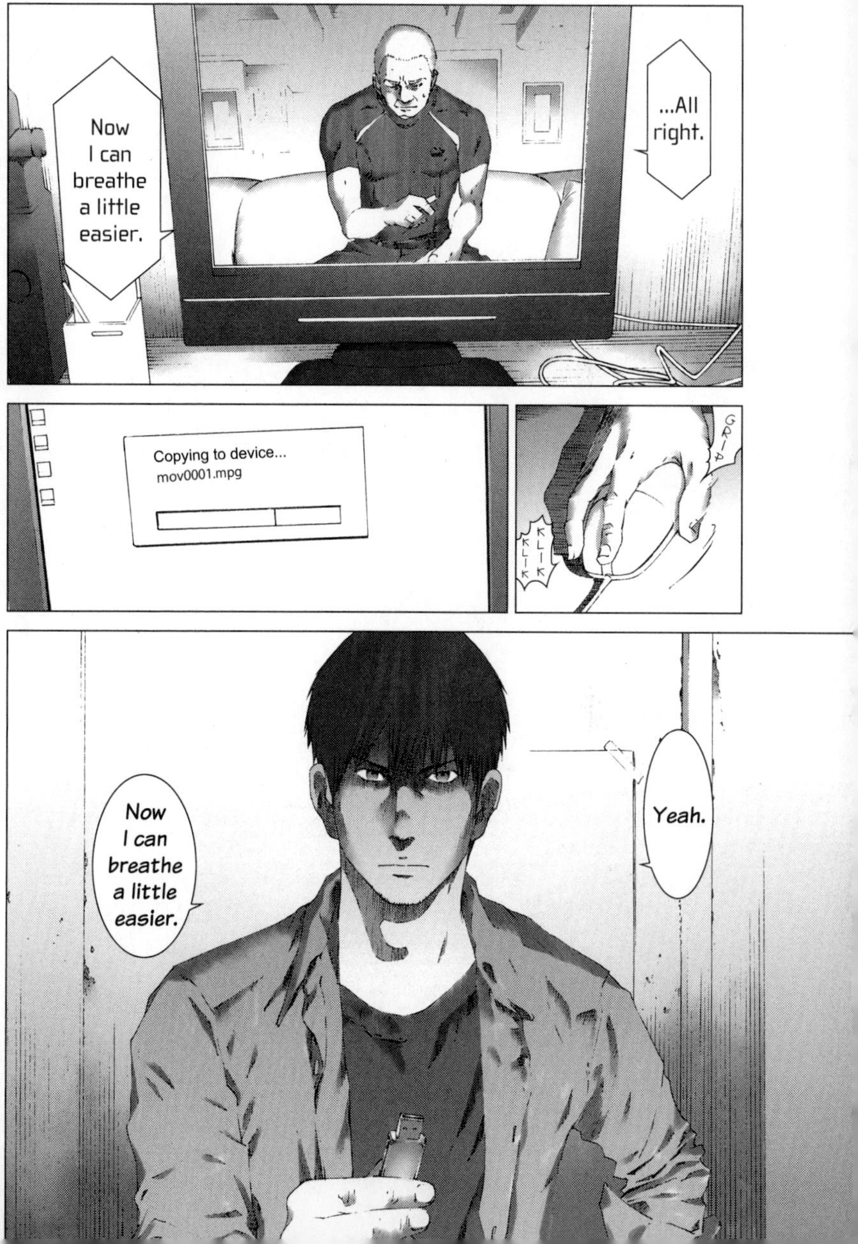
...All right.
Now I can breathe a little easier.
GRIP
KLIK KLIK
Copying to device...
mov0001.mpg
Yeah.
Now I can breathe a little easier.

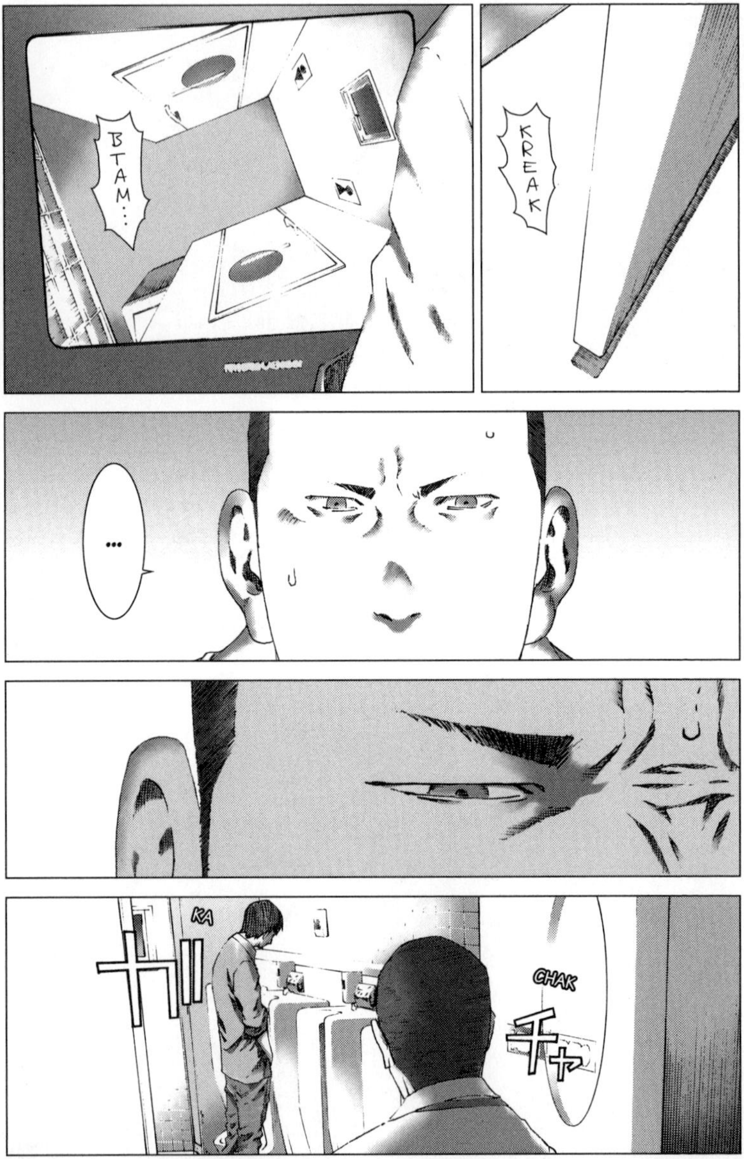
KREAK
BTAM...
...
CHAK
KA

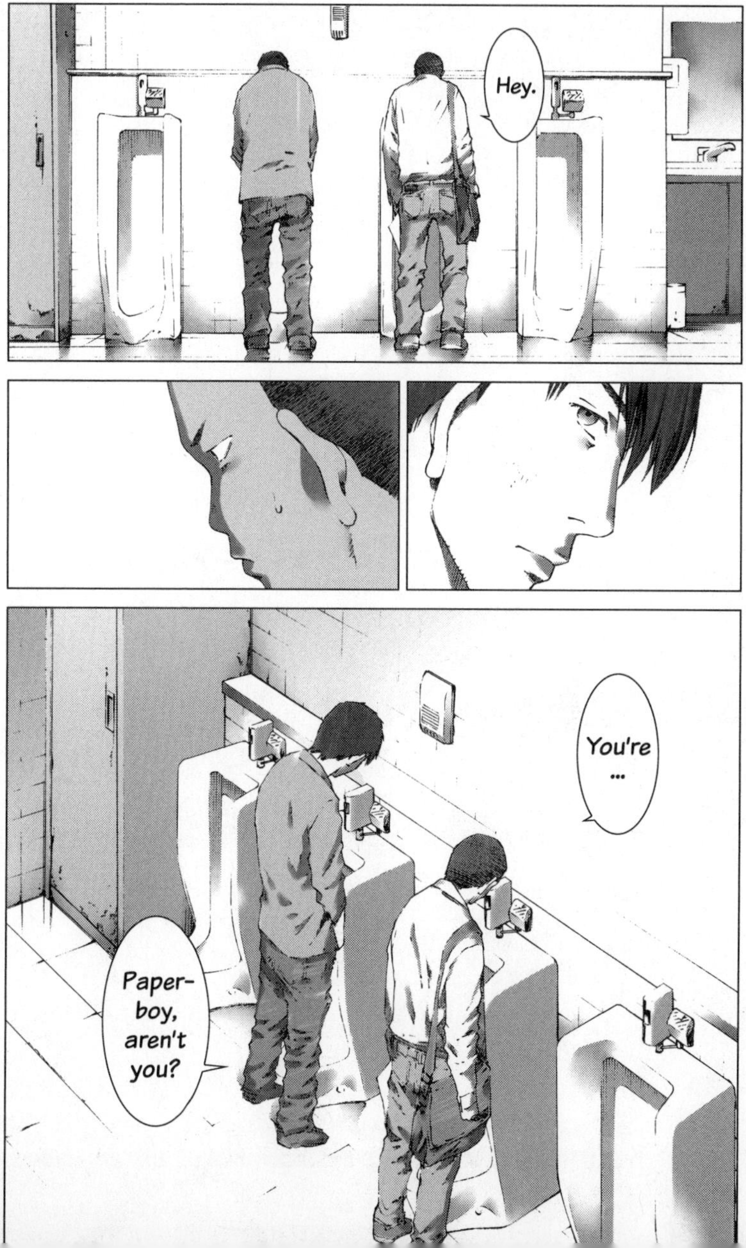
Hey.
You're ...
Paper-boy, aren't you?

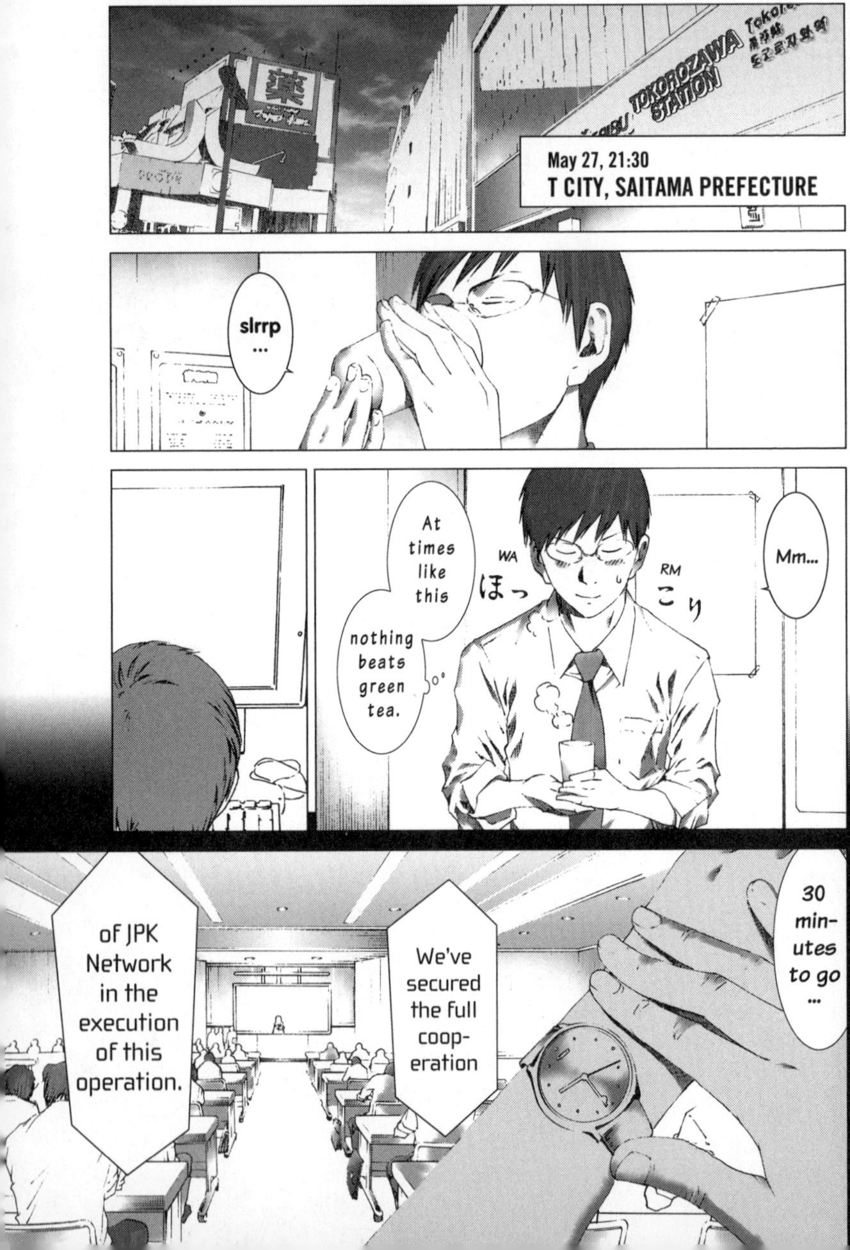
TOKOROZAWA
STATION
May 27, 21:30
T CITY, SAITAMA PREFECTURE
slrrp...
Mm...
RM こり
At times like this nothing beats green tea.
WA ほっ
30 minutes to go...
We've secured the full cooperation
of JPK Network in the execution of this operation.

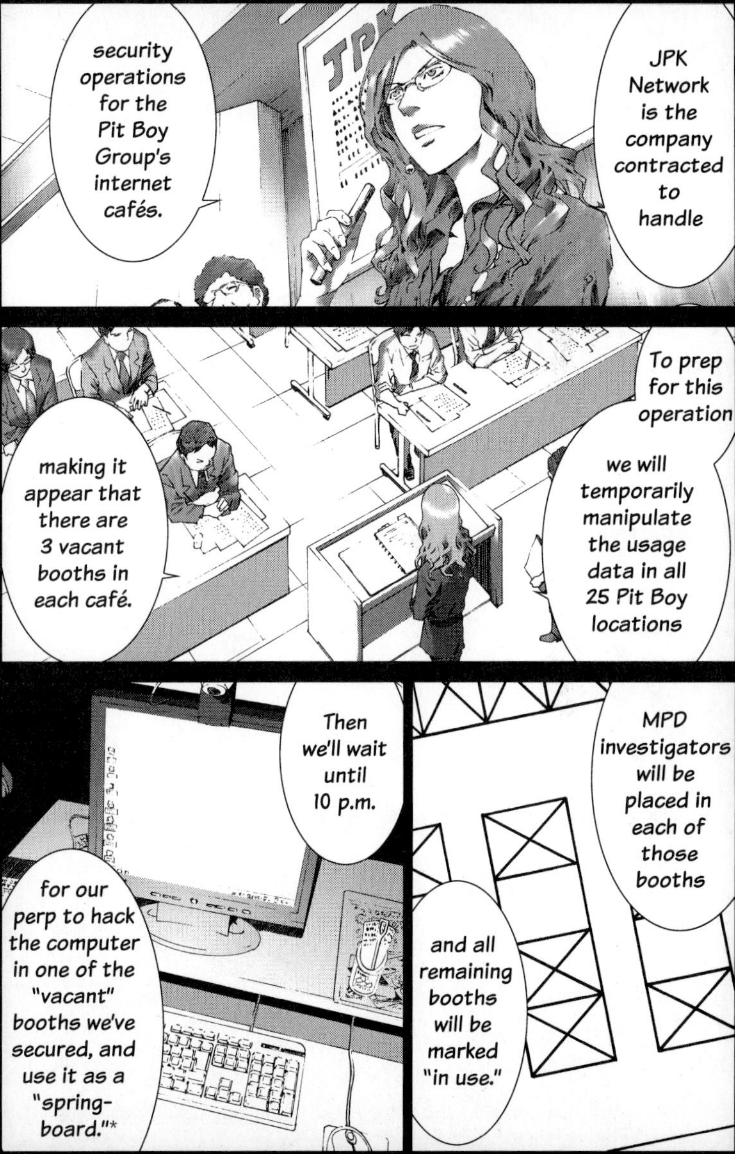
JPK Network is the company contracted to handle
security operations for the Pit Boy Group's internet cafés.
To prep for this operation
we will temporarily manipulate the usage data in all 25 Pit Boy locations
making it appear that there are 3 vacant booths in each café.
MPD investigators will be placed in each of those booths
and all remaining booths will be marked "in use."
Then we'll wait until 10 p.m.
for our perp to hack the computer in one of the "vacant" booths we've secured, and use it as a "spring-board."*

* A computer used as a relay point to conduct unlawful activity with another computer.

When the perp starts his infiltration, we'll trace the source.
When we've worked out his actual location, we'll contact the agents at that café
and the perp will be apprehended and arrested on site.
All investigators on standby
are to look for changes in the resource monitors and not touch their computers at all.
We can infer that the computer that displays network resource activity at 10 p.m.
is the one the perpetrator has selected as his "springboard."
Network Connection
CHIK
CHIK
Adapter Name Network Usage Speed Status

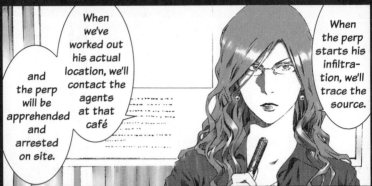

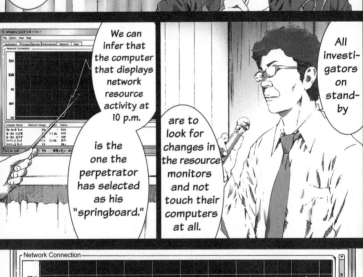

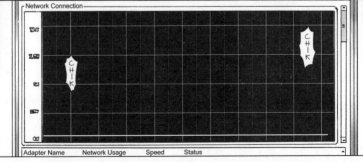

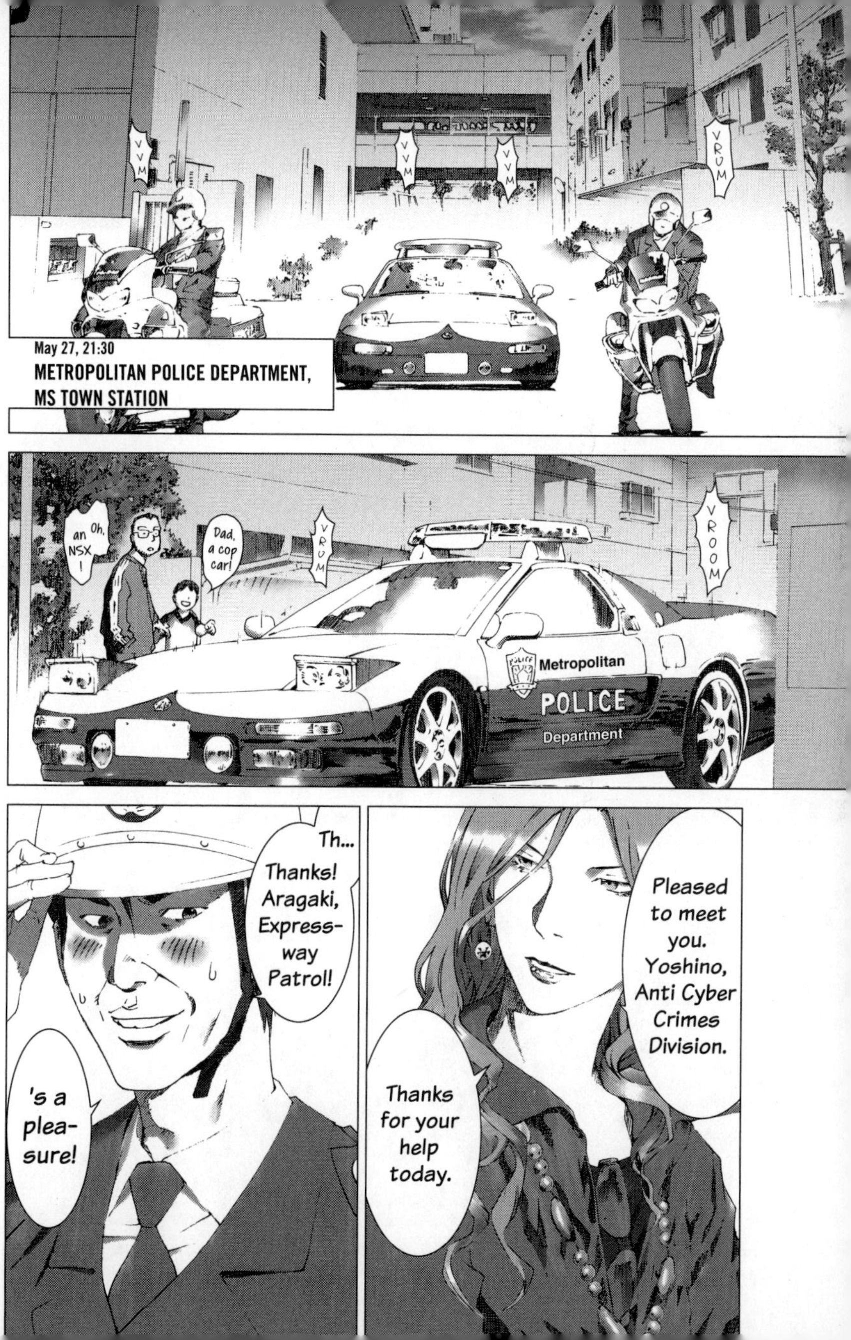

May 27, 21:30
METROPOLITAN POLICE DEPARTMENT, MS TOWN STATION
VRUM
VVM
VVM
VVM
VROOM
VRUM
Dad, a cop car!
Oh, an NSX!
Metropolitan POLICE Department
Pleased to meet you. Yoshino, Anti Cyber Crimes Division.
Thanks for your help today.
Th... Thanks! Aragaki, Express-way Patrol!
's a plea-sure!

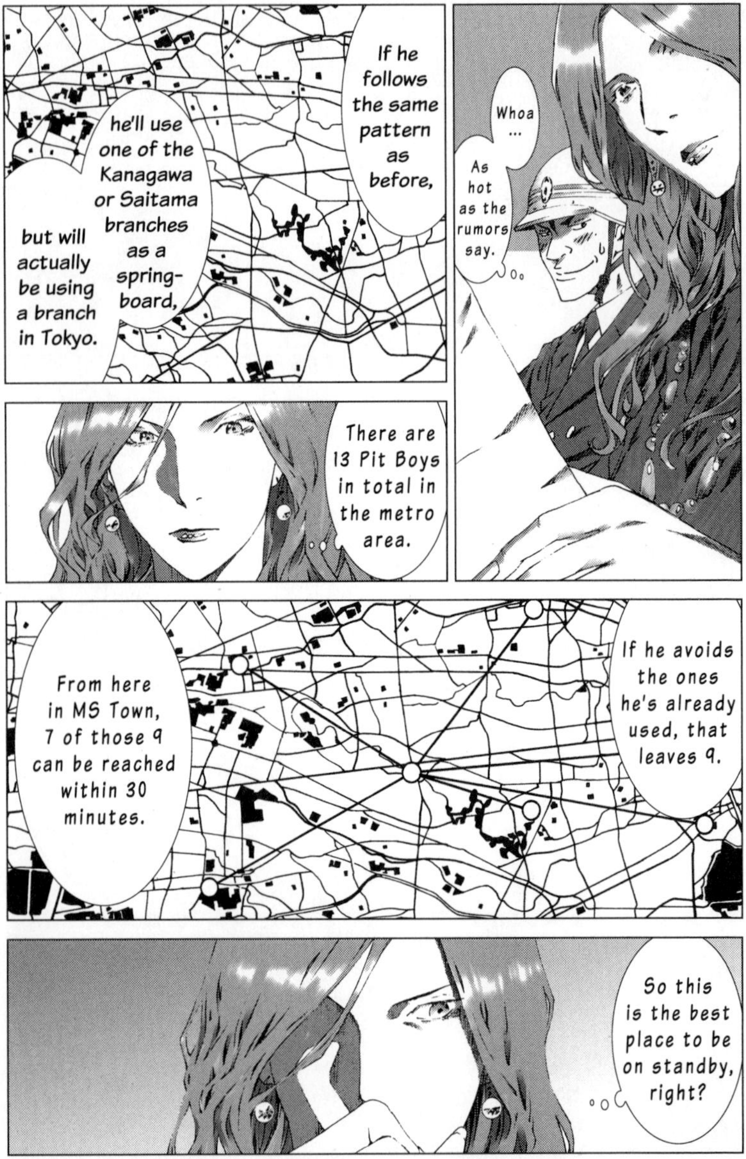
Whoa ...
As hot as the rumors say.
If he follows the same pattern as before,
he'll use one of the Kanagawa or Saitama branches as a spring-board,
but will actually be using a branch in Tokyo.
There are 13 Pit Boys in total in the metro area.
If he avoids the ones he's already used, that leaves 9.
From here in MS Town, 7 of those 9 can be reached within 30 minutes.
So this is the best place to be on standby, right?

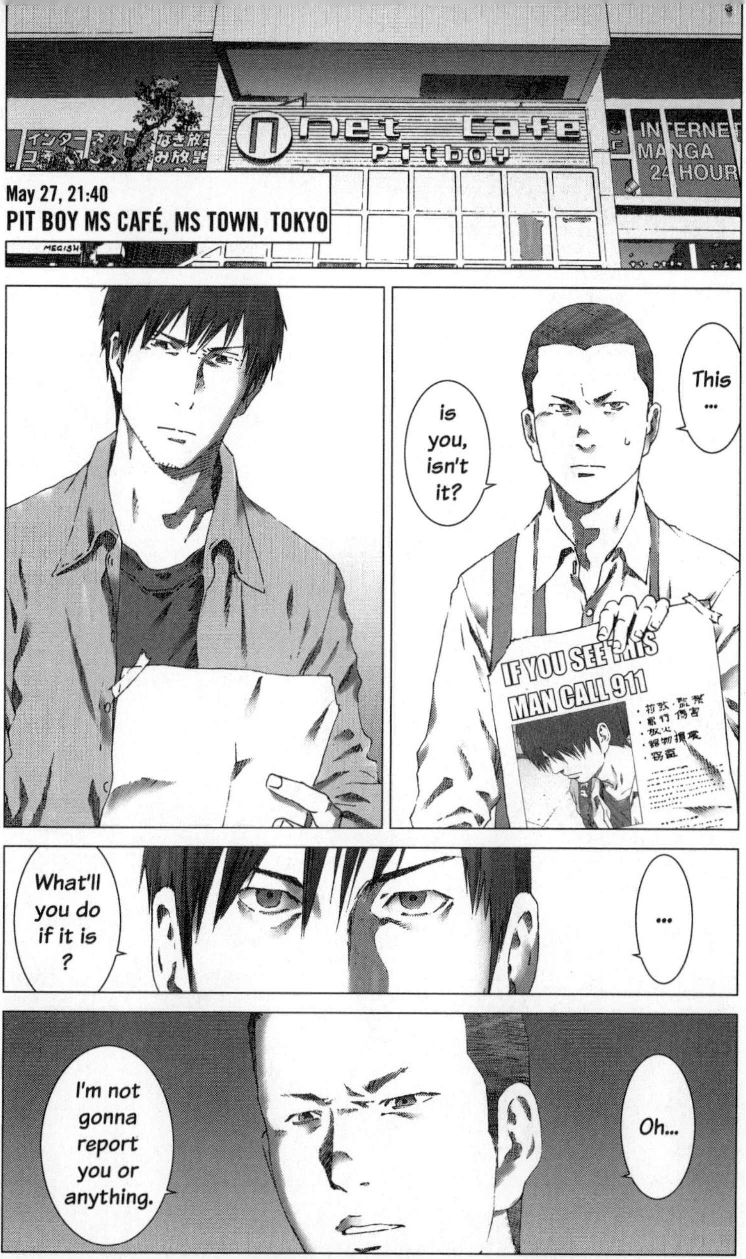
net Cafe
Pitboy
INTERNET
MANGA
24 HOUR
May 27, 21:40
PIT BOY MS CAFÉ, MS TOWN, TOKYO
This ...
is you, isn't it?
IF YOU SEE THIS MAN CALL 911
...
What'll you do if it is ?
Oh...
I'm not gonna report you or anything.

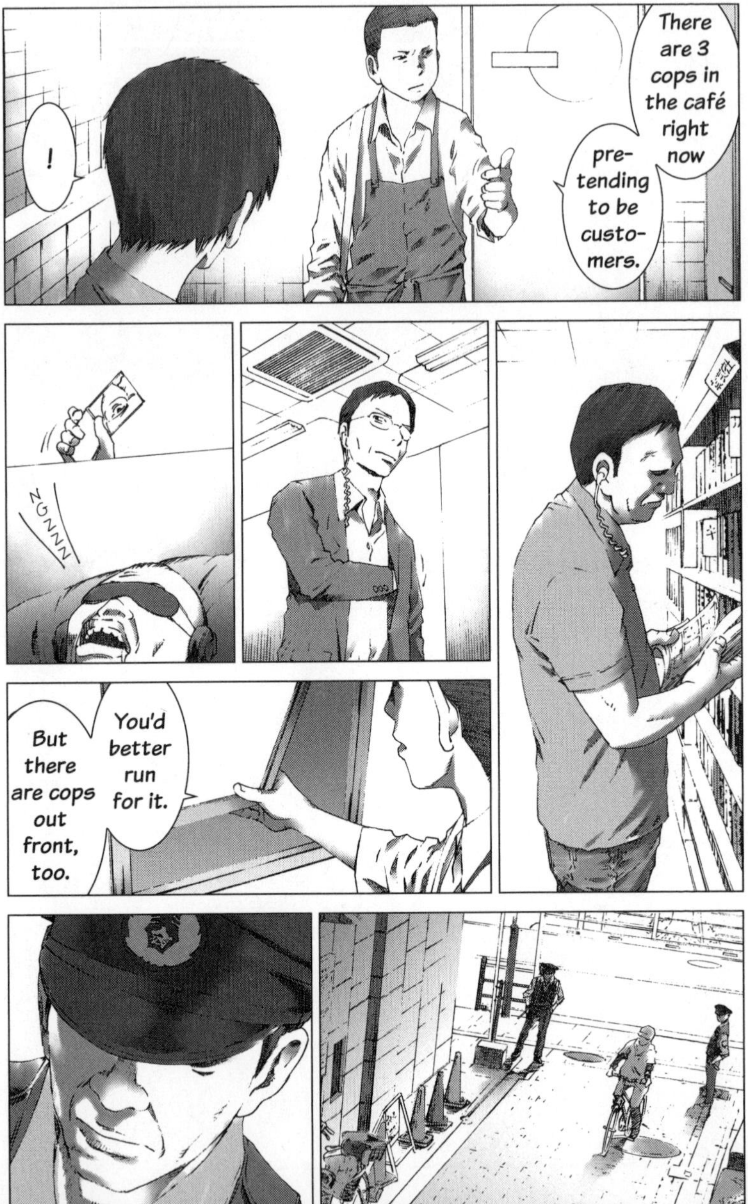
There are 3 cops in the café right now
pretending to be customers.
!
NGZZZ
You'd better run for it.
But there are cops out front, too.

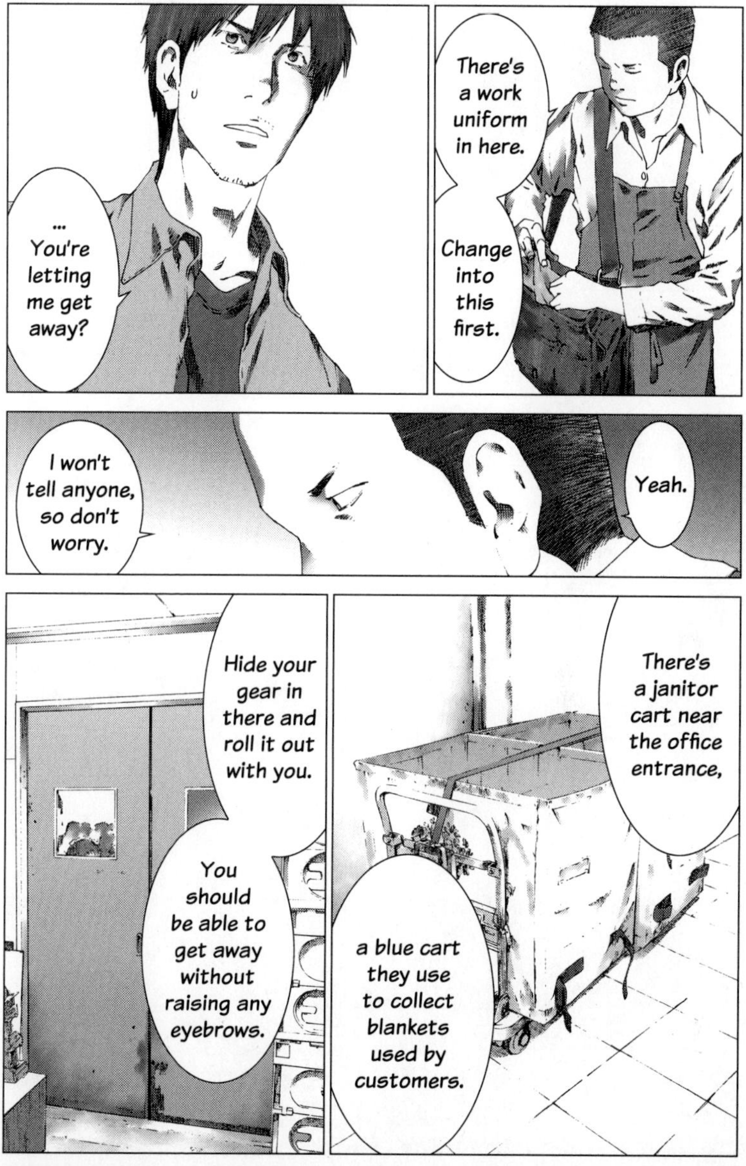
There's a work uniform in here.
Change into this first.
... You're letting me get away?
Yeah.
I won't tell anyone, so don't worry.
There's a janitor cart near the office entrance,
a blue cart they use to collect blankets used by customers.
Hide your gear in there and roll it out with you.
You should be able to get away without raising any eyebrows.

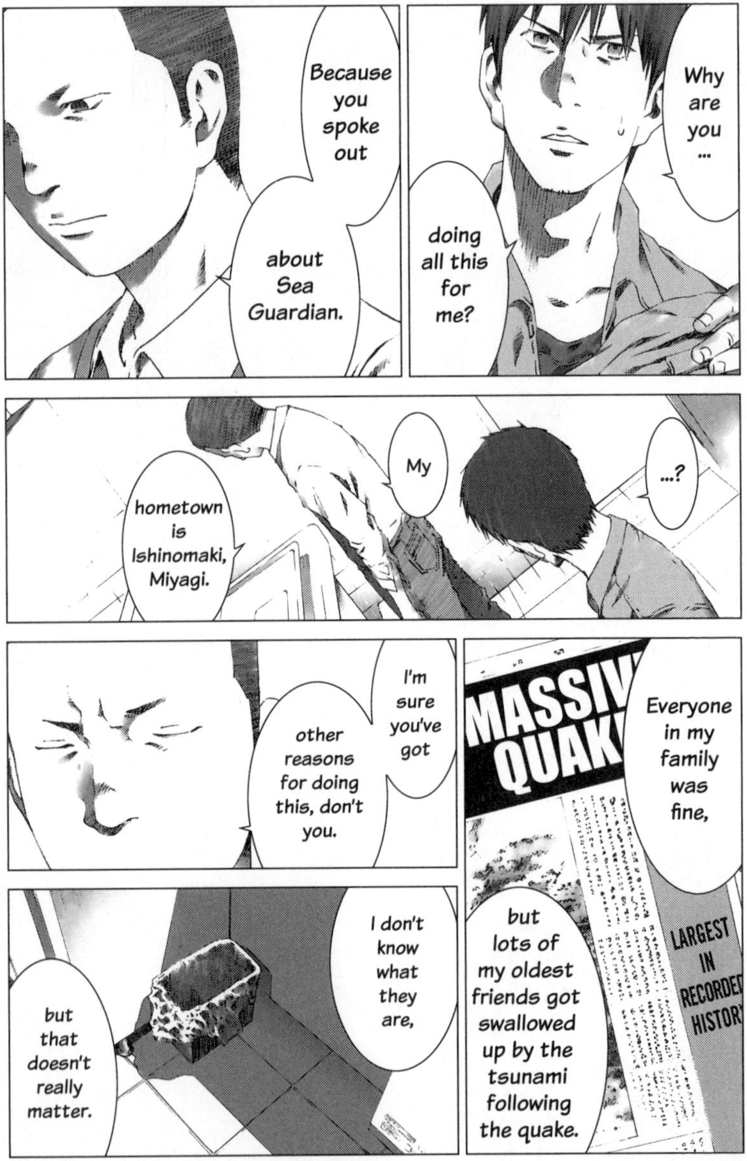
Why are you ...
doing all this for me?
Because you spoke out
about Sea Guardian.
...?
My
hometown is Ishinomaki, Miyagi.
MASSIV QUAK
LARGEST IN RECORDE HISTOR
Everyone in my family was fine,
but lots of my oldest friends got swallowed up by the tsunami following the quake.
I'm sure you've got
other reasons for doing this, don't you.
I don't know what they are,
but that doesn't really matter.

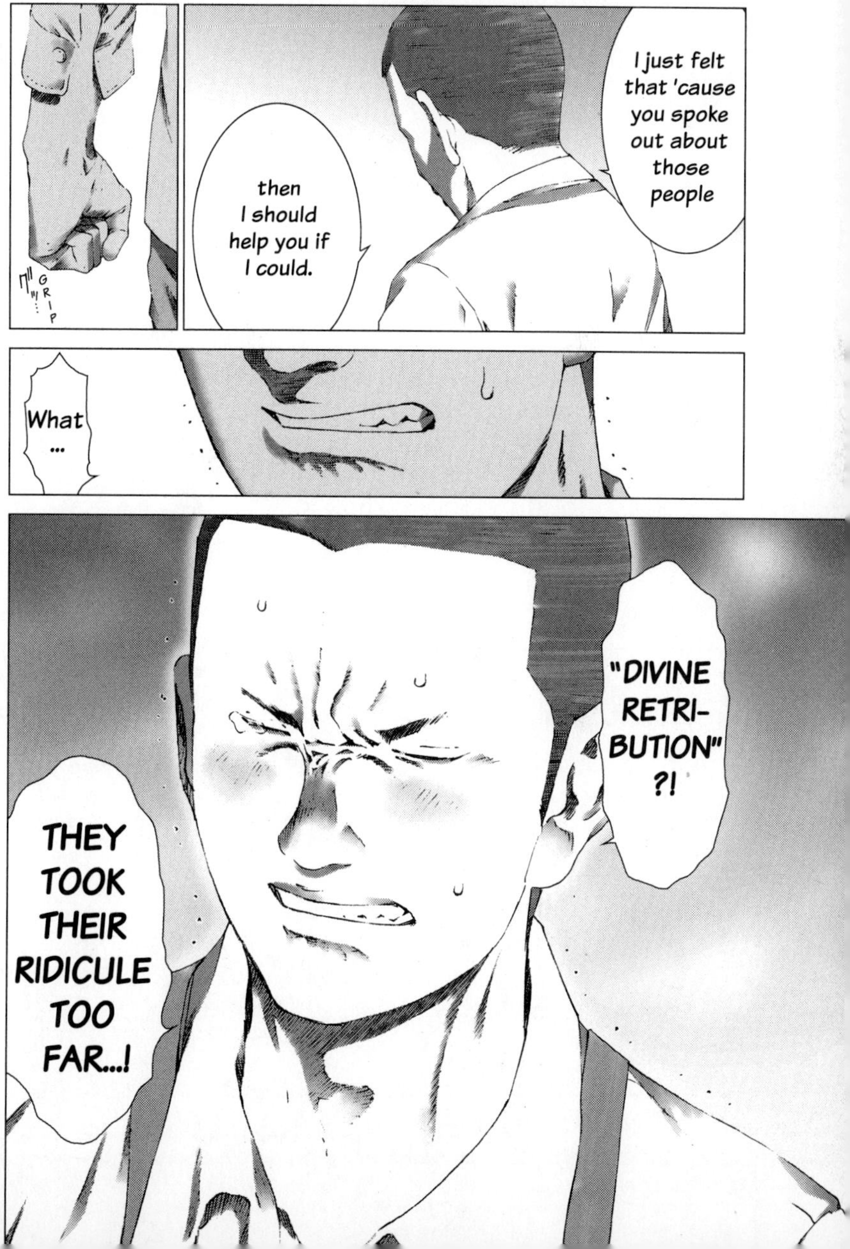
I just felt that 'cause you spoke out about those people
then I should help you if I could.
GRIP
What...
"DIVINE RETRIBUTION"?!
THEY TOOK THEIR RIDICULE TOO FAR...!

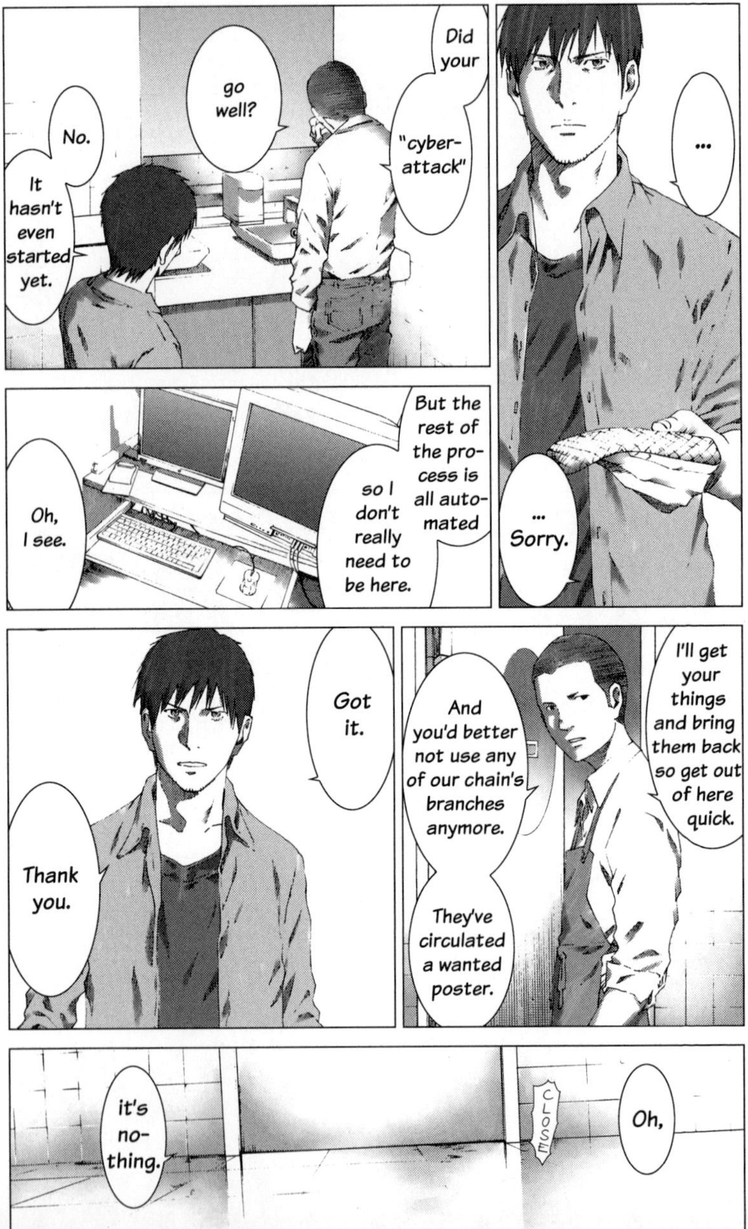
...
... Sorry.
Did your
"cyber-attack"
go well?
No.
It hasn't even started yet.
But the rest of the process is all automated
so I don't really need to be here.
Oh, I see.
I'll get your things and bring them back so get out of here quick.
And you'd better not use any of our chain's branches anymore.
They've circulated a wanted poster.
Got it.
Thank you.
Oh,
CLOSE
it's nothing.

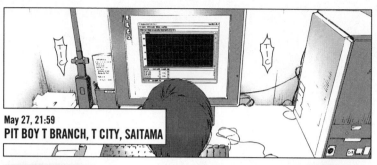

May 27, 21:59
PIT BOY T BRANCH, T CITY, SAITAMA

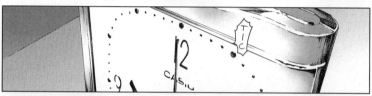

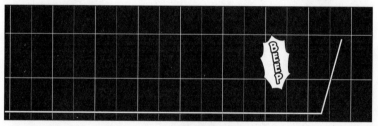

BEEP

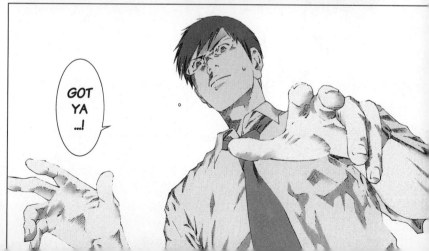

GOT YA ...!

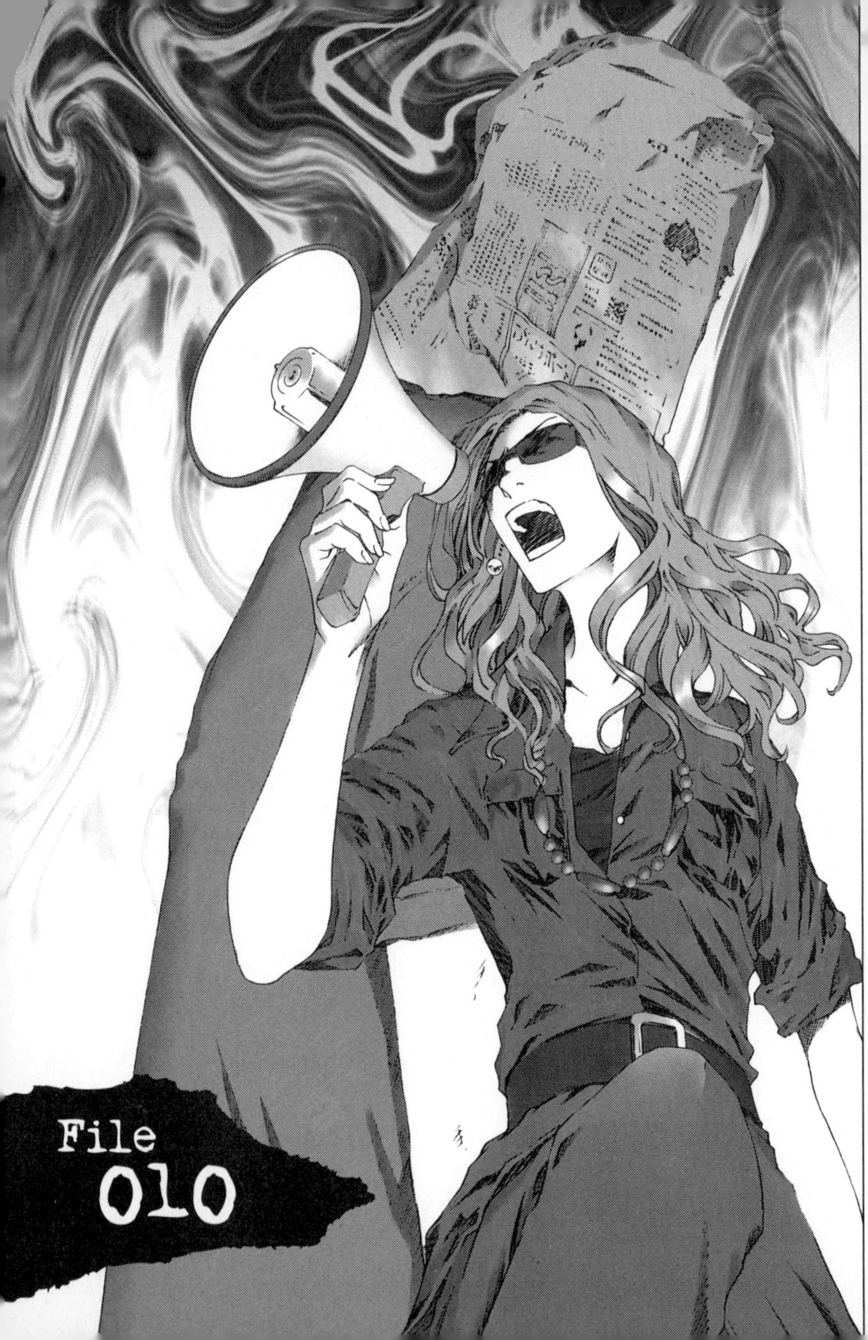
File
010

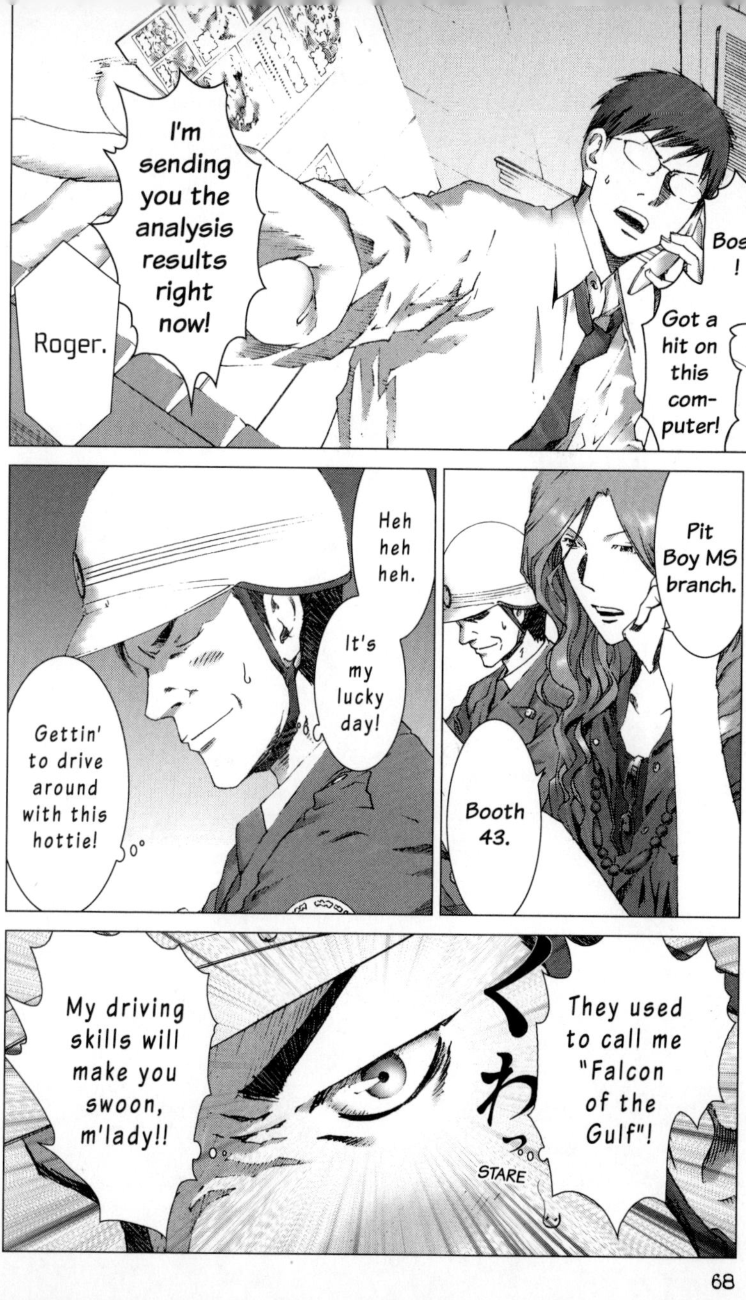
Boss!
Got a hit on this computer!
I'm sending you the analysis results right now!
Roger.
Pit Boy MS branch.
Booth 43.
Heh heh heh.
It's my lucky day!
Gettin' to drive around with this hottie!
They used to call me "Falcon of the Gulf"!
くわっ
STARE
My driving skills will make you swoon, m'lady!!

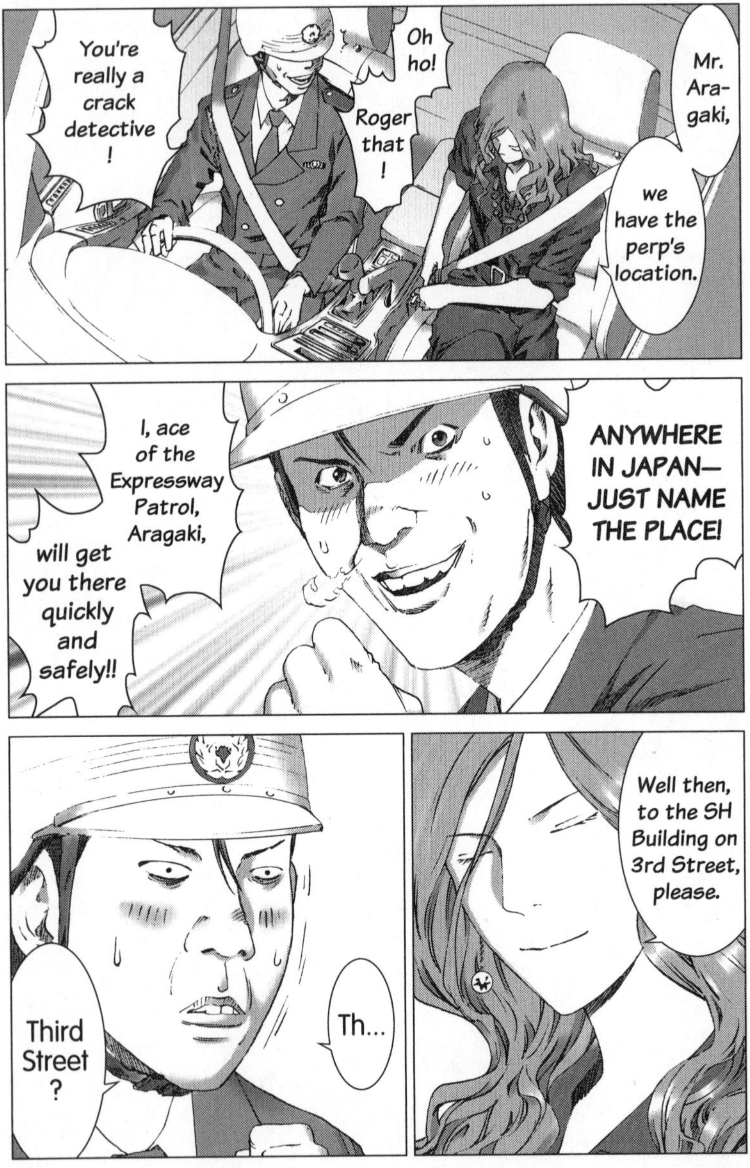
Mr. Aragaki,
we have the perp's location.
Oh ho!
Roger that!
You're really a crack detective!
ANYWHERE IN JAPAN— JUST NAME THE PLACE!
I, ace of the Expressway Patrol, Aragaki,
will get you there quickly and safely!!
Well then, to the SH Building on 3rd Street, please.
Th...
Third Street?

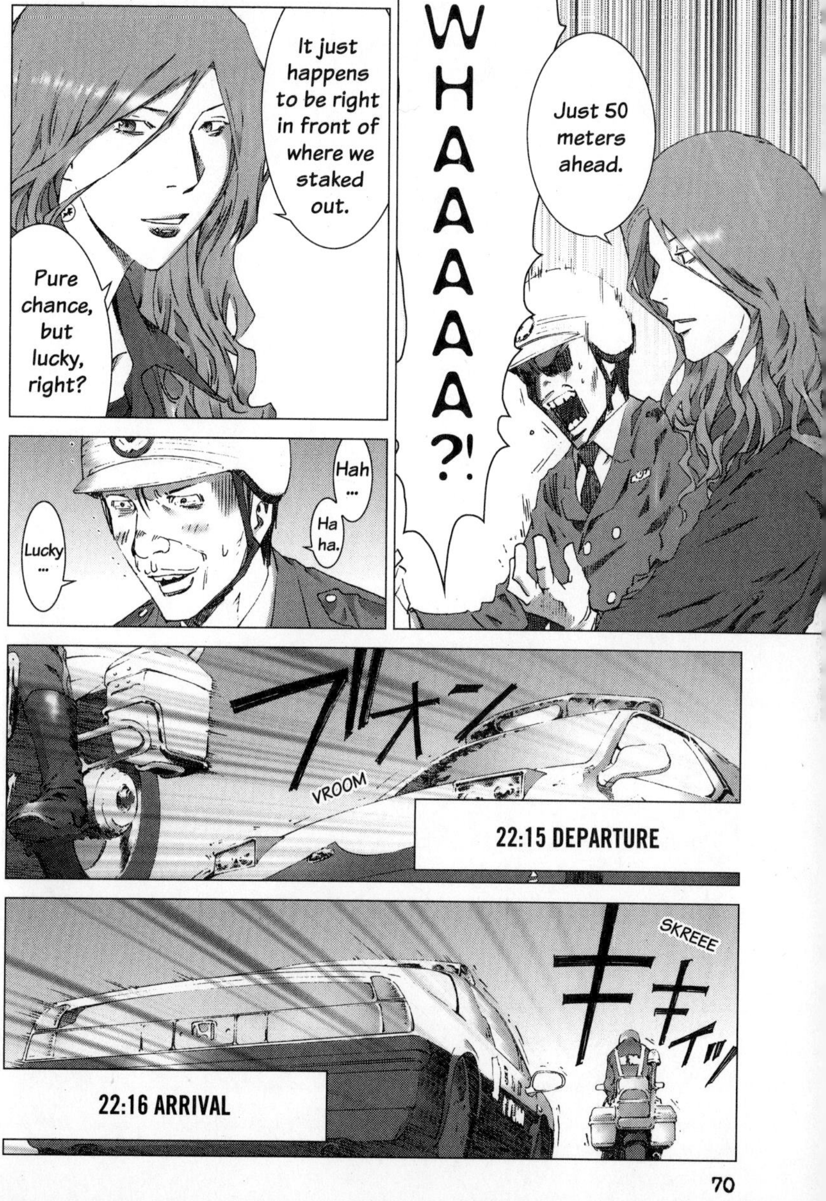
Just 50 meters ahead.
WHAAAAA?!
It just happens to be right in front of where we staked out.
Pure chance, but lucky, right?
Hah... Ha ha.
Lucky...
ブルオーン
VROOM
22:15 DEPARTURE
キキイッ
SKREEE
22:16 ARRIVAL

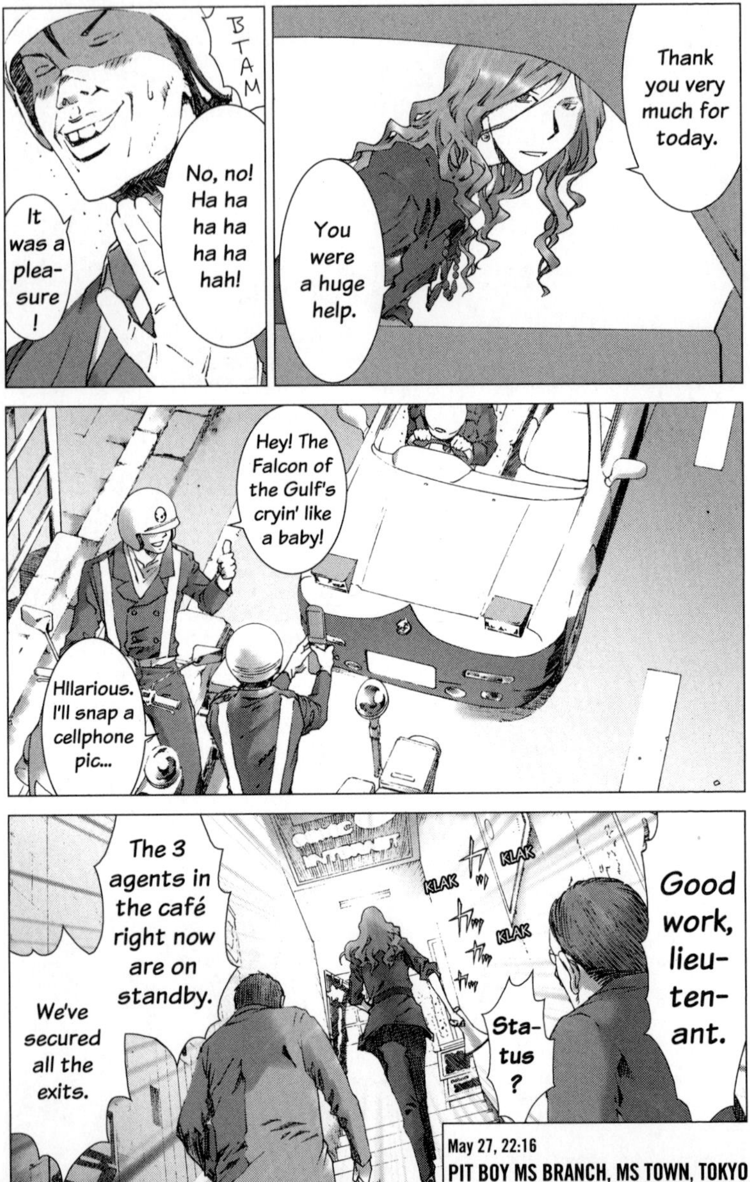

Thank you very much for today.
You were a huge help.
BTAM
No, no! Ha ha ha ha ha ha hah!
It was a plea-sure!
Hey! The Falcon of the Gulf's cryin' like a baby!
Hllarious. I'll snap a cellphone pic...
Good work, lieu-ten-ant.
Sta-tus?
KLAK
KLAK
KLAK
The 3 agents in the café right now are on standby.
We've secured all the exits.
May 27, 22:16
PIT BOY MS BRANCH, MS TOWN, TOKYO

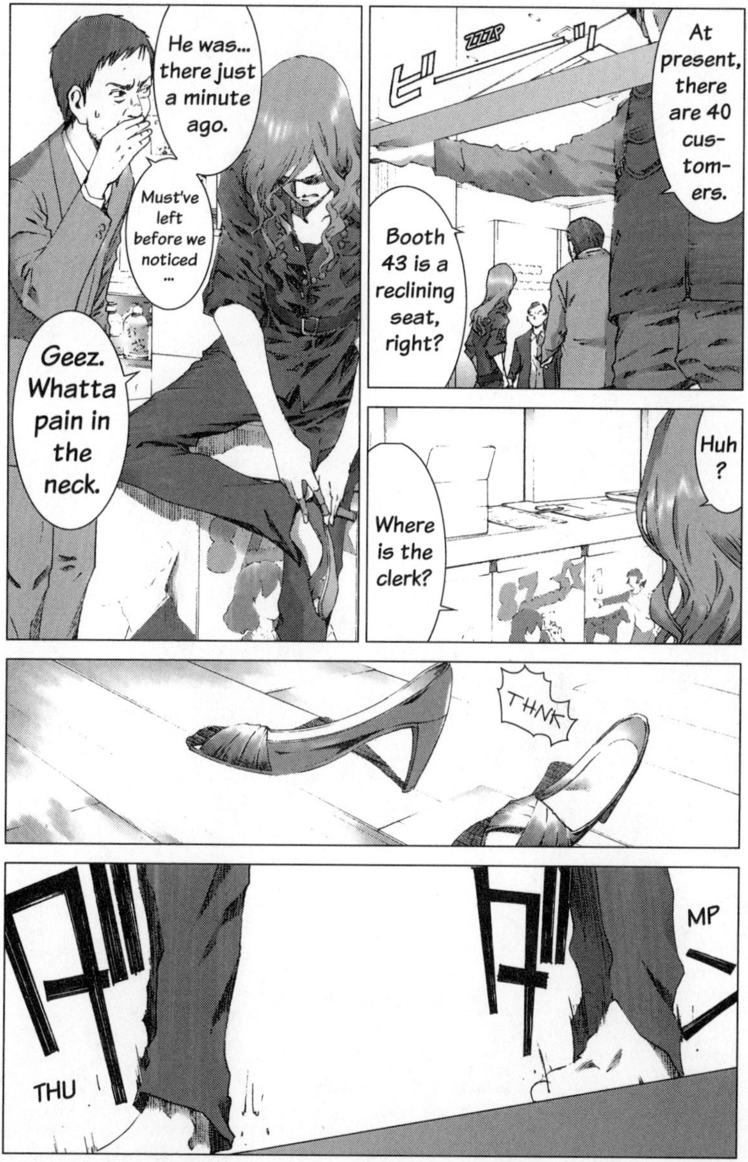
ZZZAP
At present, there are 40 cus-tom-ers.
Booth 43 is a reclining seat, right?
Huh?
Where is the clerk?
He was... there just a minute ago.
Must've left before we noticed ...
Geez. Whatta pain in the neck.
THNK
MP
THU

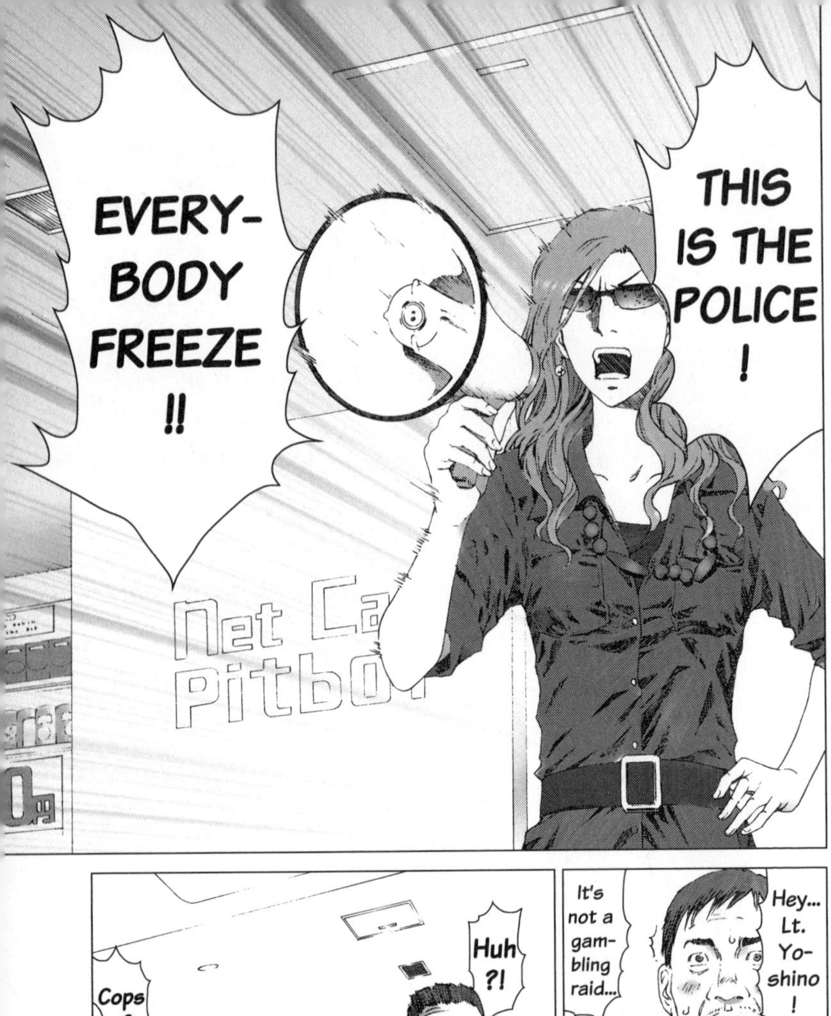
THIS IS THE POLICE !
EVERY-BODY FREEZE !!
Net Ca Pitbo
Hey... Lt. Yo-shino !
What are you doing ?!
It's not a gam-bling raid...
Huh ?!
Cops ?
39

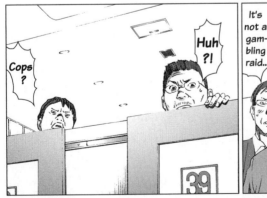

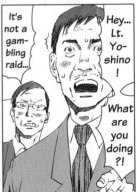

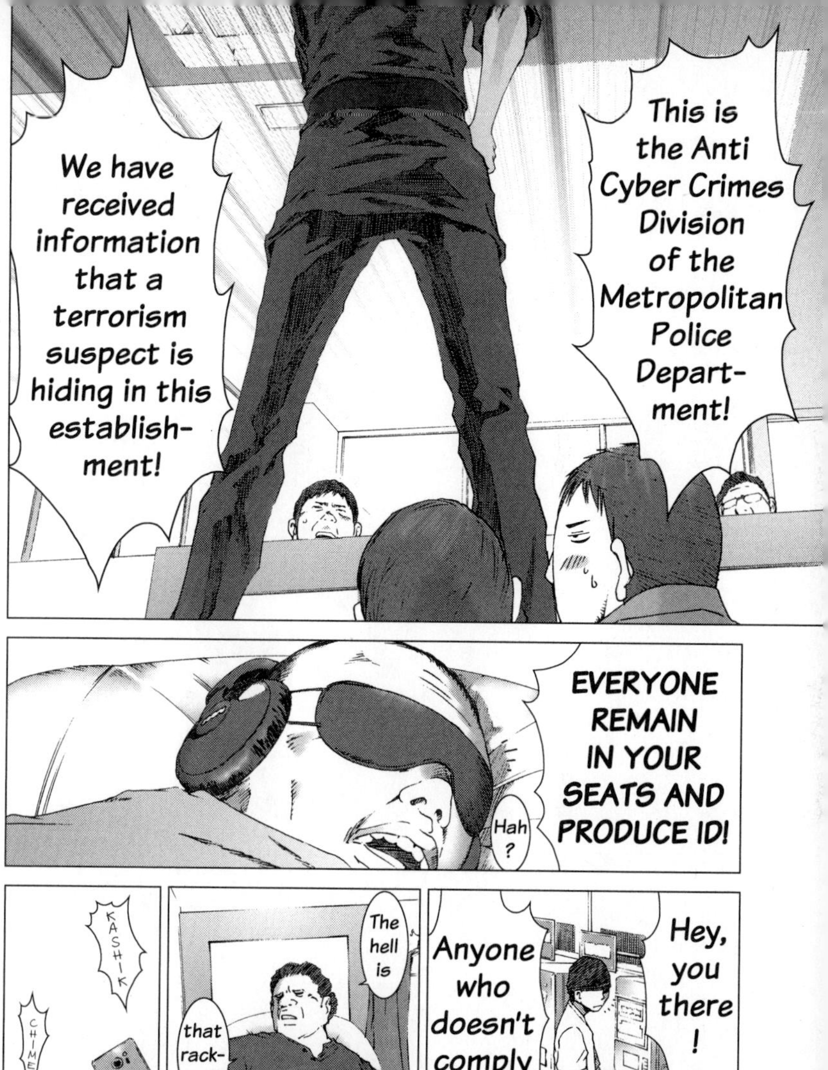
This is the Anti Cyber Crimes Division of the Metropolitan Police Department!
We have received information that a terrorism suspect is hiding in this establishment!
EVERYONE REMAIN IN YOUR SEATS AND PRODUCE ID!
Hah?
Hey, you there!
Get back to your seat!
Anyone who doesn't comply will be detained!
The hell is
that racket?
KASHIK
CHIME

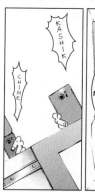

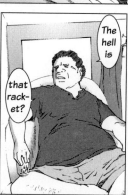

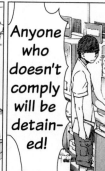

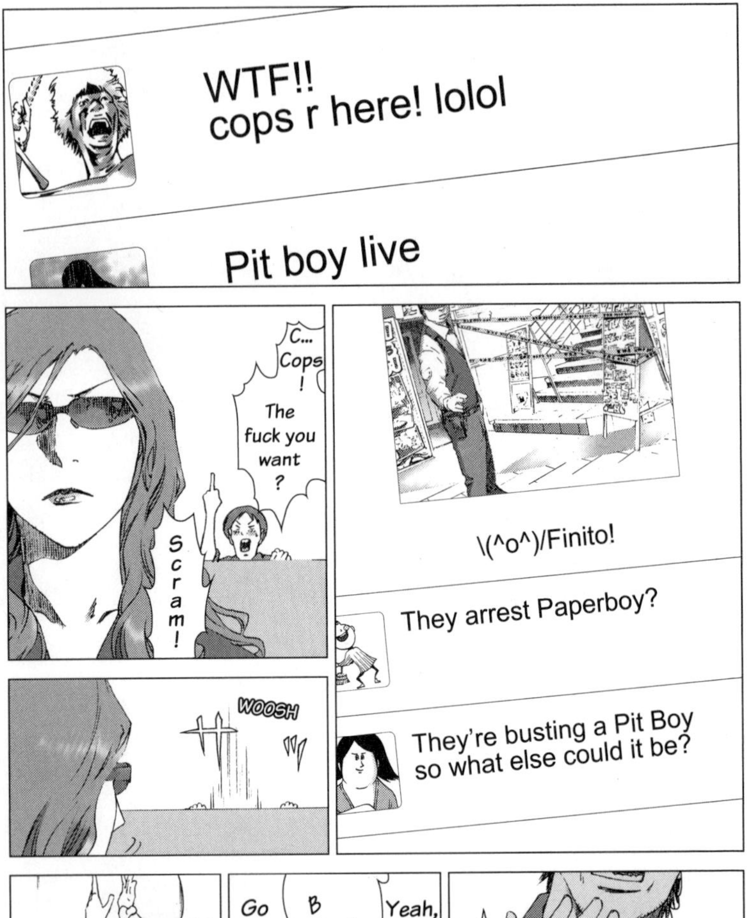
WTF!!
cops r here! lolol
Pit boy live
\(^o^)/Finito!
They arrest Paperboy?
They're busting a Pit Boy so what else could it be?
C... Cops!
The fuck you want?
Scram!
WOOSH
Go home, pigs!
No-body called you!
Yeah, yeah!
BOO
BOO
Go away!
Go away!
GO A-WAY!
GO A-WAY!

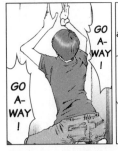

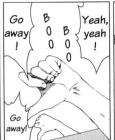

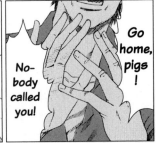

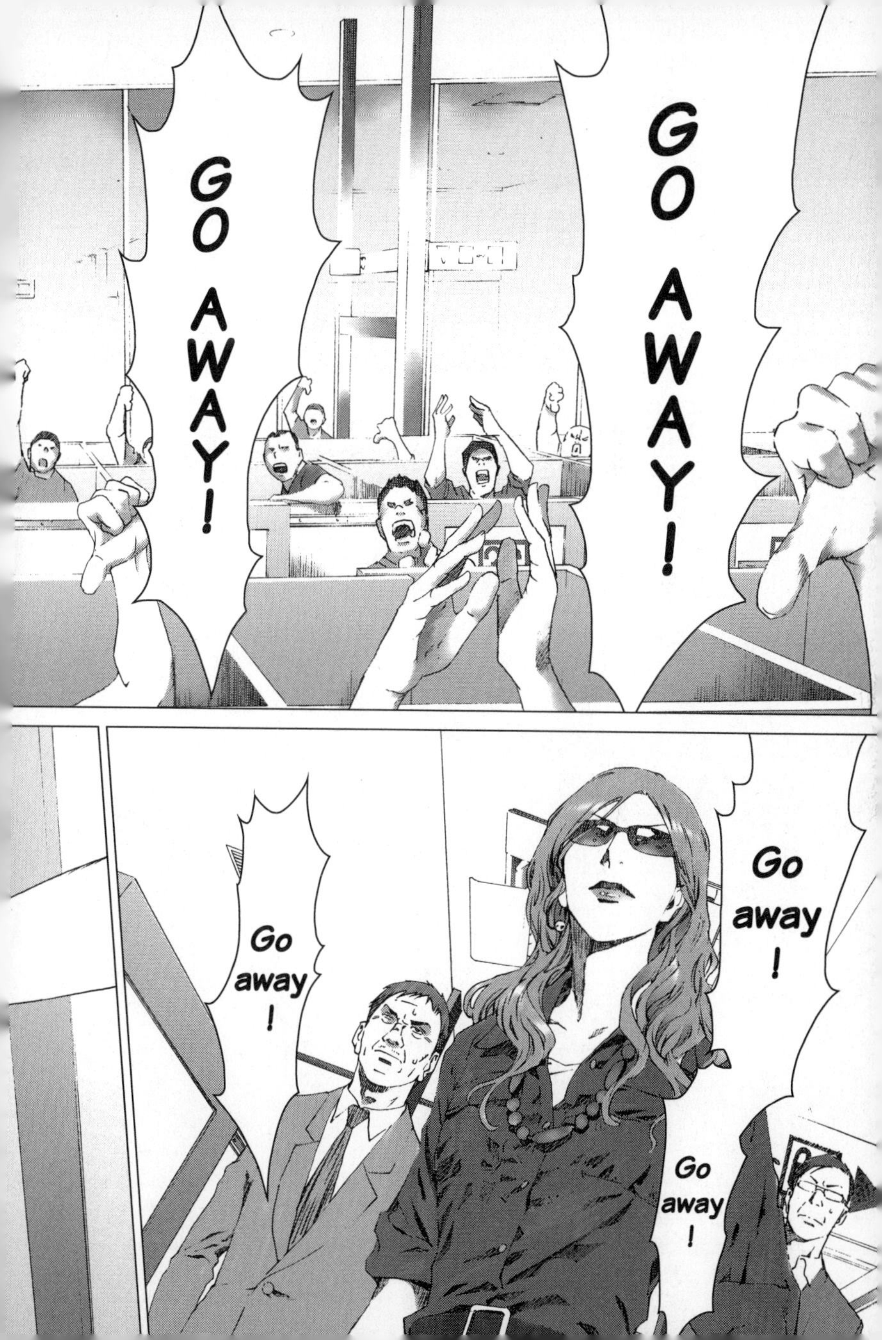
GO AWAY!
GO AWAY!
Go away!
Go away!
Go away!

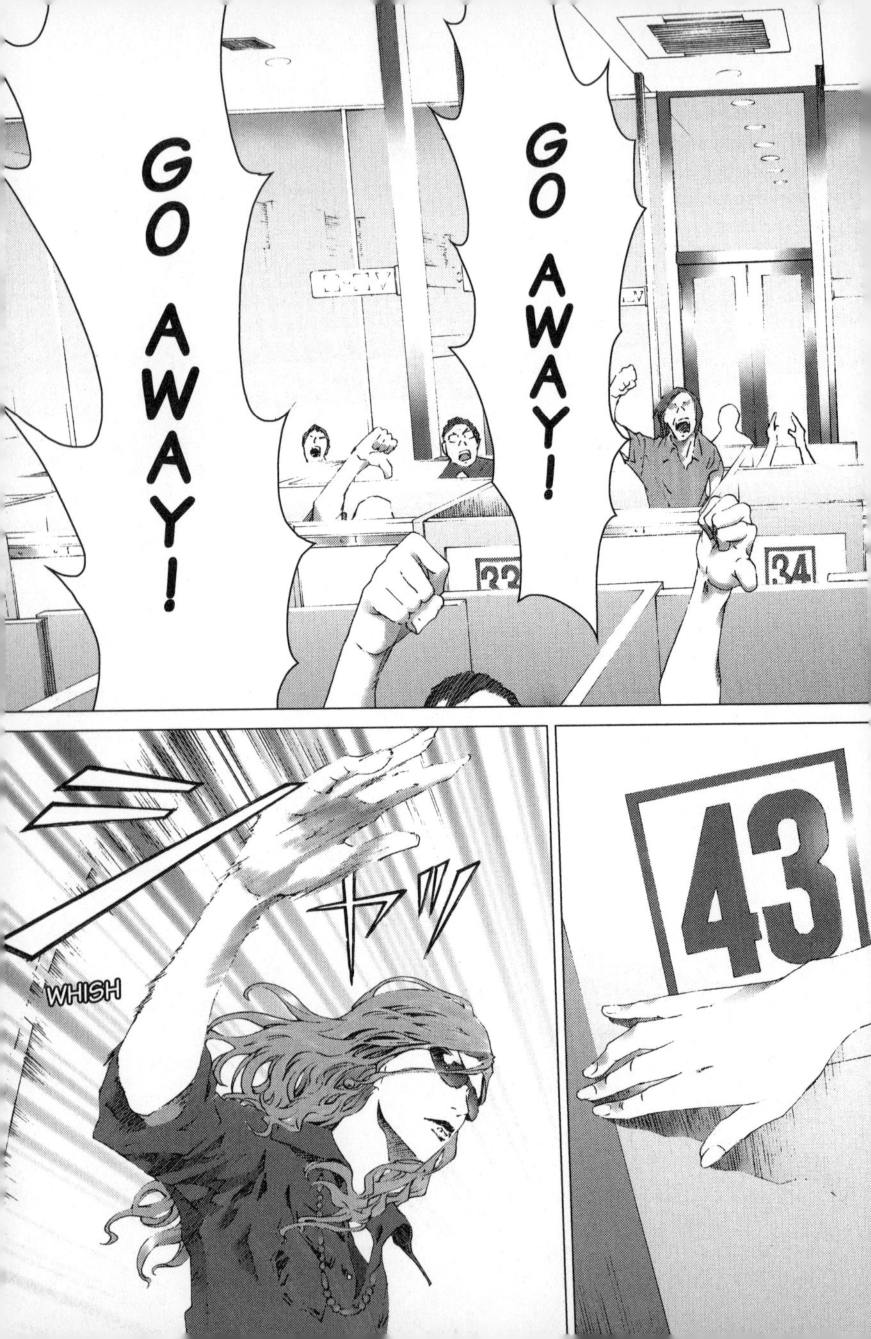
GO AWAY!
GO AWAY!
43
WHISH

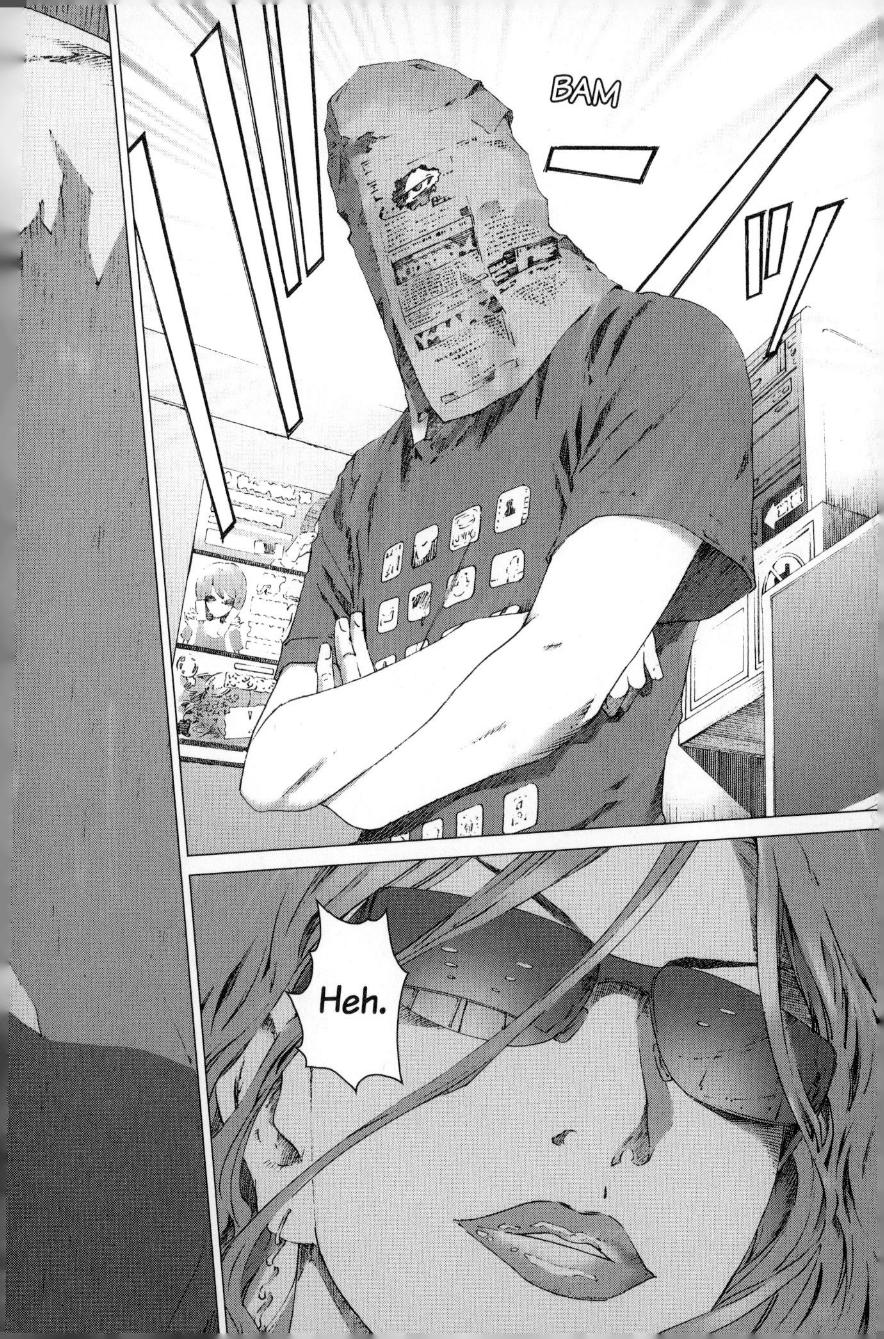
BAM
Heh.

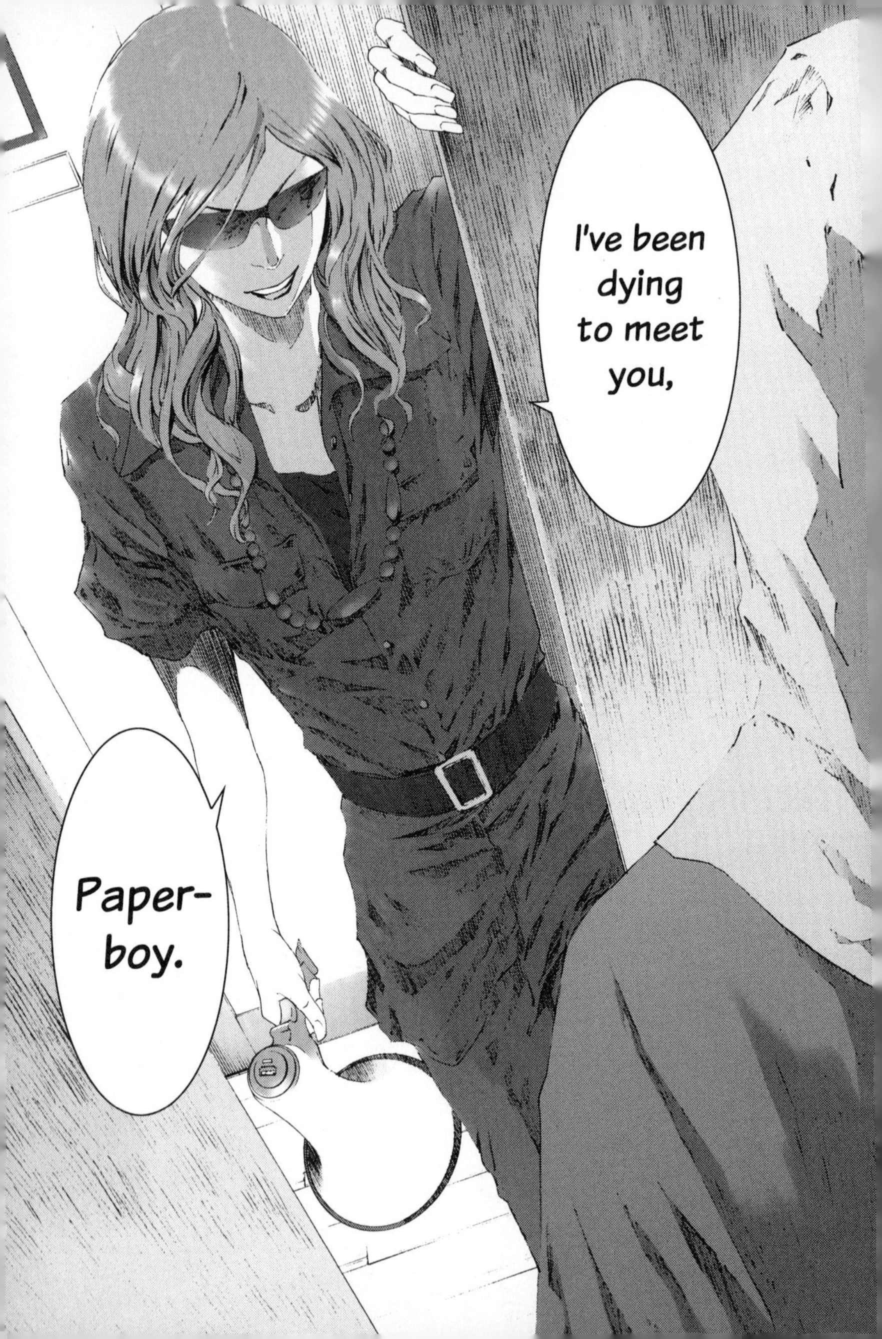
I've been dying to meet you,
Paper-boy.

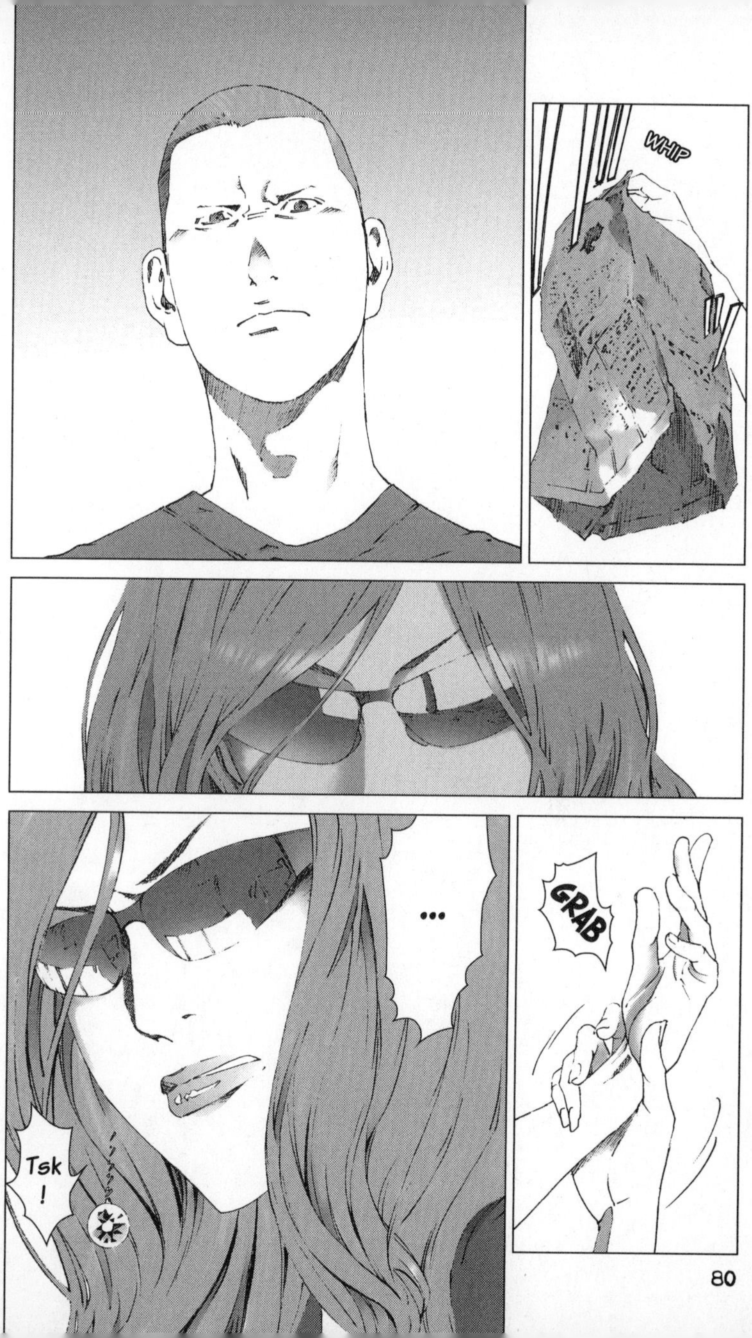
WHIP
GRAB
...
Tsk!

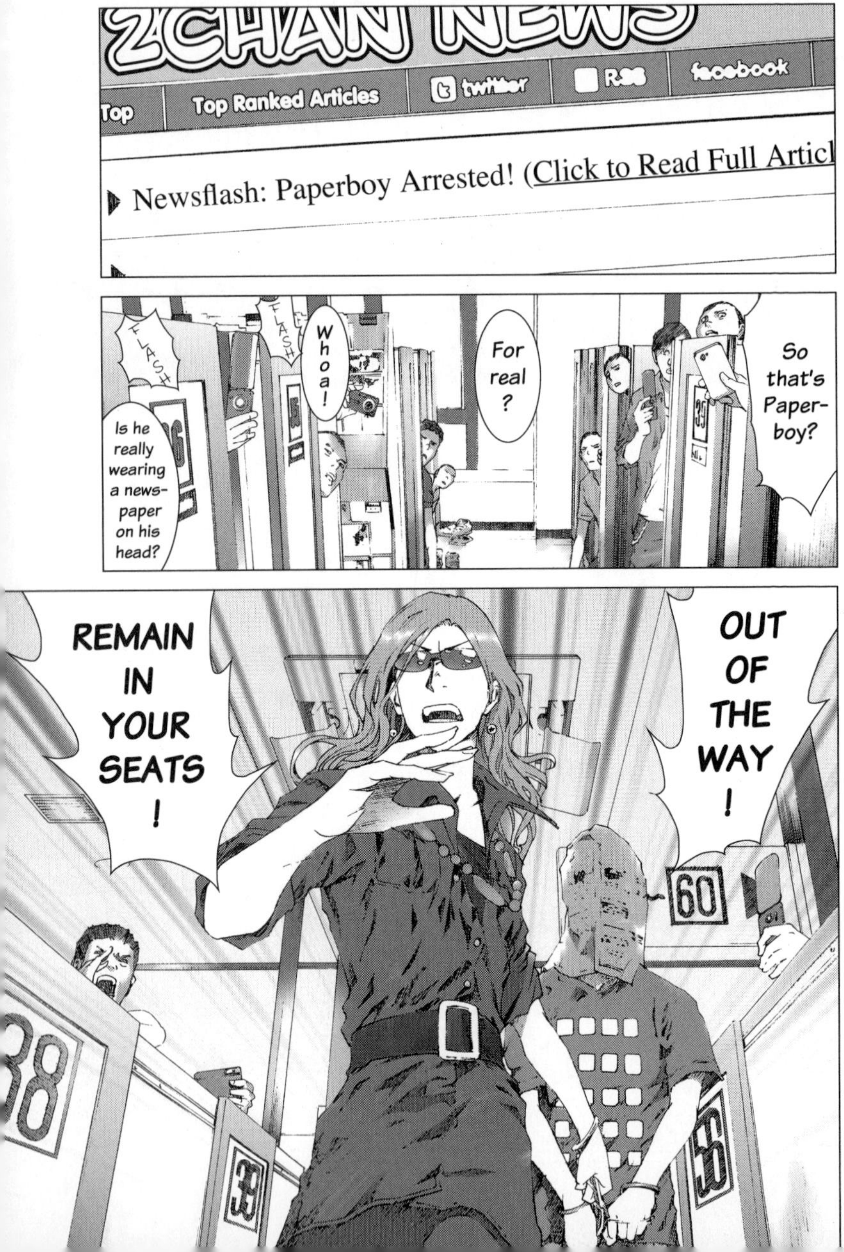
2CHAN NEWS
Top
Top Ranked Articles
twitter
RSS
facebook
Newsflash: Paperboy Arrested! (Click to Read Full Articl
So that's Paper-boy?
For real?
Whoa!
FLASH
FLASH
Is he really wearing a news-paper on his head?
OUT OF THE WAY!
REMAIN IN YOUR SEATS!

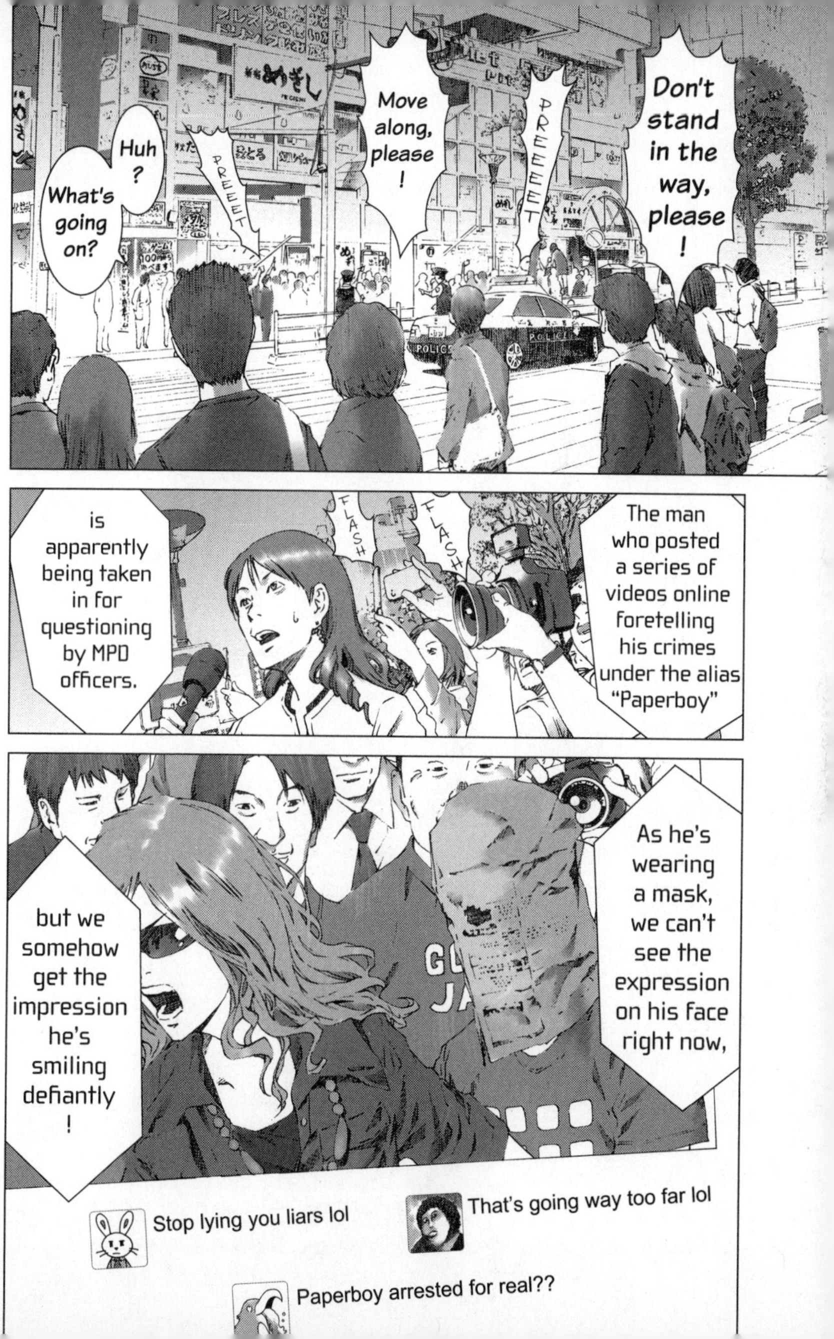
Don't stand in the way, please!
PREEEET
Move along, please!
PREEET
Huh? What's going on?
The man who posted a series of videos online foretelling his crimes under the alias "Paperboy"
FLASH
FLASH
is apparently being taken in for questioning by MPD officers.
As he's wearing a mask, we can't see the expression on his face right now,
but we somehow get the impression he's smiling defiantly!
That's going way too far lol
Stop lying you liars lol
Paperboy arrested for real??

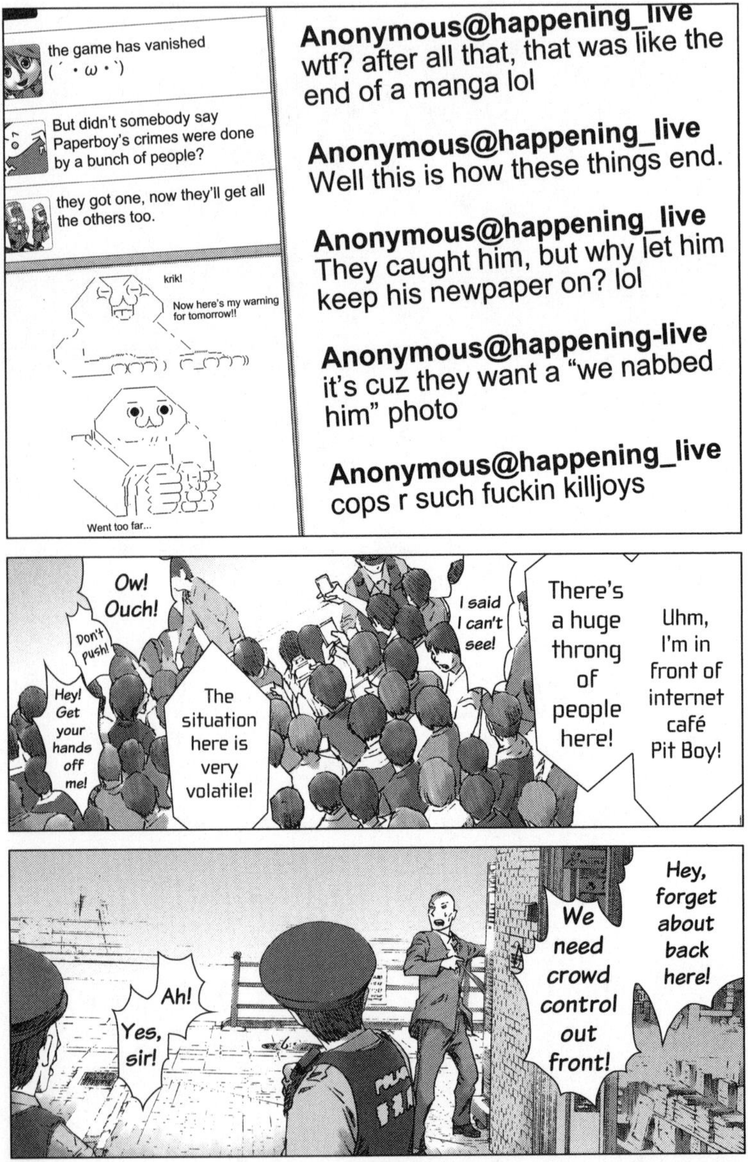

Anonymous@happening_live
wtf? after all that, that was like the end of a manga lol
Anonymous@happening_live
Well this is how these things end.
Anonymous@happening_live
They caught him, but why let him keep his newpaper on? lol
Anonymous@happening-live
it's cuz they want a "we nabbed him" photo
Anonymous@happening_live
cops r such fuckin killjoys
the game has vanished
(´・ω・`)
But didn't somebody say Paperboy's crimes were done by a bunch of people?
they got one, now they'll get all the others too.
krik!
Now here's my warning for tomorrow!!
Went too far...
Uhm, I'm in front of internet café Pit Boy!
There's a huge throng of people here!
I said I can't see!
The situation here is very volatile!
Ow! Ouch!
Don't push!
Hey! Get your hands off me!
Hey, forget about back here!
We need crowd control out front!
Ah!
Yes, sir!

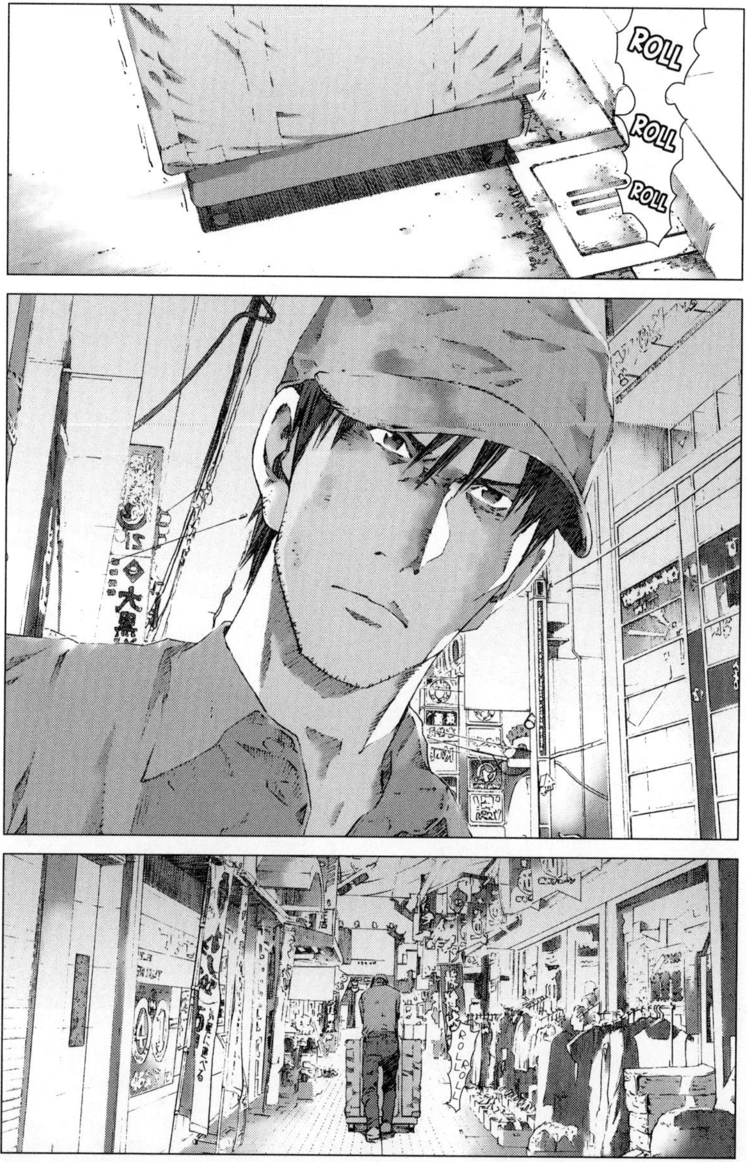
ROLL
ROLL
ROLL
ROLL
ROLL

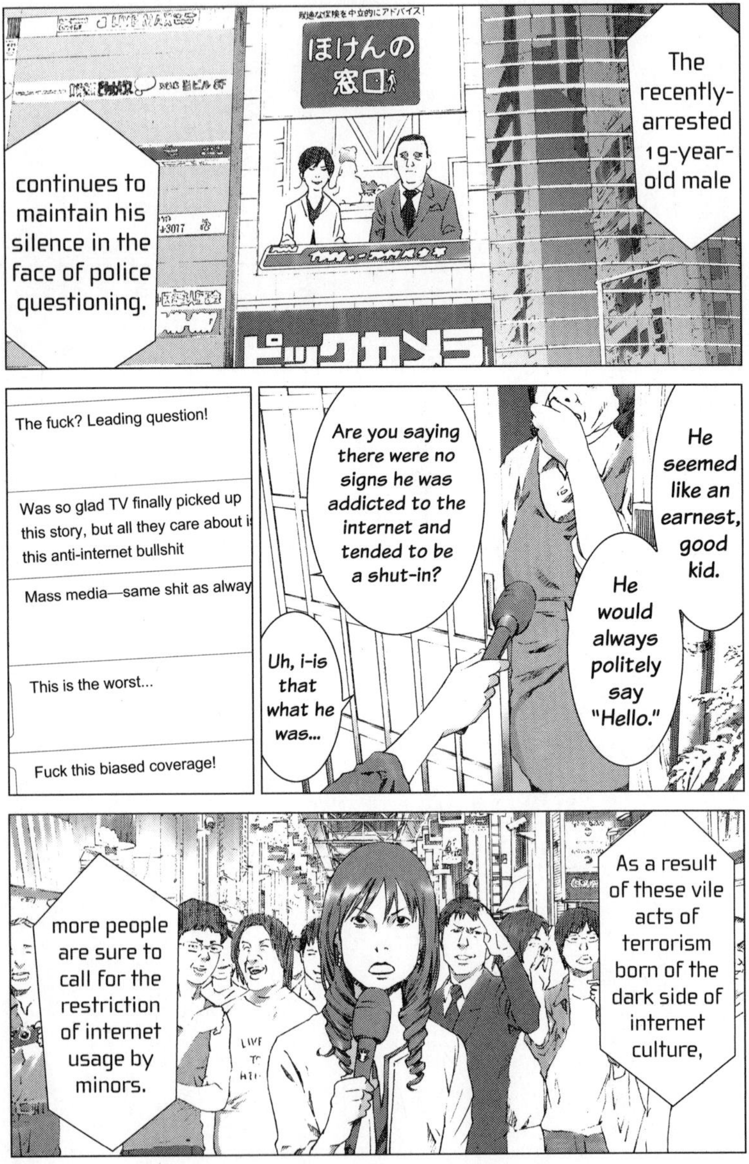

The recently-arrested 19-year-old male
ほけんの窓口
continues to maintain his silence in the face of police questioning.
He seemed like an earnest, good kid.
He would always politely say "Hello."
Are you saying there were no signs he was addicted to the internet and tended to be a shut-in?
Uh, i-is that what he was...
The fuck? Leading question!
Was so glad TV finally picked up this story, but all they care about i
this anti-internet bullshit
Mass media—same shit as alway
This is the worst...
Fuck this biased coverage!
As a result of these vile acts of terrorism born of the dark side of internet culture,
more people are sure to call for the restriction of internet usage by minors.

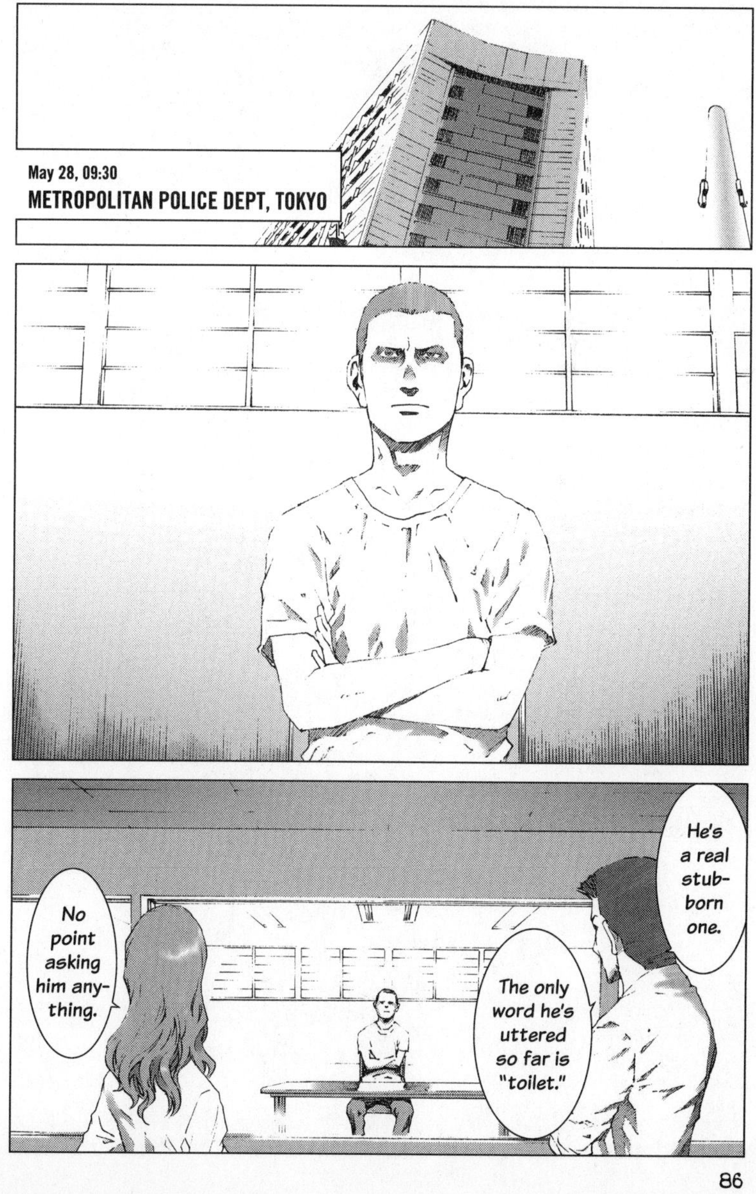
May 28, 09:30
METROPOLITAN POLICE DEPT, TOKYO
He's a real stub-born one.
The only word he's uttered so far is "toilet."
No point asking him anything.

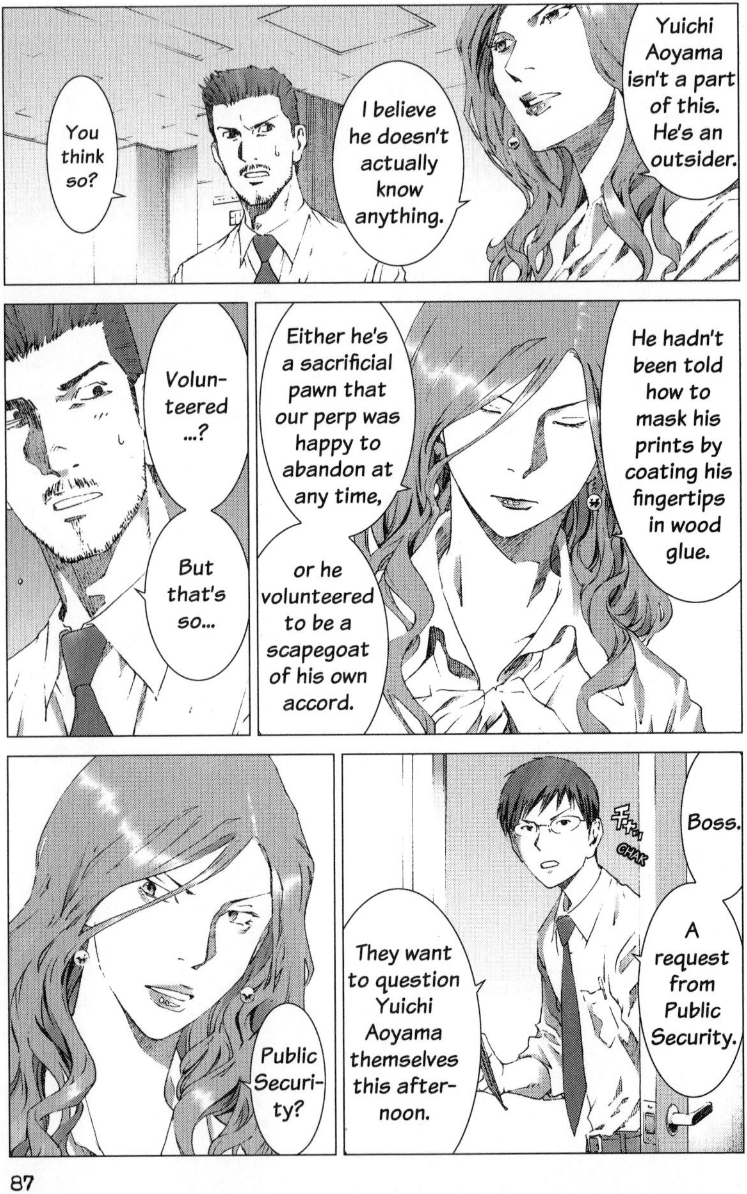
Yuichi Aoyama isn't a part of this. He's an outsider.
I believe he doesn't actually know anything.
You think so?
He hadn't been told how to mask his prints by coating his fingertips in wood glue.
Either he's a sacrificial pawn that our perp was happy to abandon at any time,
or he volunteered to be a scapegoat of his own accord.
Volun-teered ...?
But that's so...
CHAK
Boss.
A request from Public Security.
They want to question Yuichi Aoyama themselves this after-noon.
Public Securi-ty?

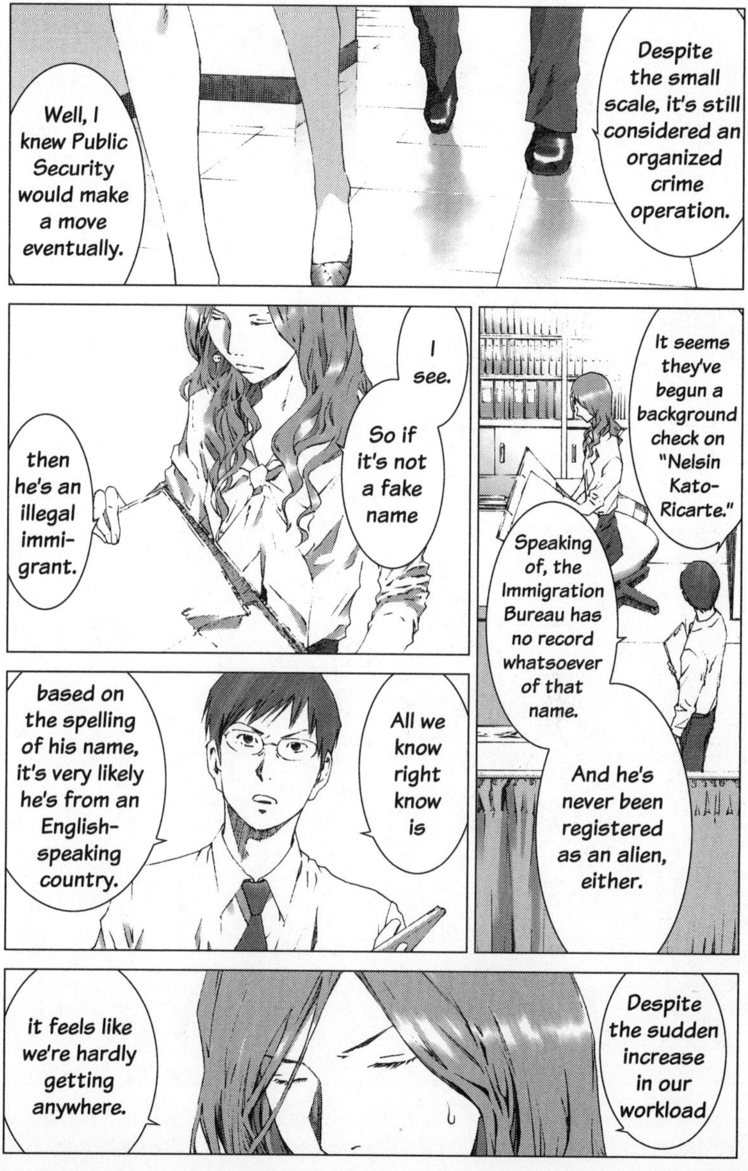
Despite the small scale, it's still considered an organized crime operation.
Well, I knew Public Security would make a move eventually.
It seems they've begun a background check on "Nelsin Kato-Ricarte."
Speaking of, the Immigration Bureau has no record whatsoever of that name.
And he's never been registered as an alien, either.
I see.
So if it's not a fake name
then he's an illegal immi-grant.
All we know right know is
based on the spelling of his name, it's very likely he's from an English-speaking country.
Despite the sudden increase in our workload
it feels like we're hardly getting anywhere.

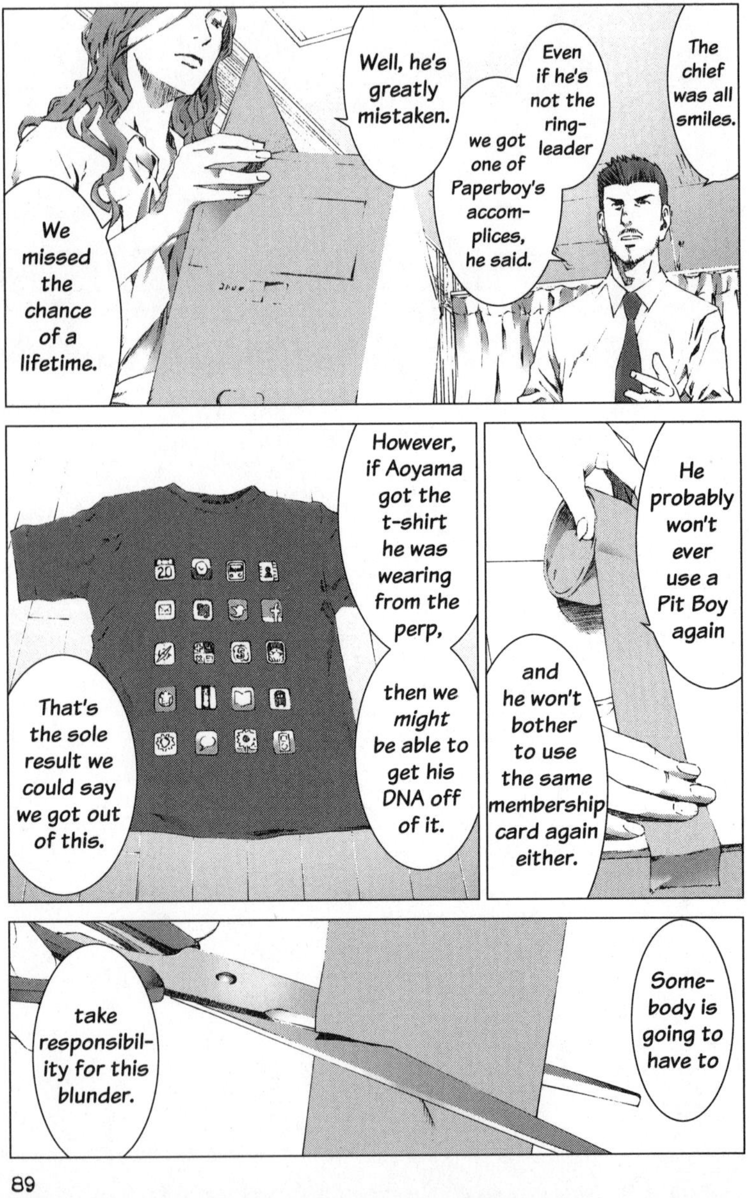
The chief was all smiles.
Even if he's not the ring-leader we got one of Paperboy's accom-plices, he said.
Well, he's greatly mistaken.
We missed the chance of a lifetime.
He probably won't ever use a Pit Boy again
and he won't bother to use the same membership card again either.
However, if Aoyama got the t-shirt he was wearing from the perp,
then we *might* be able to get his DNA off of it.
That's the sole result we could say we got out of this.
Some-body is going to have to
take responsibil-ity for this blunder.

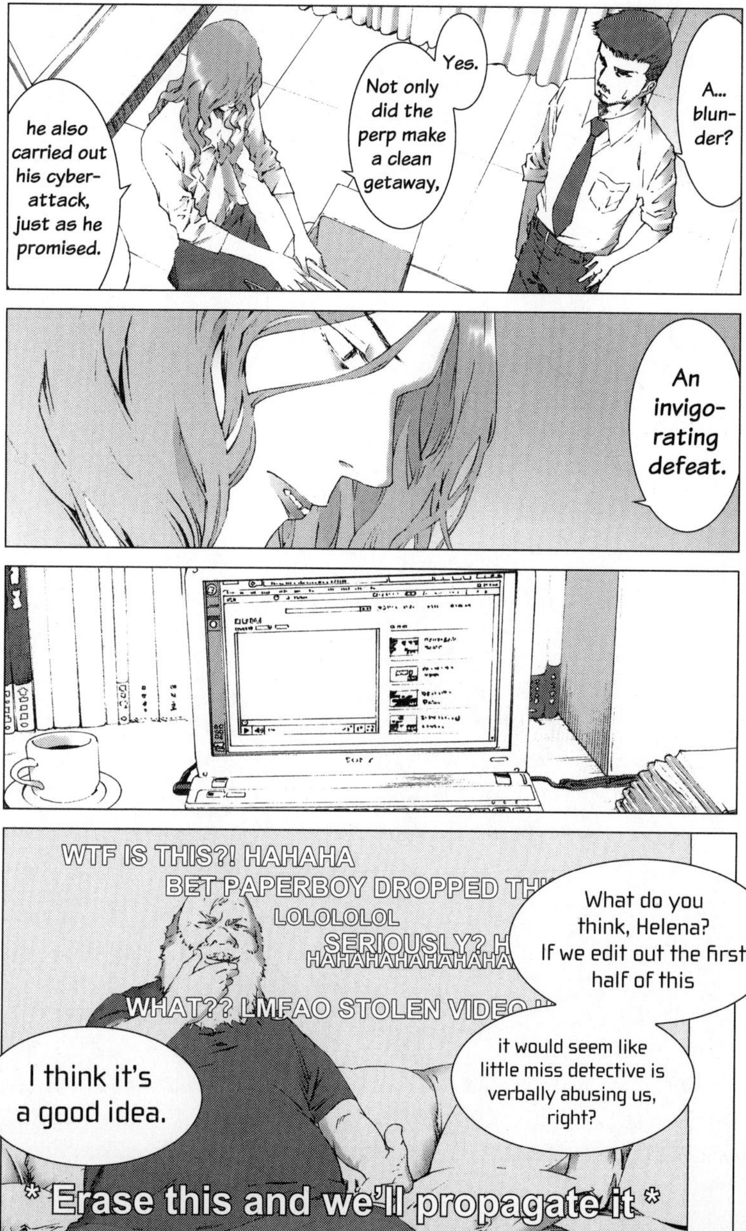
A... blunder?
Yes.
Not only did the perp make a clean getaway,
he also carried out his cyber-attack, just as he promised.
An invigorating defeat.
What do you think, Helena? If we edit out the first half of this
it would seem like little miss detective is verbally abusing us, right?
I think it's a good idea.
WTF IS THIS?! HAHAHA
BET PAPERBOY DROPPED TH
LOLOLOLOL
SERIOUSLY? H
HAHAHAHAHAHAHA
WHAT?? LMFAO STOLEN VIDEO
* Erase this and we'll propagate it *

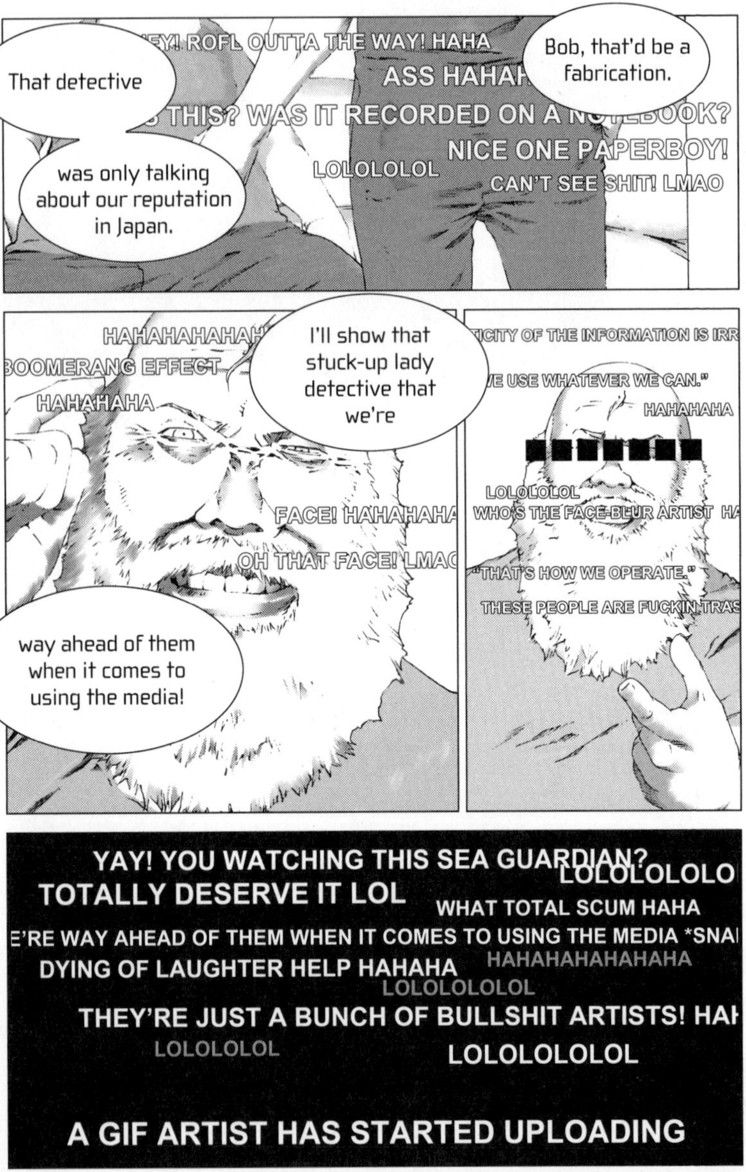
Bob, that'd be a fabrication.
EY! ROFL OUTTA THE WAY! HAHA
ASS HAHAH
That detective
THIS? WAS IT RECORDED ON A NOTEBOOK?
NICE ONE PAPERBOY!
LOLOLOLOL
CAN'T SEE SHIT! LMAO
was only talking about our reputation in Japan.
TICITY OF THE INFORMATION IS IRR
E USE WHATEVER WE CAN."
HAHAHAHA
LOLOLOLOL
WHO'S THE FACE-BLUR ARTIST HA
"THAT'S HOW WE OPERATE."
THESE PEOPLE ARE FUCKIN TRAS
HAHAHAHAHAH
I'll show that stuck-up lady detective that we're
BOOMERANG EFFECT
HAHAHAHA
FACE! HAHAHAHA
OH THAT FACE! LMAO
way ahead of them when it comes to using the media!
YAY! YOU WATCHING THIS SEA GUARDIAN?
LOLOLOLOLO
TOTALLY DESERVE IT LOL
WHAT TOTAL SCUM HAHA
E'RE WAY AHEAD OF THEM WHEN IT COMES TO USING THE MEDIA *SNA
DYING OF LAUGHTER HELP HAHAHA
HAHAHAHAHAHAHA
LOLOLOLOLOL
THEY'RE JUST A BUNCH OF BULLSHIT ARTISTS! HA
LOLOLOLOL
LOLOLOLOLOL
A GIF ARTIST HAS STARTED UPLOADING

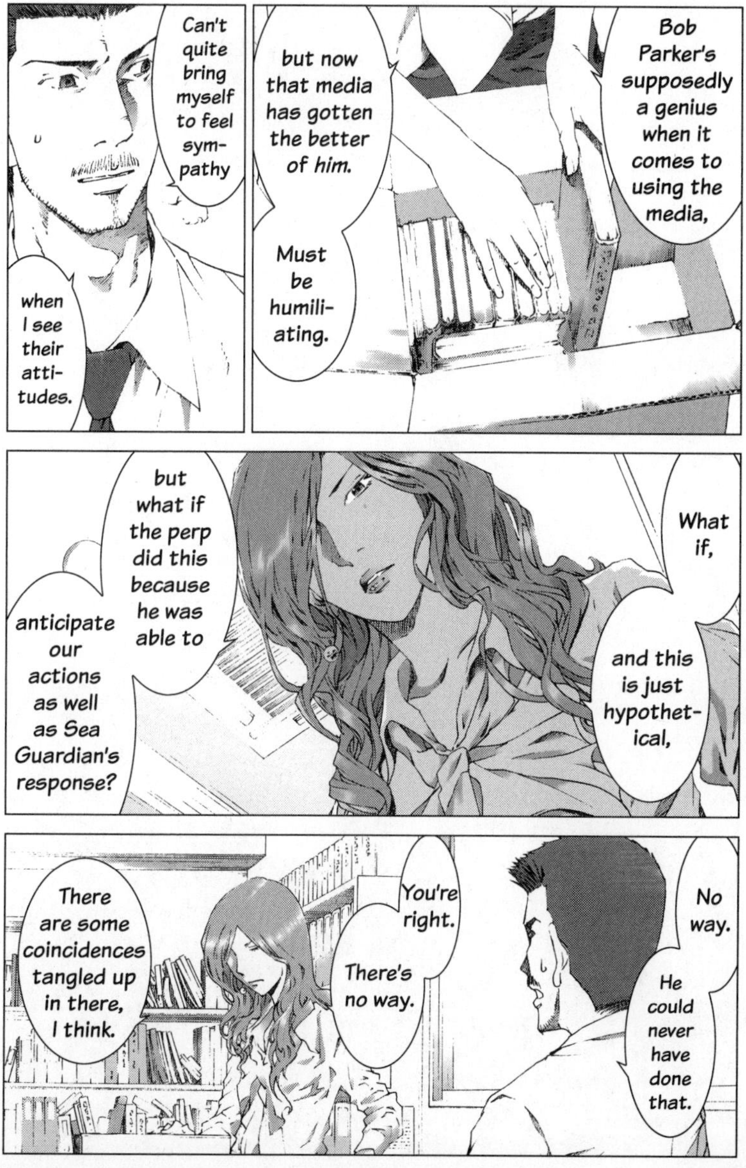
Bob Parker's supposedly a genius when it comes to using the media,
but now that media has gotten the better of him.
Must be humiliating.
Can't quite bring myself to feel sympathy
when I see their attitudes.
What if,
and this is just hypothetical,
but what if the perp did this because he was able to
anticipate our actions as well as Sea Guardian's response?
No way.
He could never have done that.
You're right.
There's no way.
There are some coincidences tangled up in there, I think.

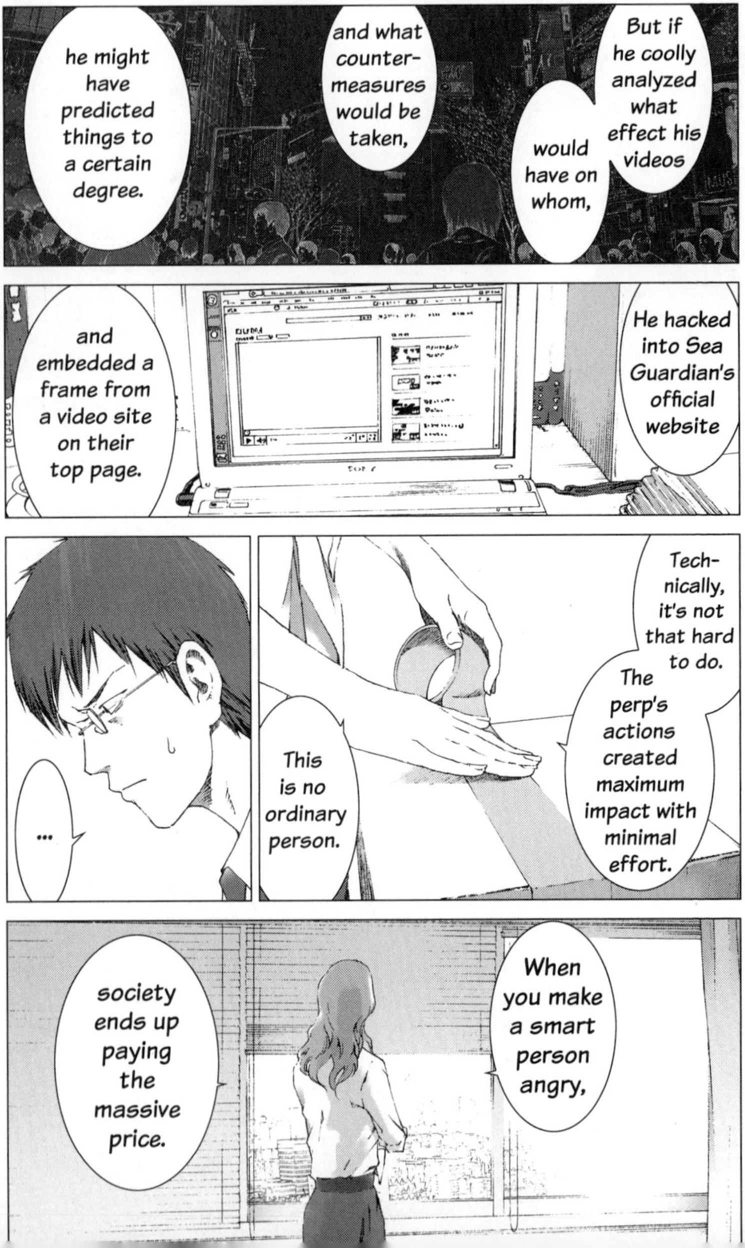
But if he coolly analyzed what effect his videos
would have on whom,
and what counter-measures would be taken,
he might have predicted things to a certain degree.
He hacked into Sea Guardian's official website
and embedded a frame from a video site on their top page.
Tech-nically, it's not that hard to do.
The perp's actions created maximum impact with minimal effort.
This is no ordinary person.
...
When you make a smart person angry,
society ends up paying the massive price.

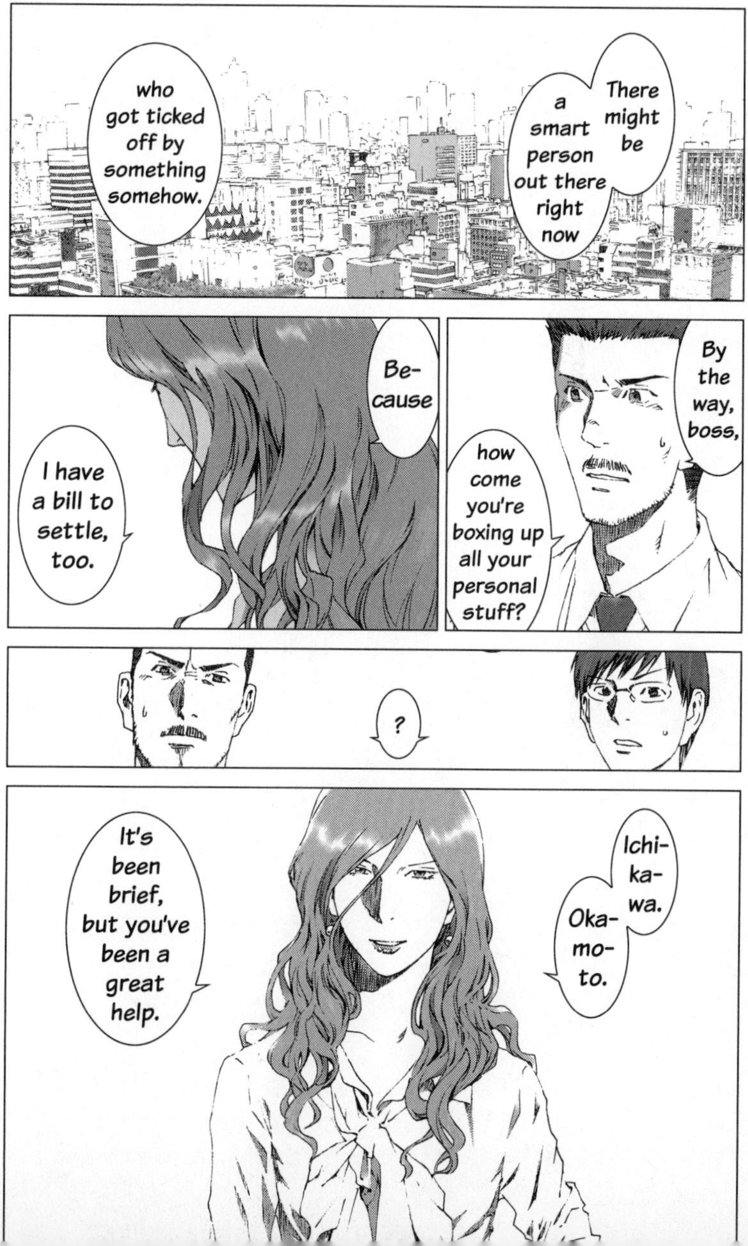
There might be
a smart person out there right now
who got ticked off by something somehow.
By the way, boss,
how come you're boxing up all your personal stuff?
Be-cause
I have a bill to settle, too.
?
Ichi-ka-wa.
Oka-mo-to.
It's been brief, but you've been a great help.

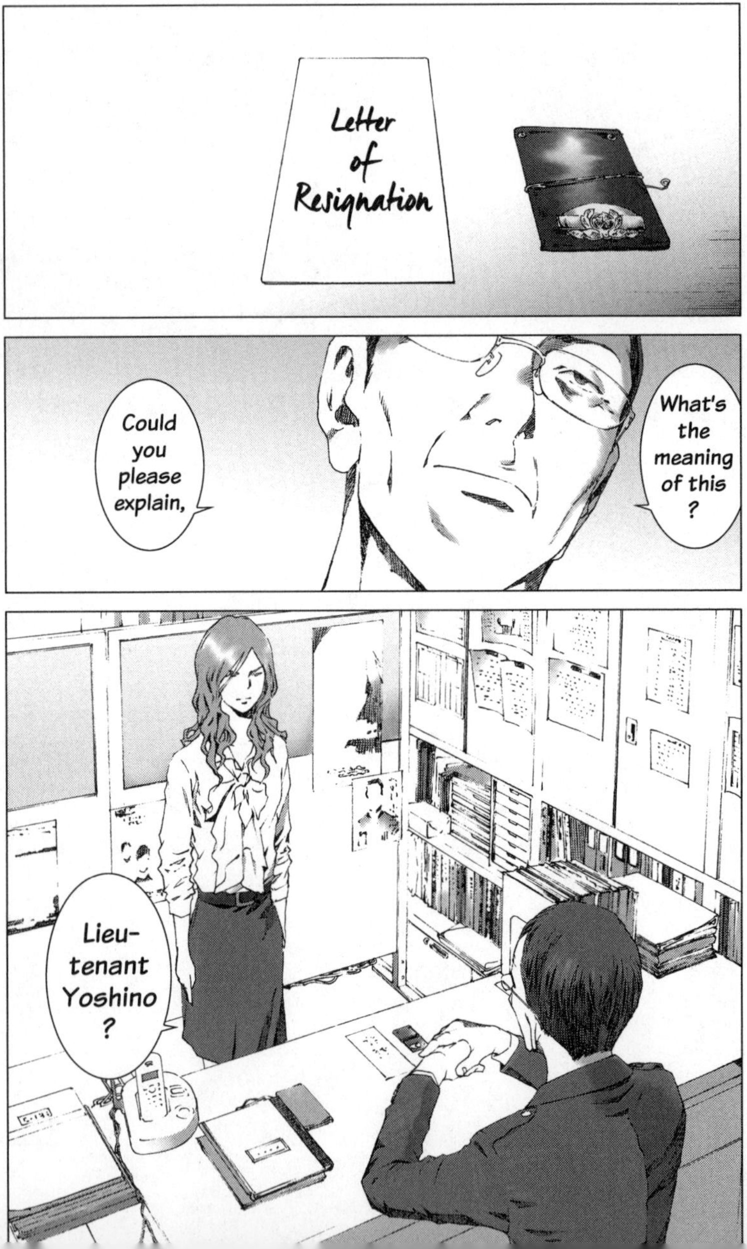
Letter of Resignation
What's the meaning of this?
Could you please explain,
Lieu-tenant Yoshino?

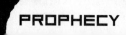
PROPHECY

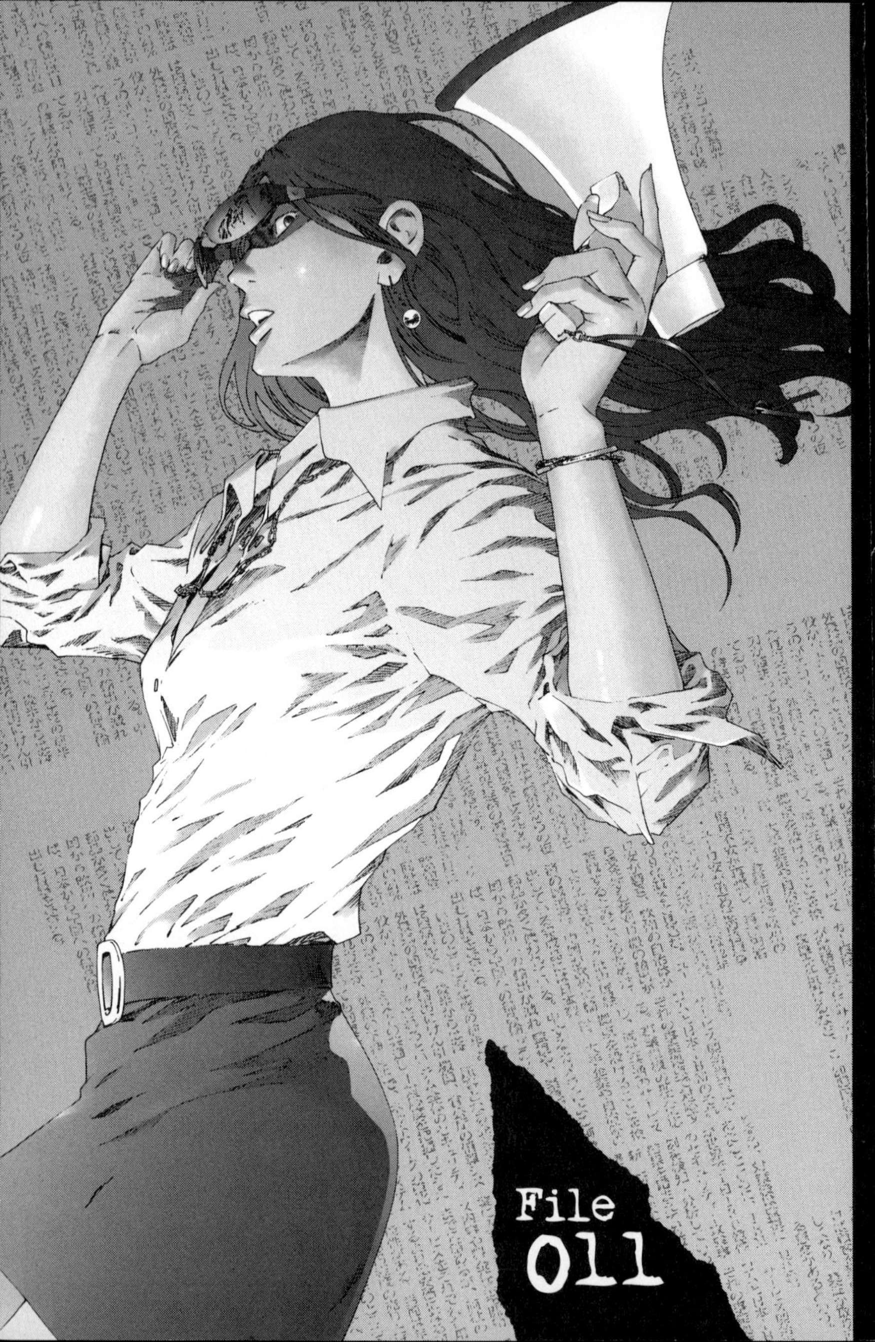
File
011

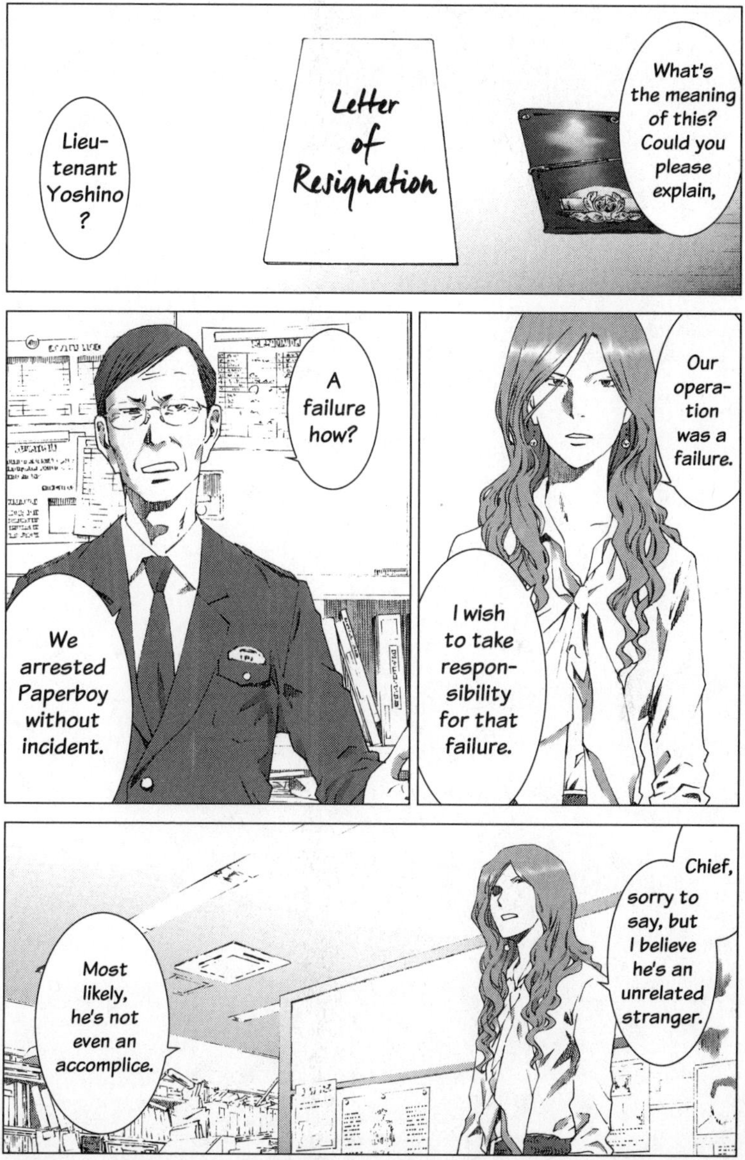

What's the meaning of this? Could you please explain,
Letter of Resignation
Lieu-tenant Yoshino?
Our opera-tion was a failure.
I wish to take respon-sibility for that failure.
A failure how?
We arrested Paperboy without incident.
Chief, sorry to say, but I believe he's an unrelated stranger.
Most likely, he's not even an accomplice.

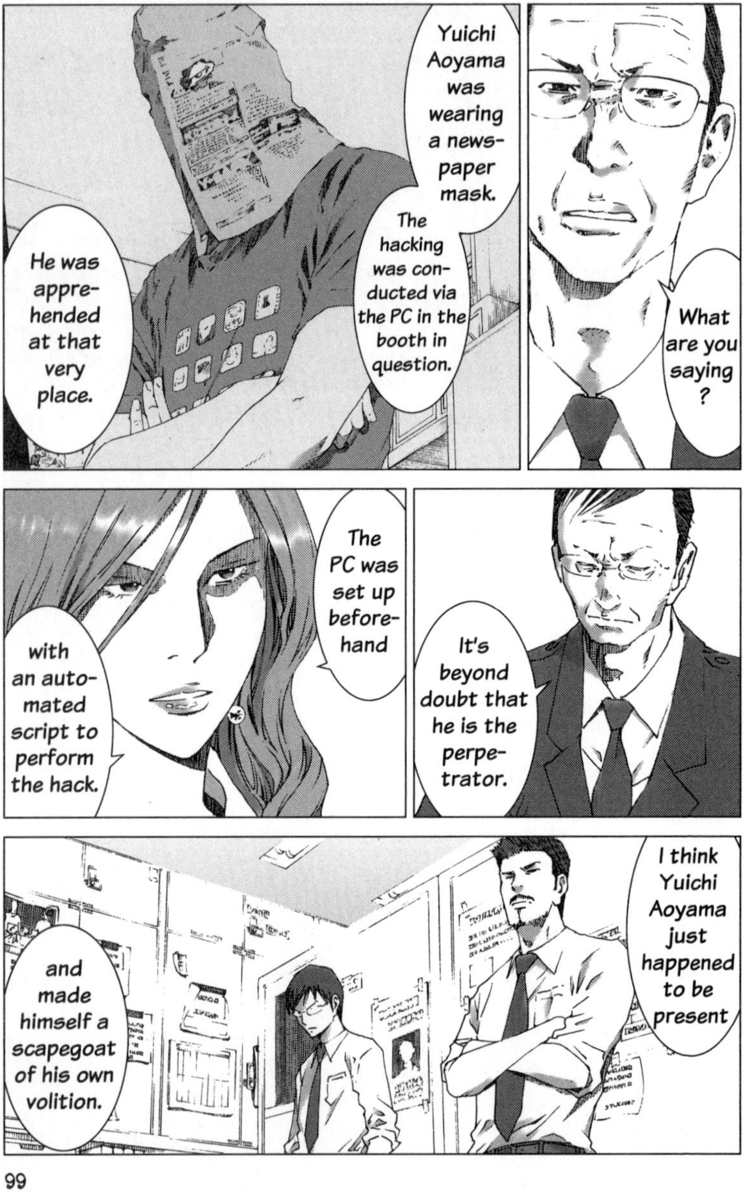
What are you saying?
Yuichi Aoyama was wearing a newspaper mask.
The hacking was conducted via the PC in the booth in question.
He was apprehended at that very place.
It's beyond doubt that he is the perpetrator.
The PC was set up beforehand
with an automated script to perform the hack.
I think Yuichi Aoyama just happened to be present
and made himself a scapegoat of his own volition.

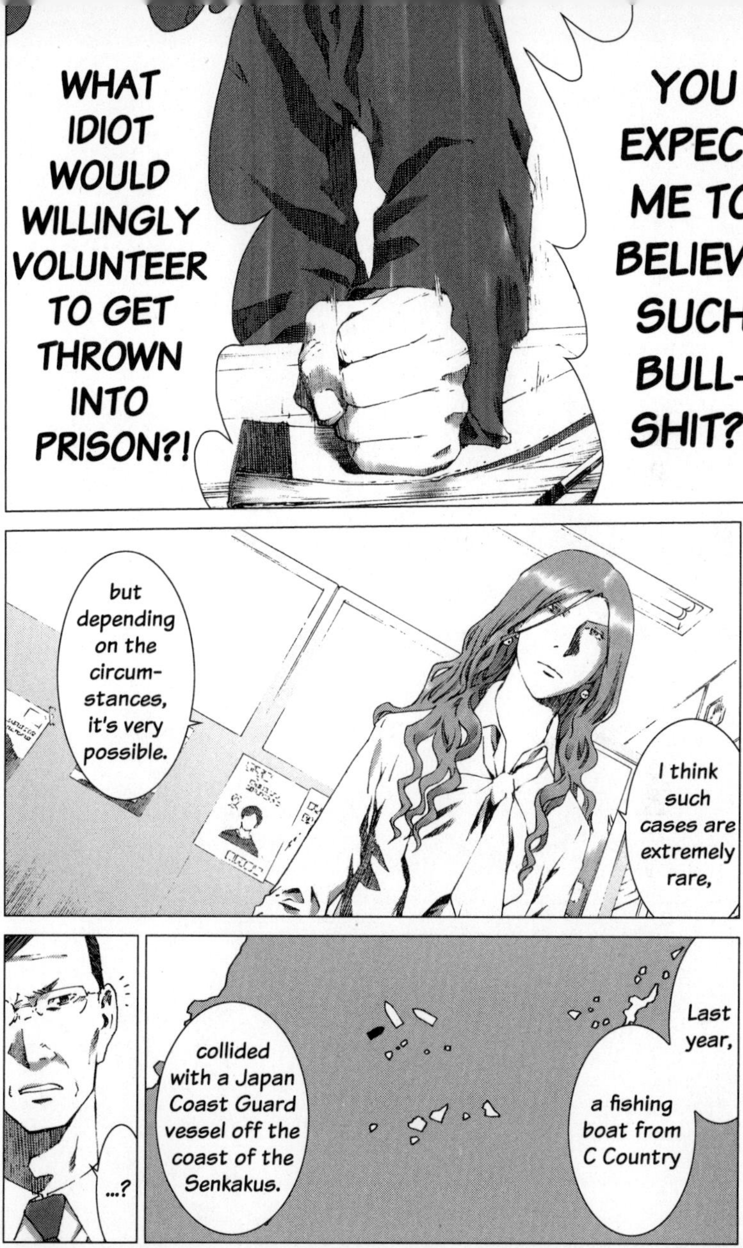
YOU EXPECT ME TO BELIEVE SUCH BULL-SHIT?!
WHAT IDIOT WOULD WILLINGLY VOLUNTEER TO GET THROWN INTO PRISON?!
I think such cases are extremely rare,
but depending on the circum-stances, it's very possible.
Last year,
a fishing boat from C Country
collided with a Japan Coast Guard vessel off the coast of the Senkakus.
...?

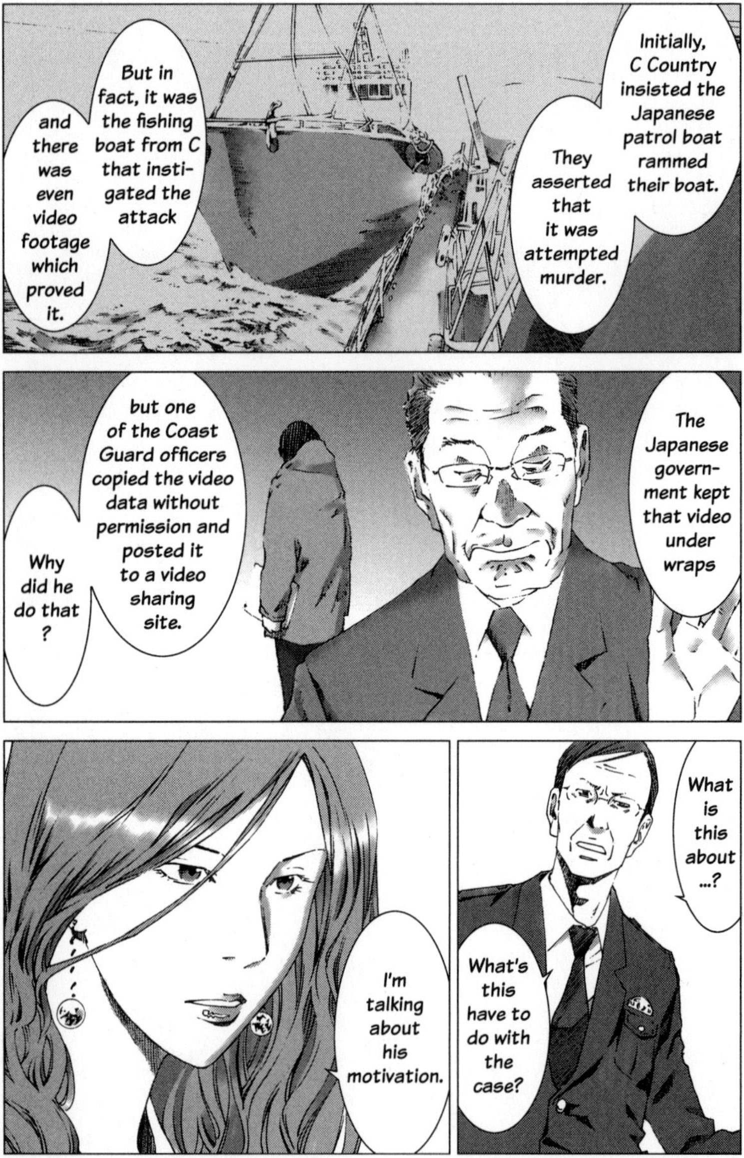
Initially, C Country insisted the Japanese patrol boat rammed their boat.
They asserted that it was attempted murder.
But in fact, it was the fishing boat from C that instigated the attack
and there was even video footage which proved it.
The Japanese government kept that video under wraps
but one of the Coast Guard officers copied the video data without permission and posted it to a video sharing site.
Why did he do that?
What is this about ...?
What's this have to do with the case?
I'm talking about his motivation.

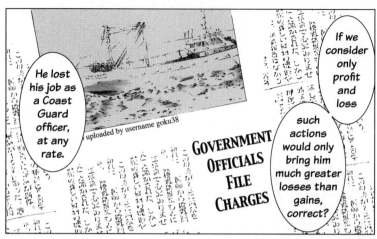

If we consider only profit and loss
such actions would only bring him much greater losses than gains, correct?
GOVERNMENT OFFICIALS FILE CHARGES
uploaded by username goku38
He lost his job as a Coast Guard officer, at any rate.
On the other hand,
he was able to prove to the world the honor and legitimacy
JAPAN COAST GUAR
of the Japan Coast Guard, who were being called murderers.
...
Here's what I think.

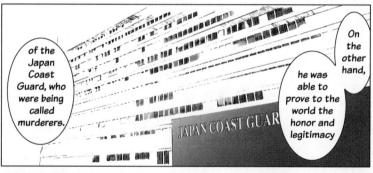

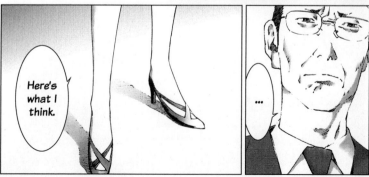

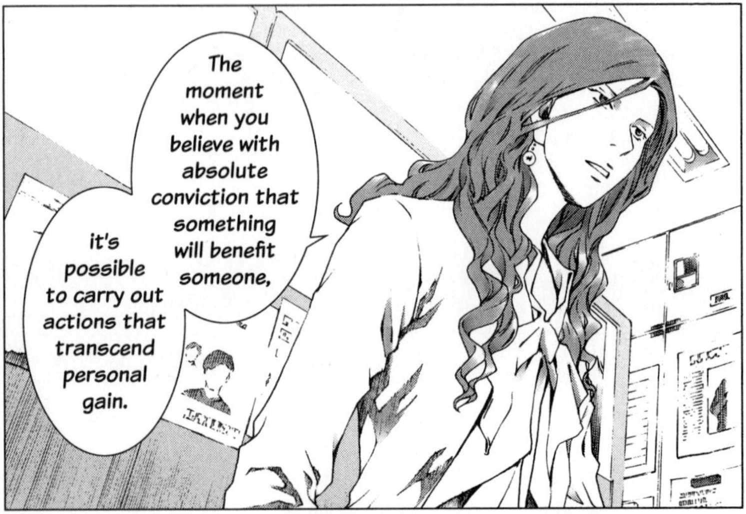
The moment when you believe with absolute conviction that something will benefit someone,
it's possible to carry out actions that transcend personal gain.
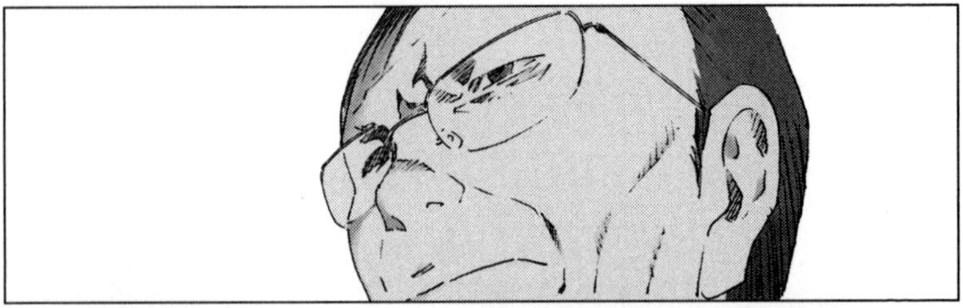
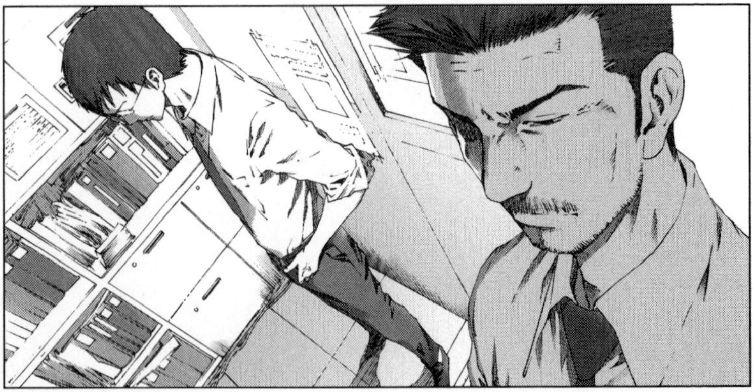

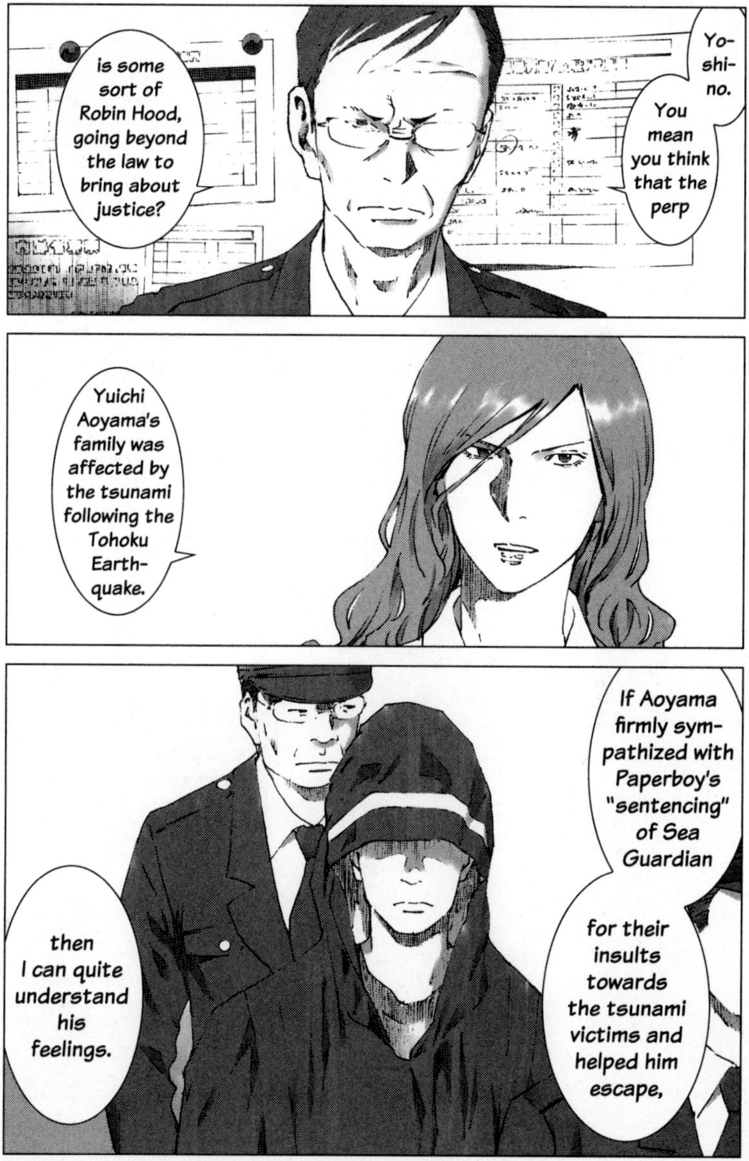
Yo-shi-no. You mean you think that the perp
is some sort of Robin Hood, going beyond the law to bring about justice?
Yuichi Aoyama's family was affected by the tsunami following the Tohoku Earth-quake.
If Aoyama firmly sym-pathized with Paperboy's "sentencing" of Sea Guardian
for their insults towards the tsunami victims and helped him escape,
then I can quite understand his feelings.

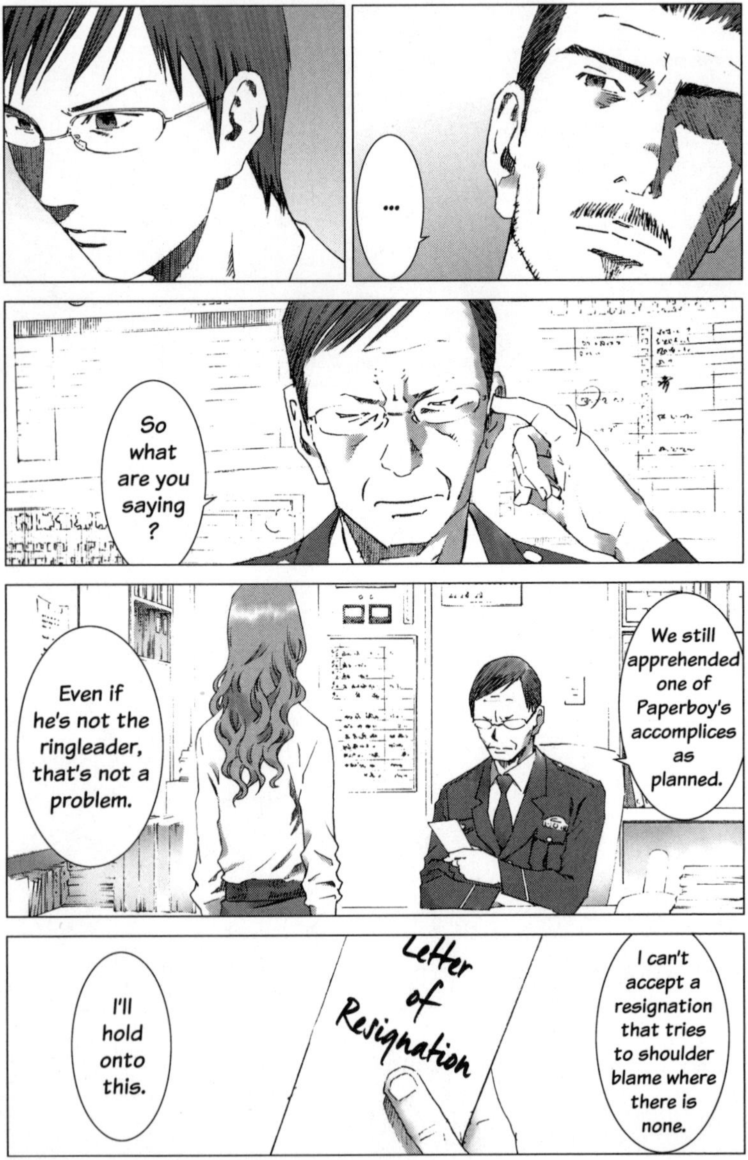
...
So what are you saying ?
We still apprehended one of Paperboy's accomplices as planned.
Even if he's not the ringleader, that's not a problem.
I can't accept a resignation that tries to shoulder blame where there is none.
Letter of Resignation
I'll hold onto this.

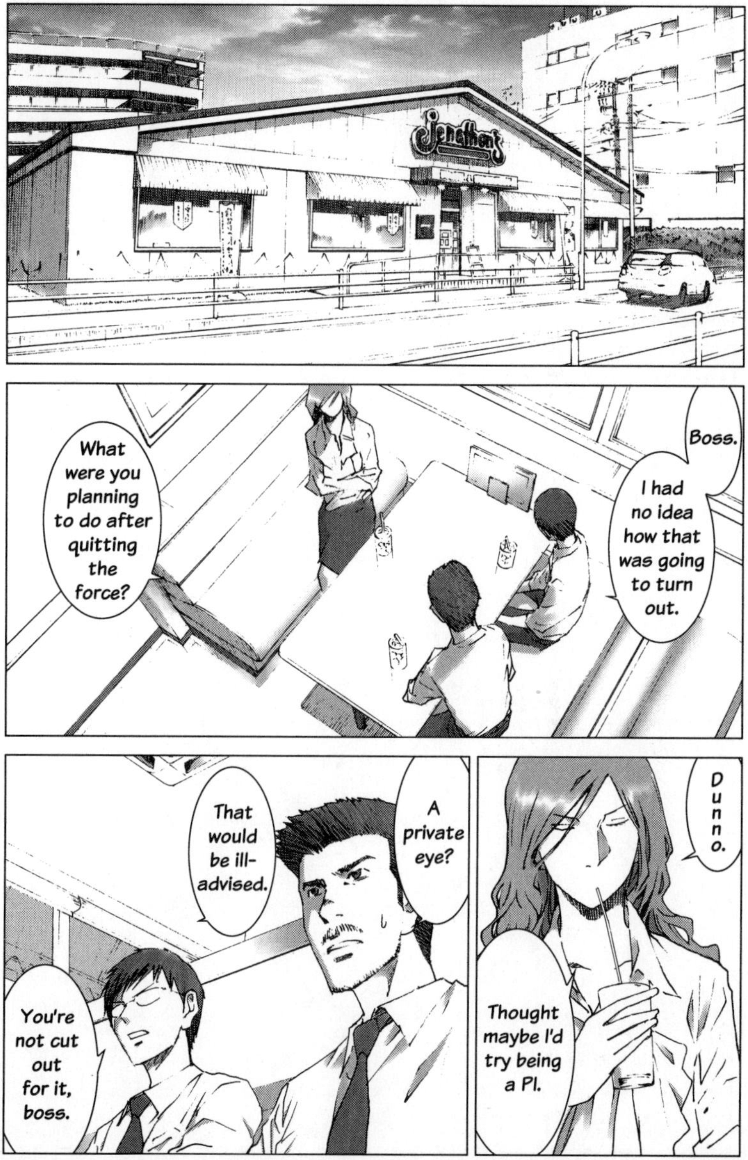
Boss.
I had no idea how that was going to turn out.
What were you planning to do after quitting the force?
Dunno.
Thought maybe I'd try being a PI.
A private eye?
That would be ill-advised.
You're not cut out for it, boss.

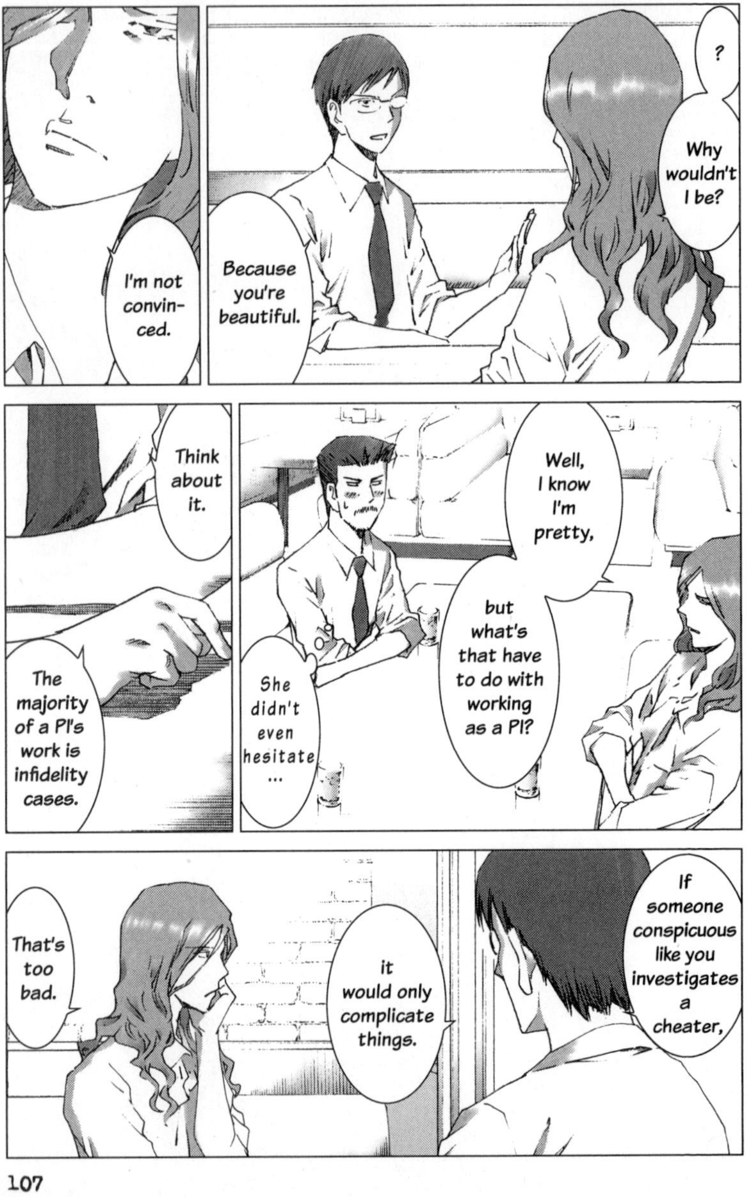
?
Why wouldn't I be?
Because you're beautiful.
I'm not convin-ced.
Well, I know I'm pretty,
but what's that have to do with working as a PI?
She didn't even hesitate ...
Think about it.
The majority of a PI's work is infidelity cases.
If someone conspicuous like you investigates a cheater,
it would only complicate things.
That's too bad.

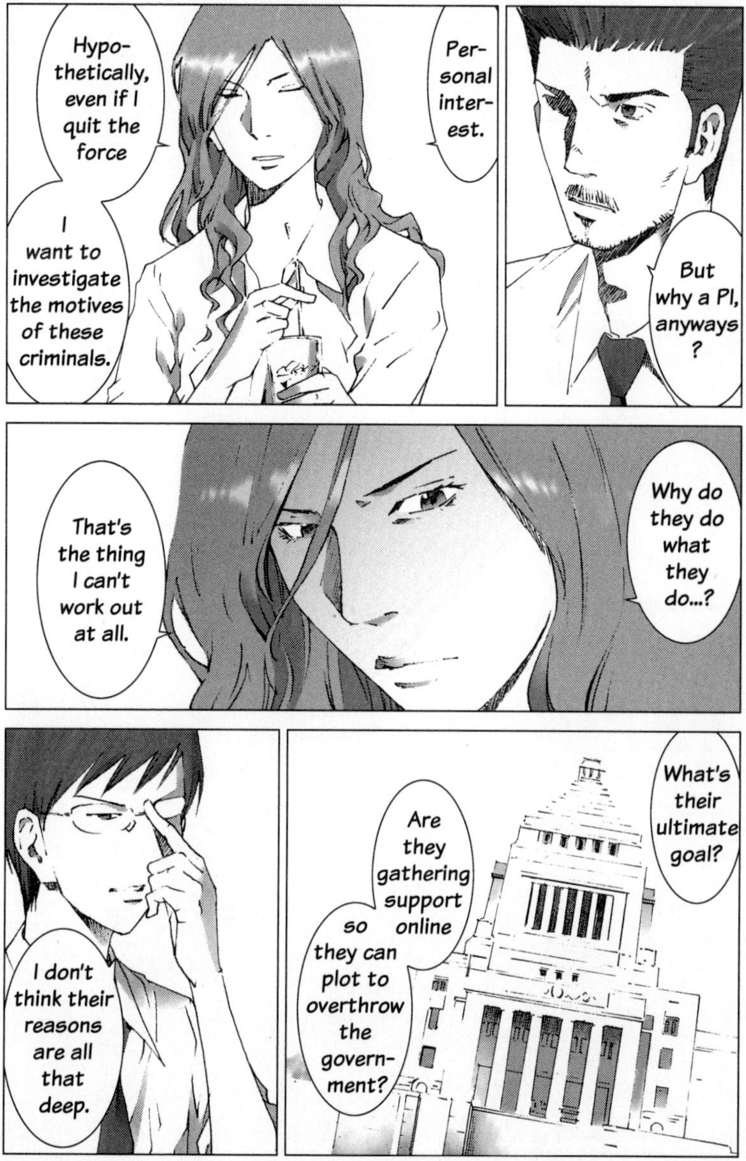
But why a PI, anyways?
Personal interest.
Hypothetically, even if I quit the force
I want to investigate the motives of these criminals.
Why do they do what they do...?
That's the thing I can't work out at all.
What's their ultimate goal?
Are they gathering support online so they can plot to overthrow the government?
I don't think their reasons are all that deep.

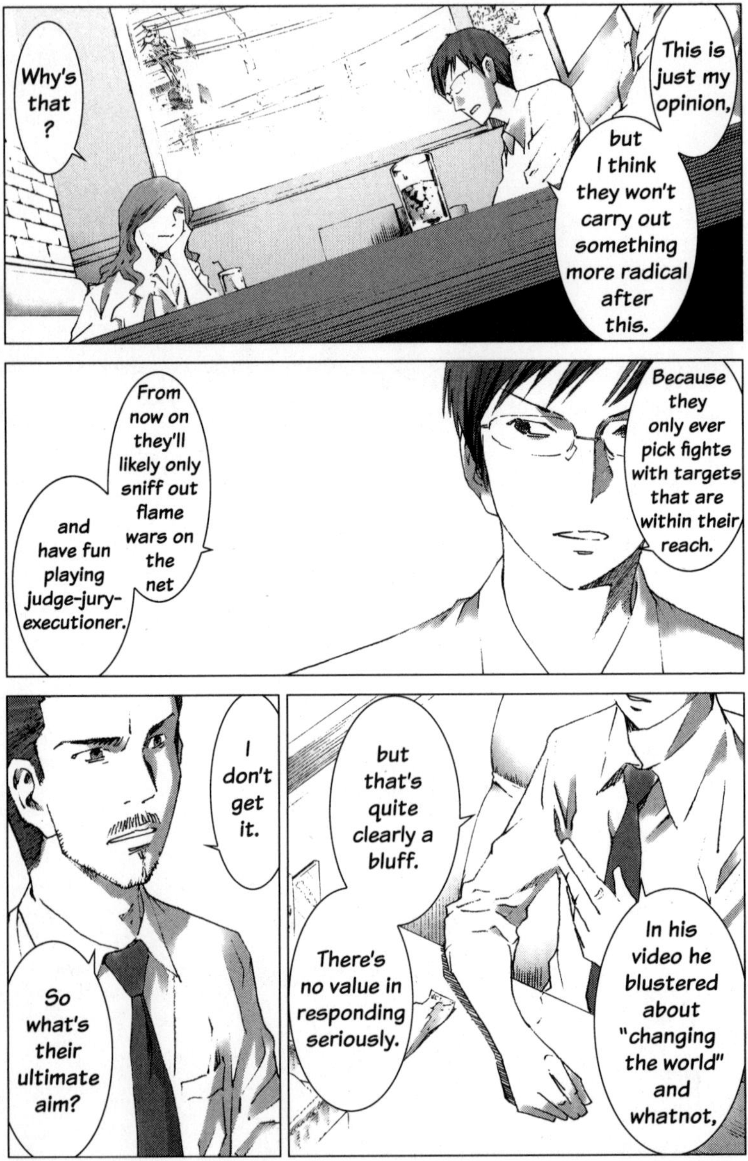
This is just my opinion,
but I think they won't carry out something more radical after this.
Why's that?
Because they only ever pick fights with targets that are within their reach.
From now on they'll likely only sniff out flame wars on the net
and have fun playing judge-jury-executioner.
In his video he blustered about "changing the world" and whatnot,
but that's quite clearly a bluff.
There's no value in responding seriously.
I don't get it.
So what's their ultimate aim?

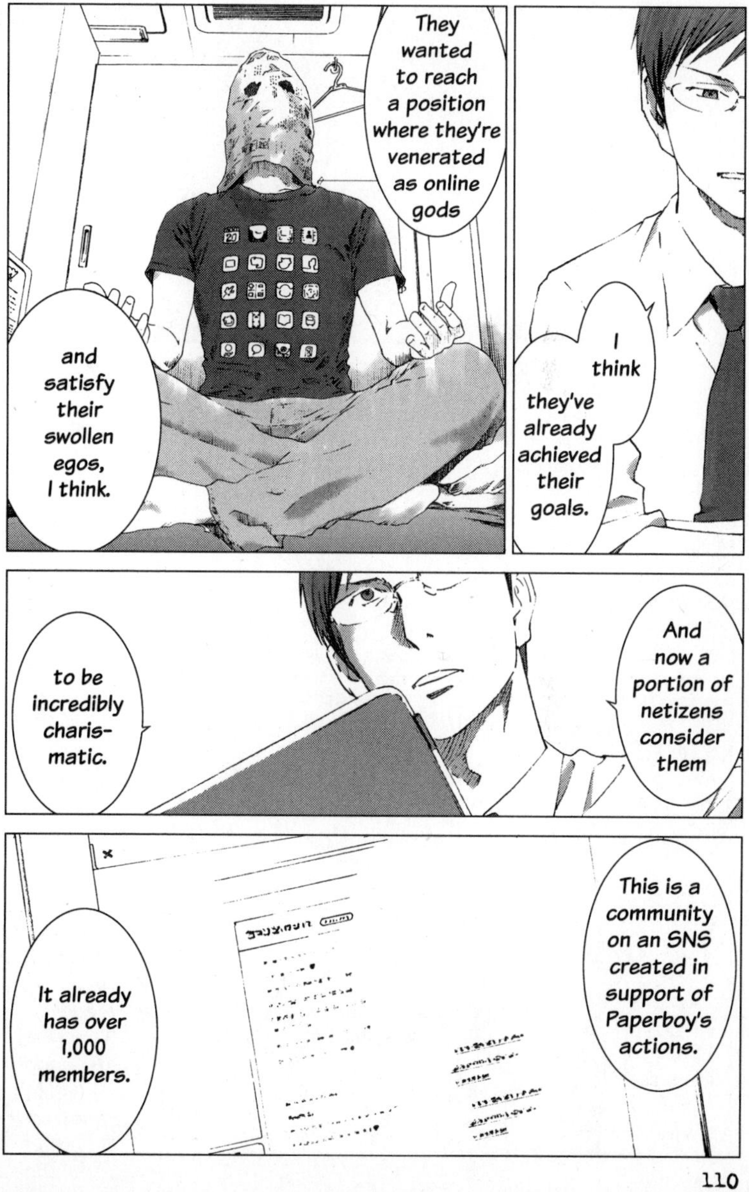
I think they've already achieved their goals.
They wanted to reach a position where they're venerated as online gods
and satisfy their swollen egos, I think.
And now a portion of netizens consider them
to be incredibly charis-matic.
This is a community on an SNS created in support of Paperboy's actions.
It already has over 1,000 members.

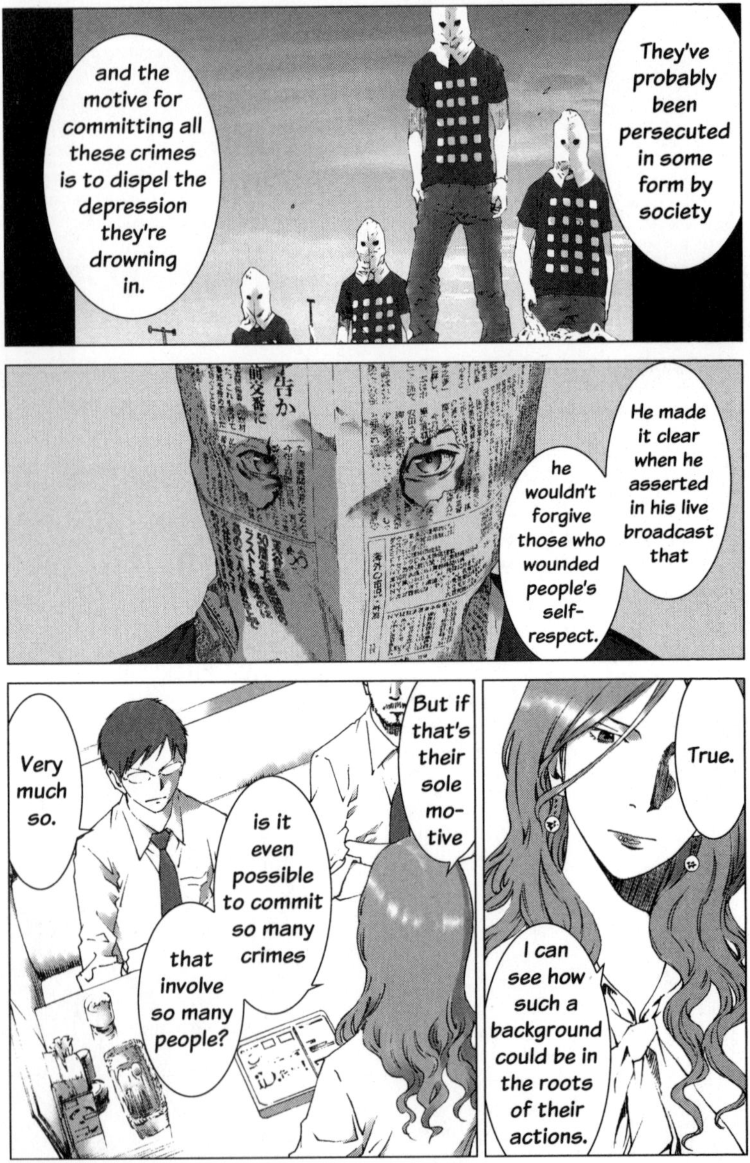
They've probably been persecuted in some form by society
and the motive for committing all these crimes is to dispel the depression they're drowning in.
He made it clear when he asserted in his live broadcast that
he wouldn't forgive those who wounded people's self-respect.
True.
I can see how such a background could be in the roots of their actions.
But if that's their sole mo-tive
is it even possible to commit so many crimes
that involve so many people?
Very much so.

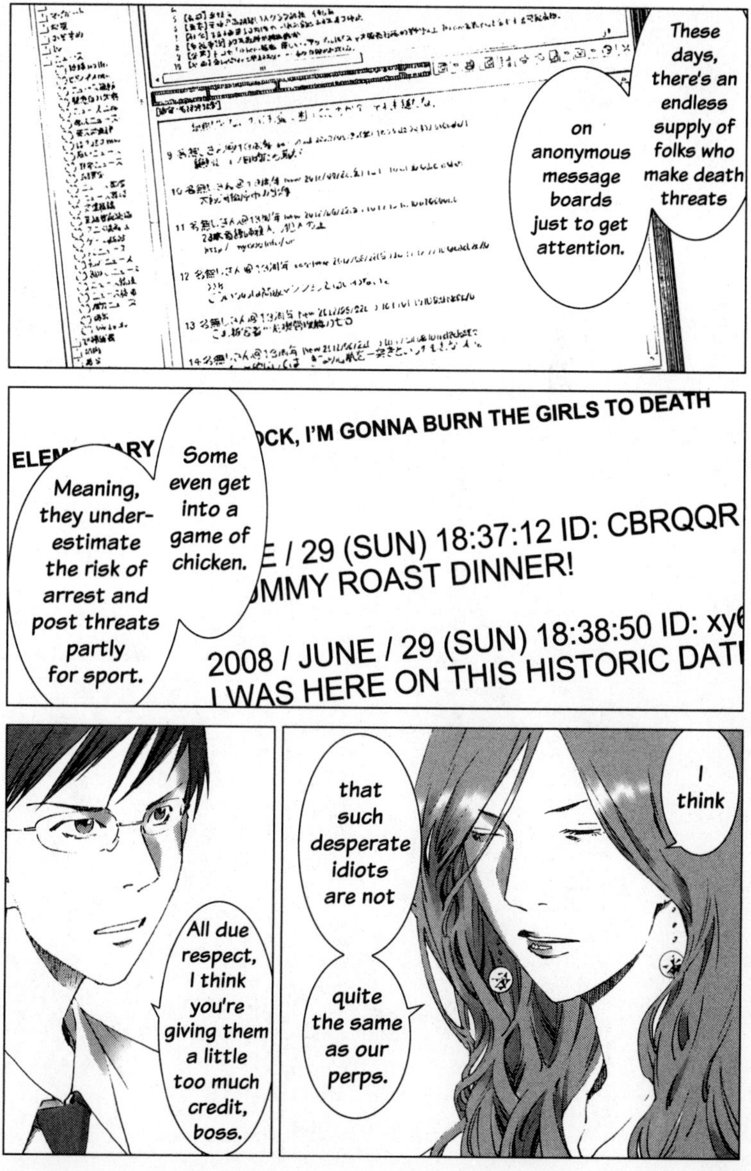
These days, there's an endless supply of folks who make death threats
on anonymous message boards just to get attention.
Some even get into a game of chicken.
Meaning, they under-estimate the risk of arrest and post threats partly for sport.
ELEM ARY
CK, I'M GONNA BURN THE GIRLS TO DEATH
E / 29 (SUN) 18:37:12 ID: CBRQQR
MMY ROAST DINNER!
2008 / JUNE / 29 (SUN) 18:38:50 ID: xy
I WAS HERE ON THIS HISTORIC DAT
I think
that such desperate idiots are not
quite the same as our perps.
All due respect, I think you're giving them a little too much credit, boss.

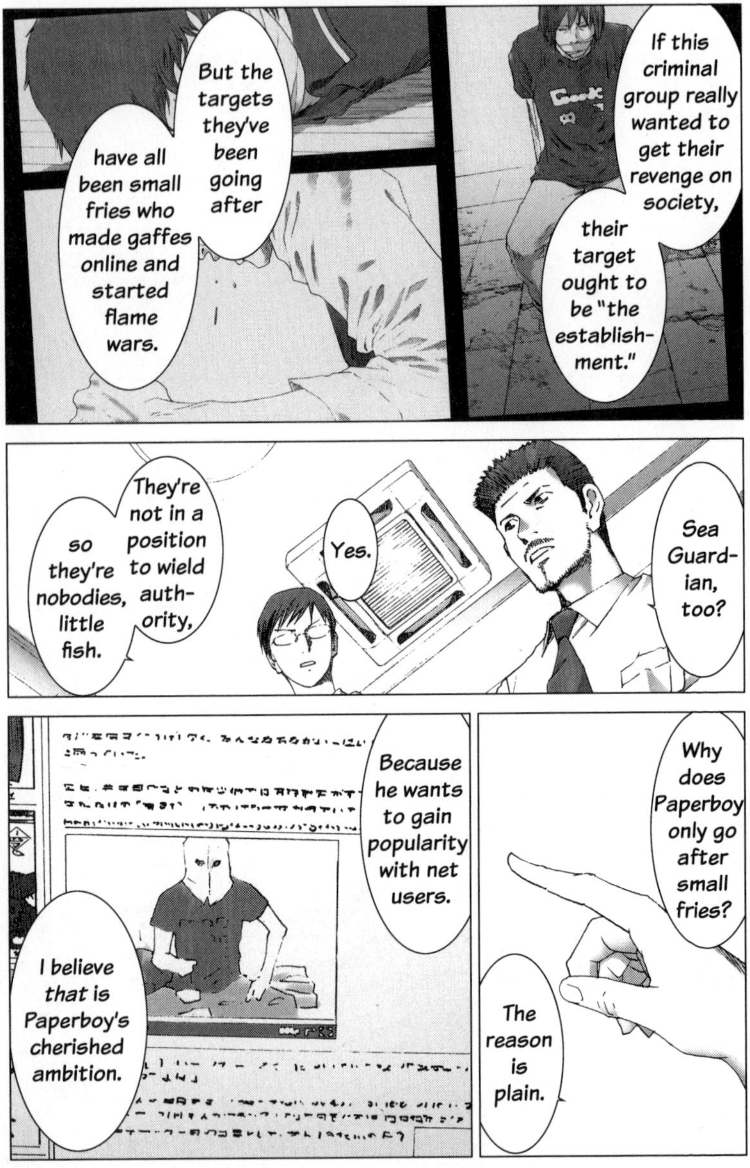
If this criminal group really wanted to get their revenge on society,
their target ought to be "the establishment."
But the targets they've been going after
have all been small fries who made gaffes online and started flame wars.
Sea Guardian, too?
Yes.
They're not in a position to wield authority,
so they're nobodies, little fish.
Why does Paperboy only go after small fries?
The reason is plain.
Because he wants to gain popularity with net users.
I believe *that* is Paperboy's cherished ambition.

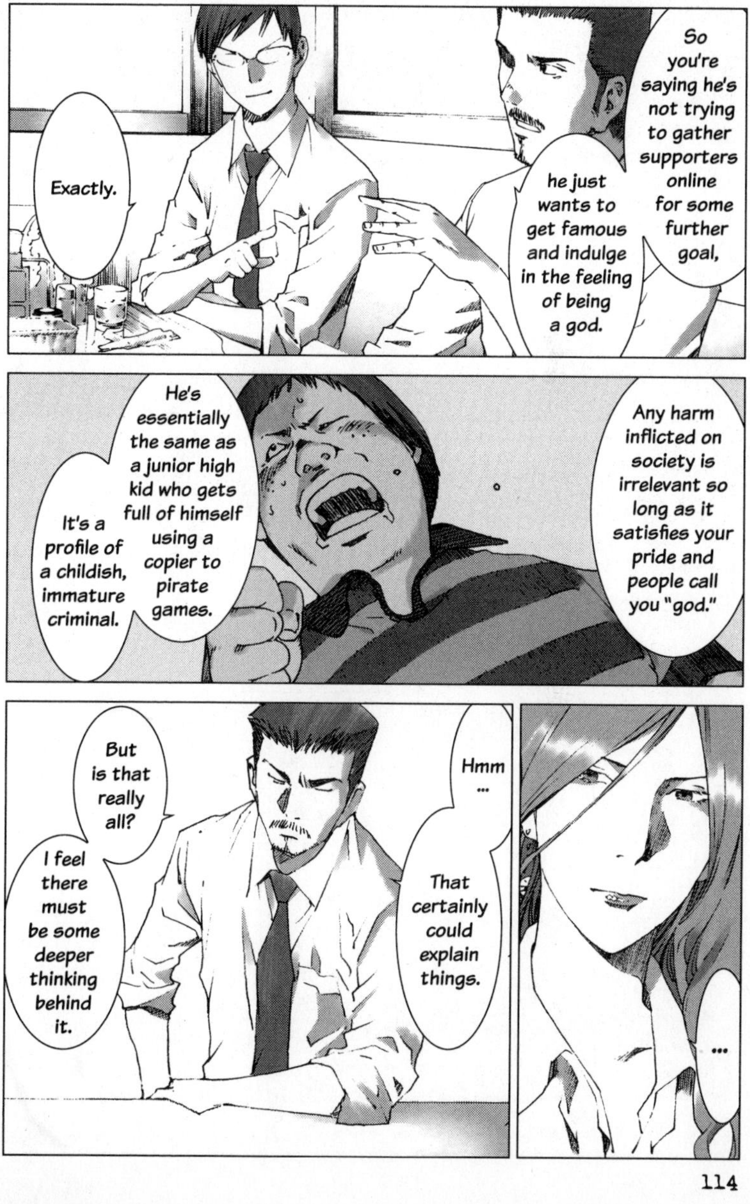

So you're saying he's not trying to gather supporters online for some further goal,
he just wants to get famous and indulge in the feeling of being a god.
Exactly.
Any harm inflicted on society is irrelevant so long as it satisfies your pride and people call you "god."
He's essentially the same as a junior high kid who gets full of himself using a copier to pirate games.
It's a profile of a childish, immature criminal.
...
Hmm ...
That certainly could explain things.
But is that really all?
I feel there must be some deeper thinking behind it.

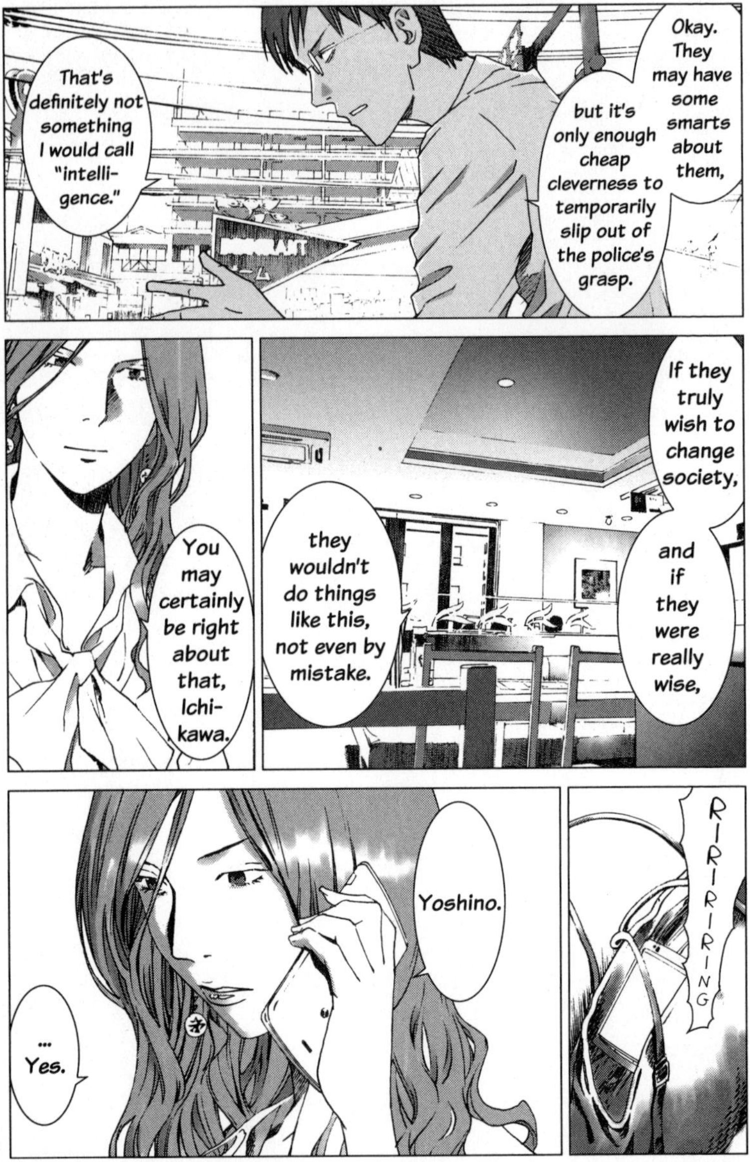
Okay. They may have some smarts about them,
but it's only enough cheap cleverness to temporarily slip out of the police's grasp.
That's definitely not something I would call "intelligence."
If they truly wish to change society,
and if they were really wise,
they wouldn't do things like this, not even by mistake.
You may certainly be right about that, Ichikawa.
RIRIRIRIRING
Yoshino.
... Yes.

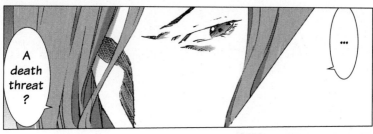

A death threat?

...

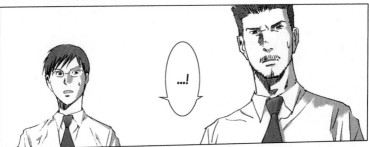

...!

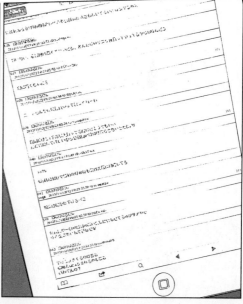

385 Anonymous
this is just empty words

386 Anonymous
If no one else'll do it I
Fuckn seriously

387 Anonymous
@386 Aaah!

388 Anonymous
@386 im reporting

389 Anonymous
@386 Yer out!

390 Anonymous

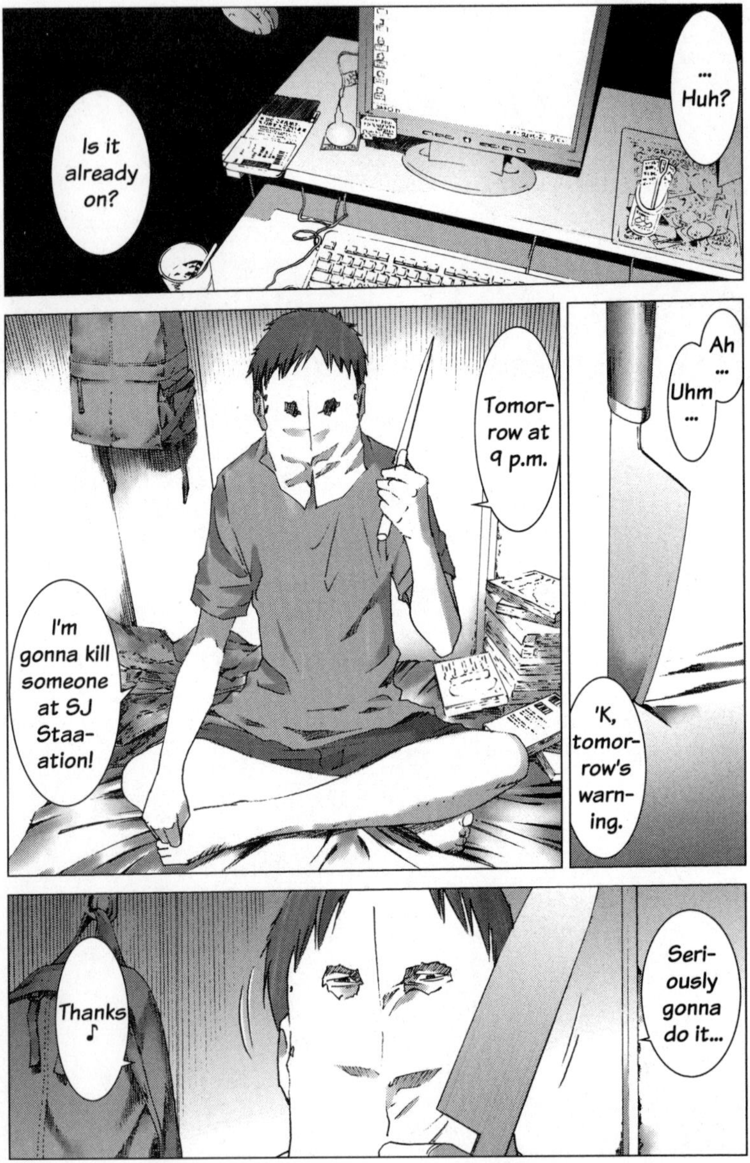
... Huh?
Is it already on?
Ah ... Uhm ...
'K, tomor-row's warn-ing.
Tomor-row at 9 p.m.
I'm gonna kill someone at SJ Staa-ation!
Seri-ously gonna do it...
Thanks ♪

PROPHECY

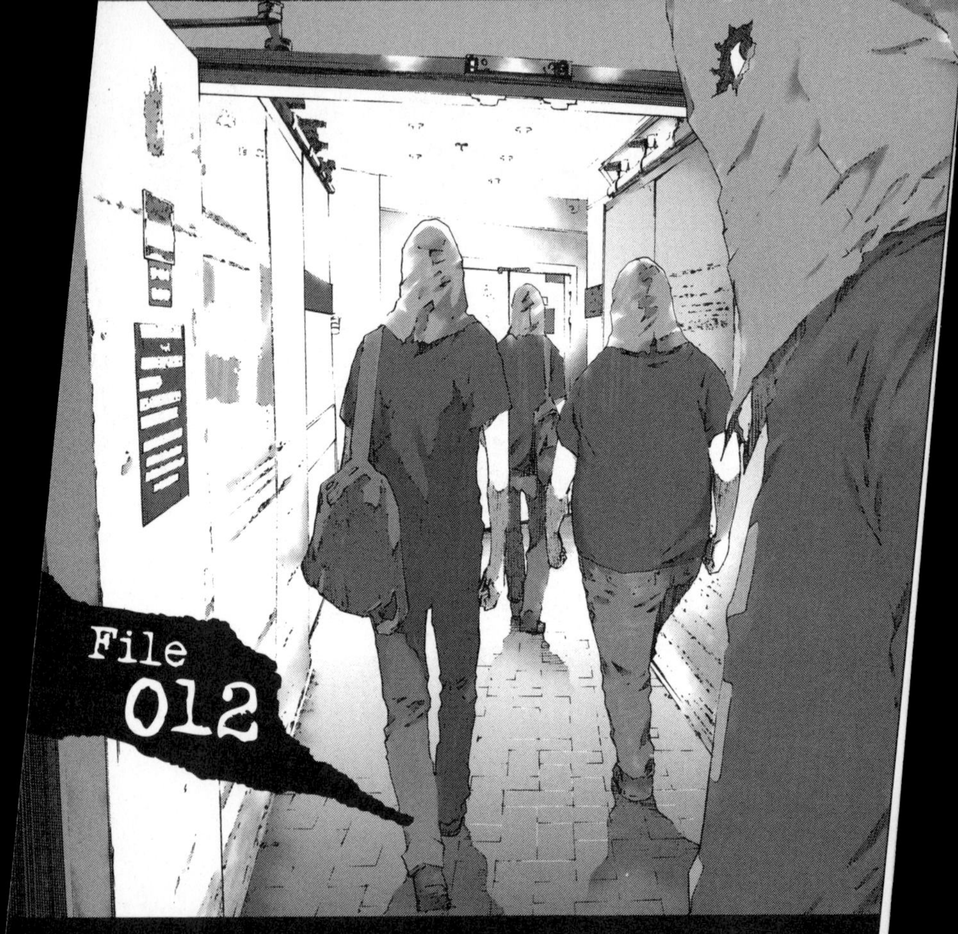
File
012

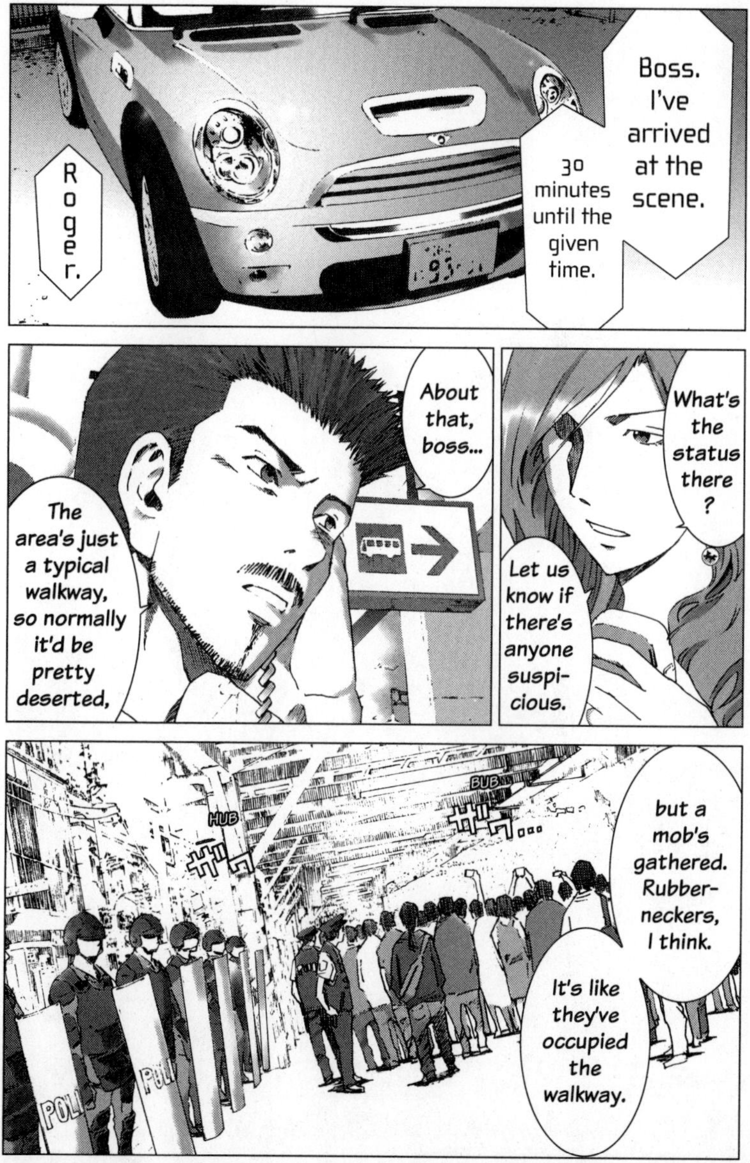
Boss. I've arrived at the scene.
30 minutes until the given time.
Roger.
What's the status there?
Let us know if there's anyone suspicious.
About that, boss...
The area's just a typical walkway, so normally it'd be pretty deserted,
but a mob's gathered. Rubber-neckers, I think.
It's like they've occupied the walkway.
BUB
HUB

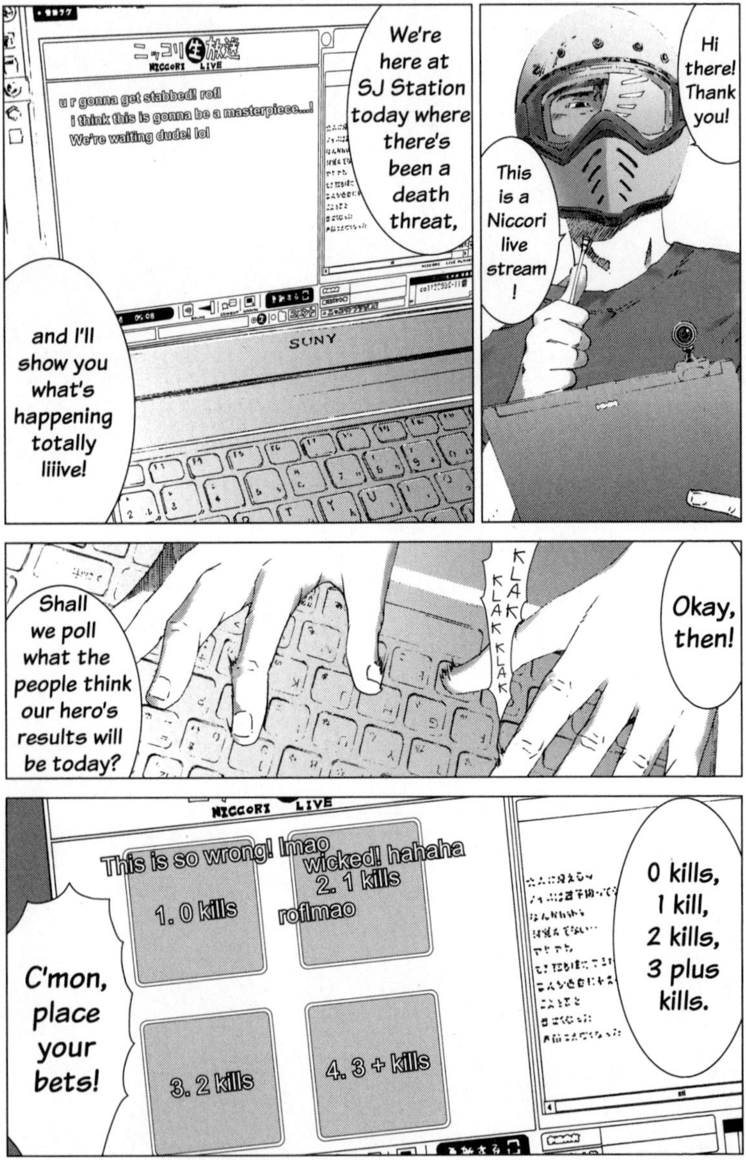
Hi there! Thank you!
This is a Niccori live stream!
We're here at SJ Station today where there's been a death threat,
ニッコリ生放送
NICCORI LIVE
u r gonna get stabbed! rofl
i think this is gonna be a masterpiece...!
We're waiting dude! lol
and I'll show you what's happening totally liiive!
SUNY
Okay, then!
KLAK KLAK KLAK KLAK
Shall we poll what the people think our hero's results will be today?
0 kills, 1 kill, 2 kills, 3 plus kills.
NICCORI LIVE
This is so wrong! lmao
wicked! hahaha
rofImao
1. 0 kills
2. 1 kills
3. 2 kills
4. 3 + kills
C'mon, place your bets!

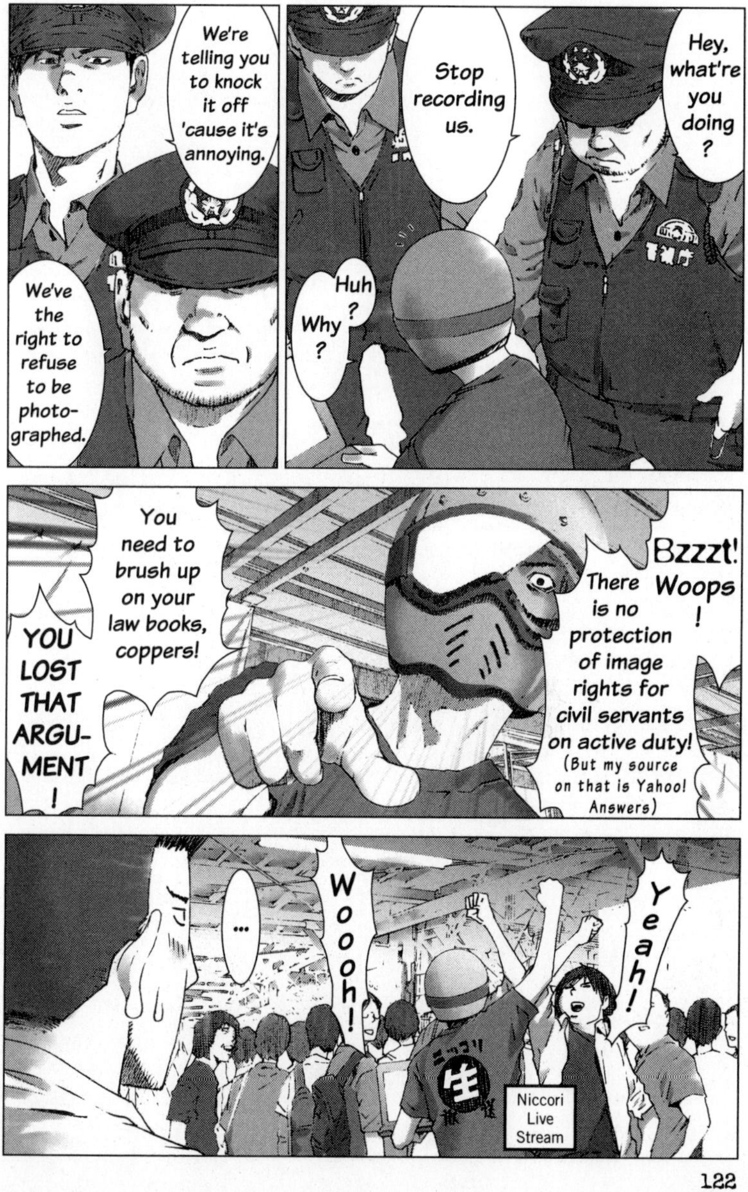
Hey, what're you doing?
Stop recording us.
Huh? Why?
We're telling you to knock it off 'cause it's annoying.
We've the right to refuse to be photo-graphed.
Bzzzt! Woops!
There is no protection of image rights for civil servants on active duty! (But my source on that is Yahoo! Answers)
You need to brush up on your law books, coppers!
YOU LOST THAT ARGU-MENT!
Yeah!
Woooh!
...
Niccori Live Stream

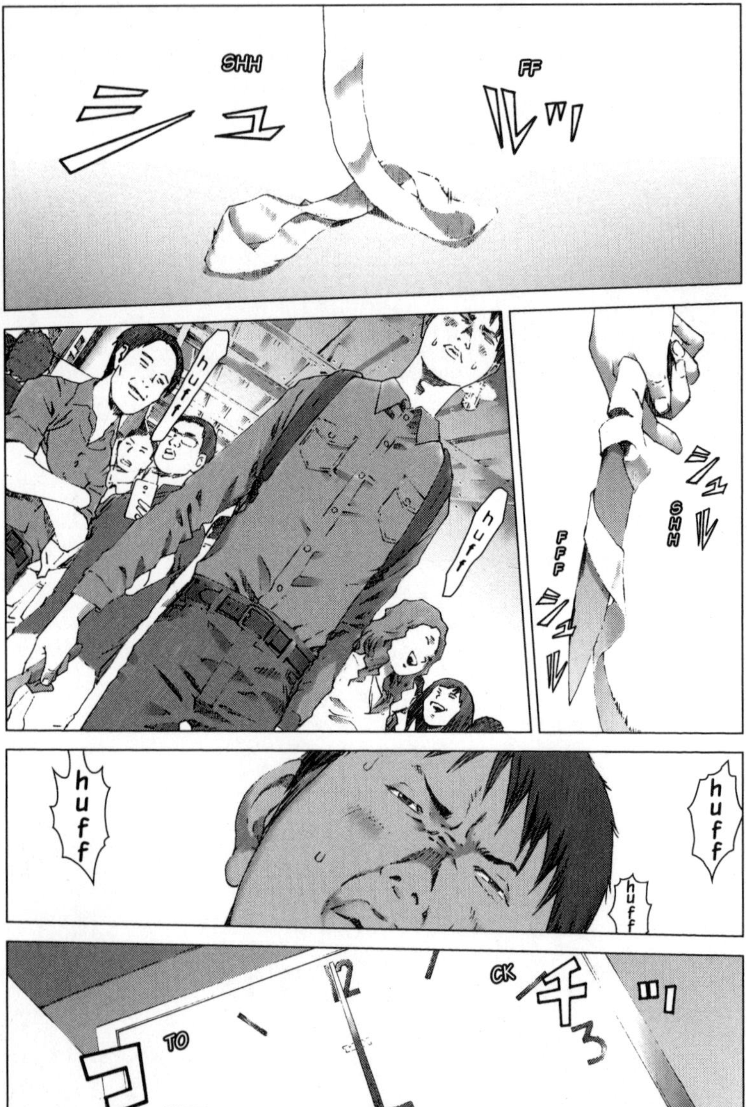
FF
ルッ
SHH
シュ
シュ
SHH
ル
FFF
シュル
huff
huff
huff
huff
huff
CK
チョッ
TO
コ

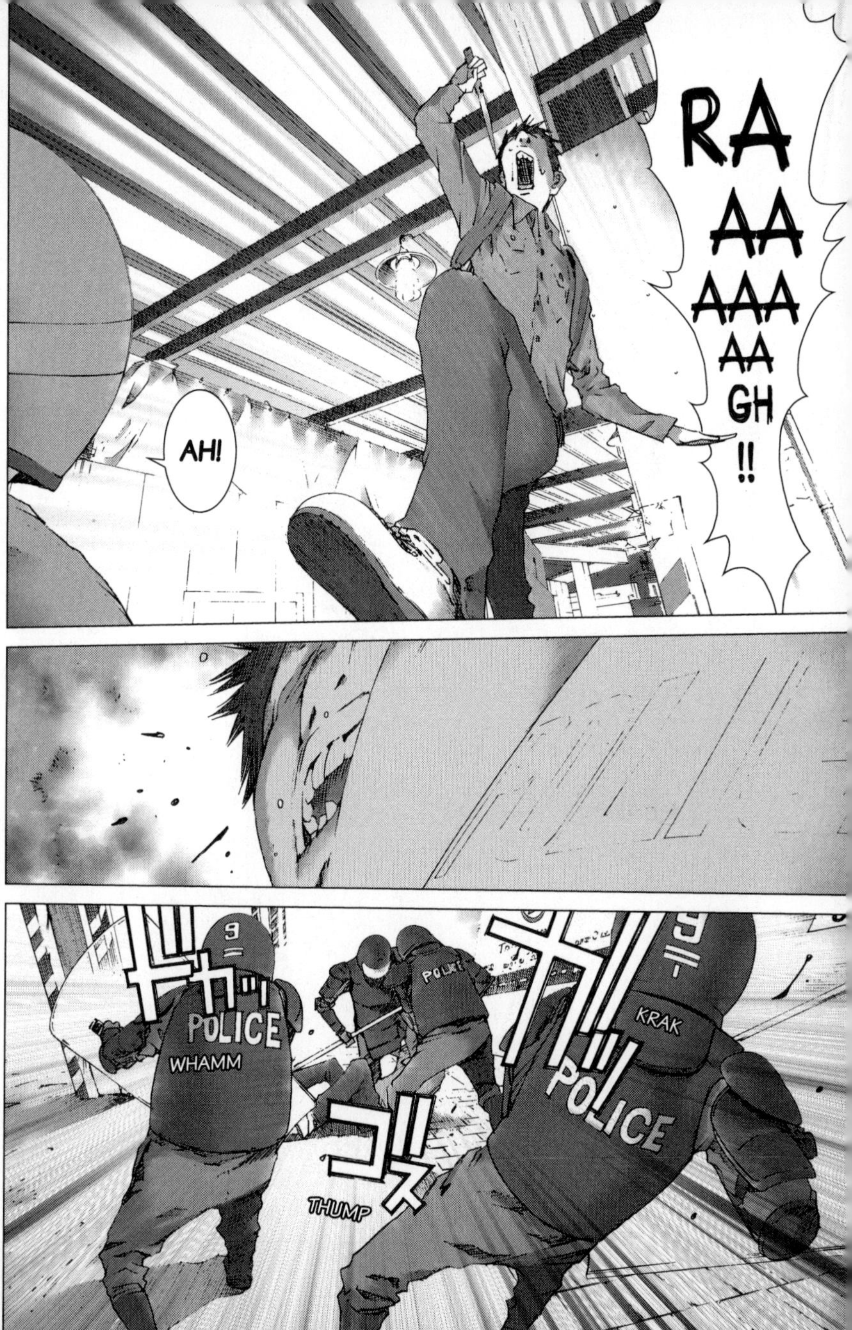
RA AA AAA AA GH !!
AH!
POLICE
KRAK
POLICE
WHAMM
POLICE
POLICE
THUMP

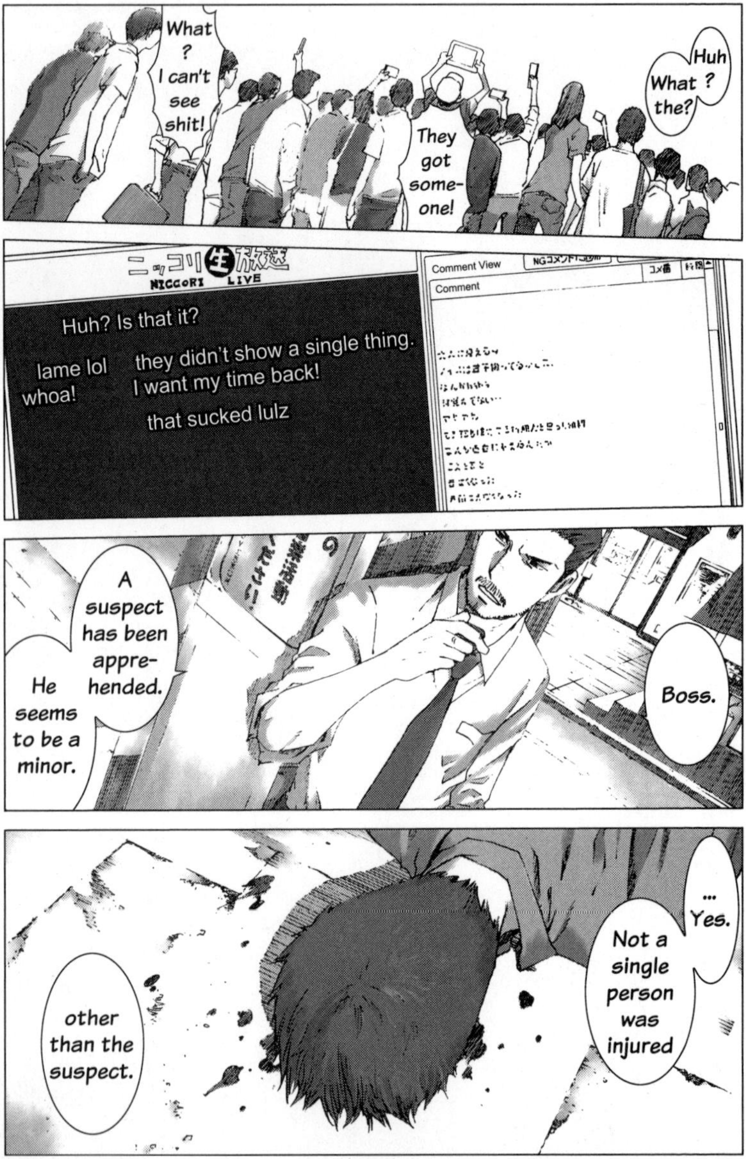
Huh What ? the?
They got some-one!
What ? I can't see shit!
ニッコリ生放送
NICCORI LIVE
Comment View
Comment
コメ番
Huh? Is that it?
they didn't show a single thing.
I want my time back!
lame lol
whoa!
that sucked lulz
Boss.
A suspect has been appre-hended.
He seems to be a minor.
... Yes.
Not a single person was injured
other than the suspect.

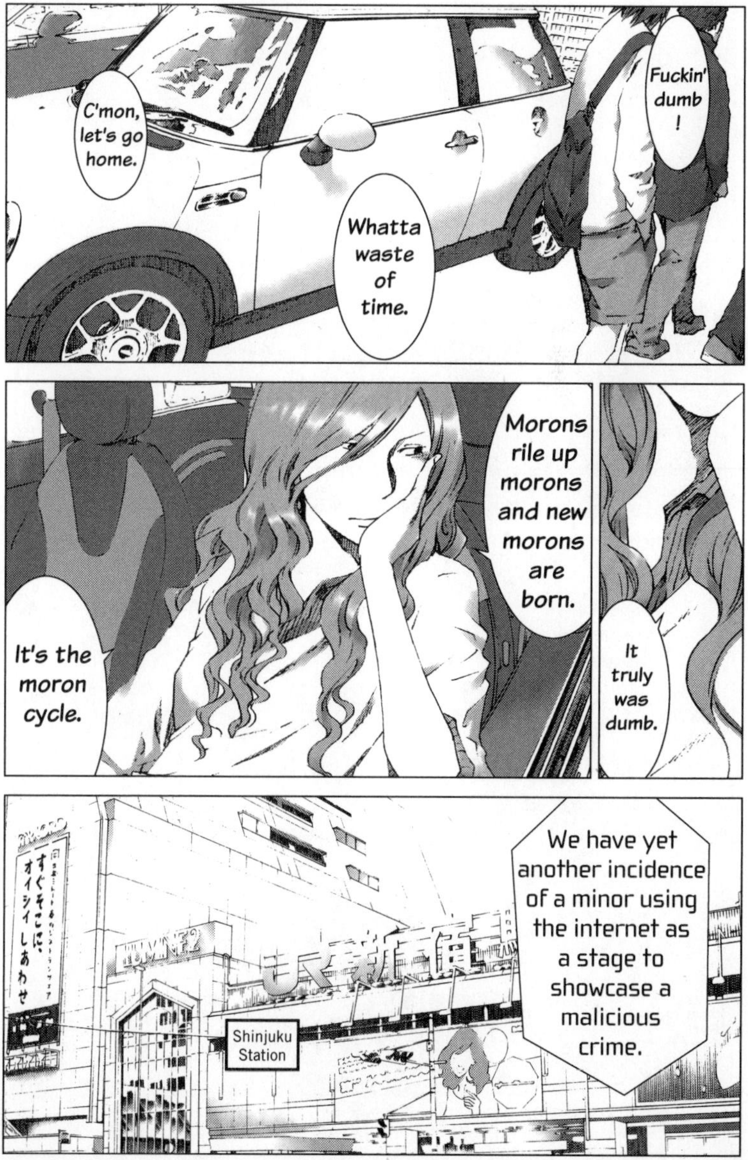
Fuckin' dumb!
Whatta waste of time.
C'mon, let's go home.
It truly was dumb.
Morons rile up morons and new morons are born.
It's the moron cycle.
We have yet another incidence of a minor using the internet as a stage to showcase a malicious crime.
Shinjuku Station
すぐそこに、オイシイしあわせ

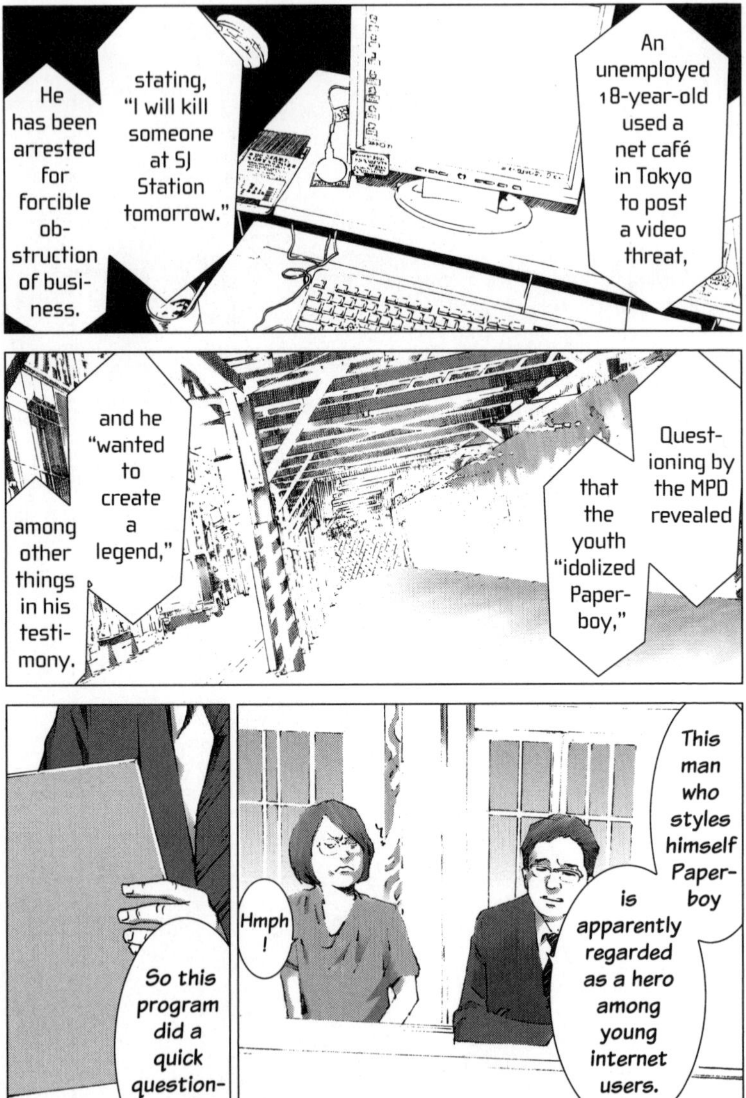

An unemployed 18-year-old used a net café in Tokyo to post a video threat,
stating, "I will kill someone at SJ Station tomorrow."
He has been arrested for forcible obstruction of business.
Questioning by the MPD revealed
that the youth "idolized Paperboy,"
and he "wanted to create a legend,"
among other things in his testimony.
This man who styles himself Paperboy
is apparently regarded as a hero among young internet users.
Hmph!
So this program did a quick questionnaire.

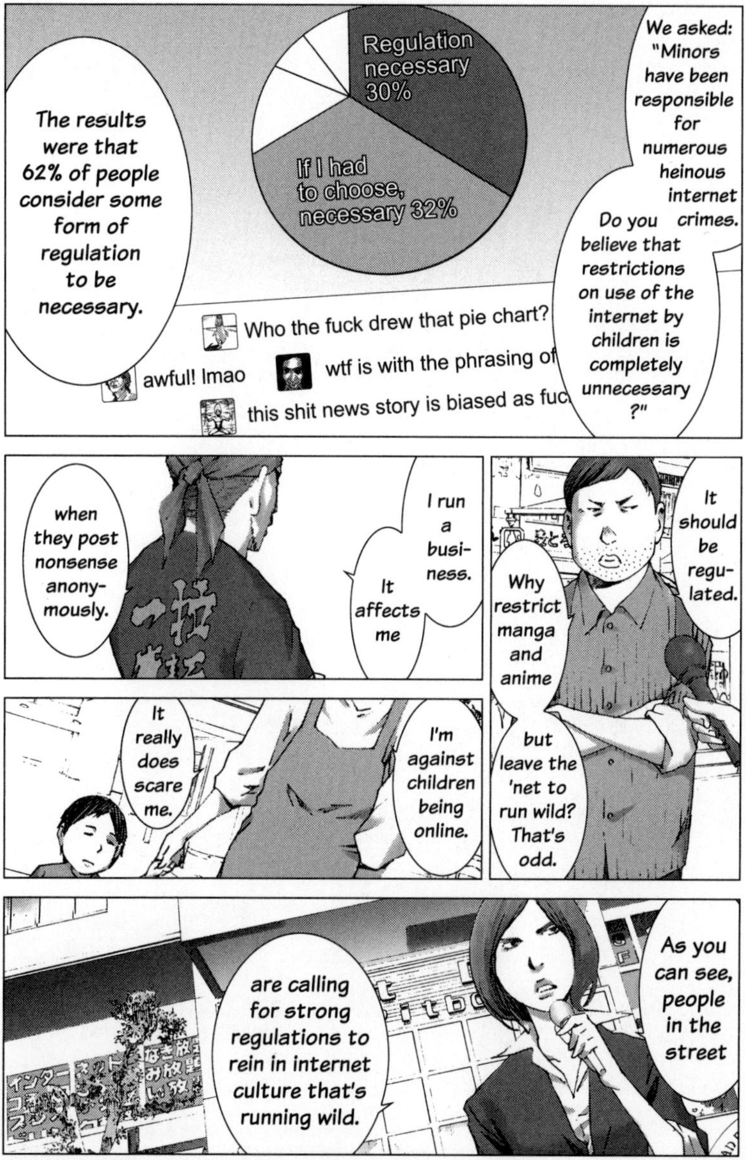
We asked: "Minors have been responsible for numerous heinous internet crimes. Do you believe that restrictions on use of the internet by children is completely unnecessary?"
Regulation necessary 30%
If I had to choose, necessary 32%
The results were that 62% of people consider some form of regulation to be necessary.
Who the fuck drew that pie chart?
wtf is with the phrasing of
awful! lmao
this shit news story is biased as fuc
It should be regulated.
Why restrict manga and anime
but leave the 'net to run wild? That's odd.
I run a business.
It affects me
when they post nonsense anonymously.
I'm against children being online.
It really does scare me.
As you can see, people in the street
are calling for strong regulations to rein in internet culture that's running wild.

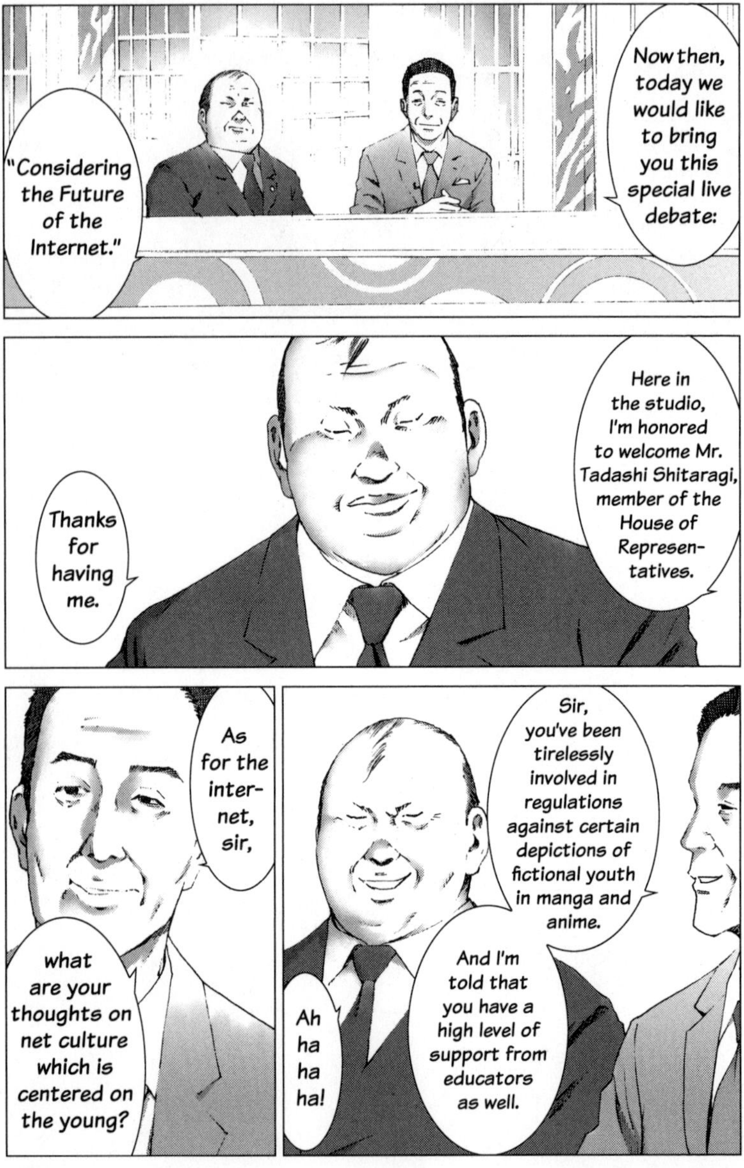
Now then, today we would like to bring you this special live debate:
"Considering the Future of the Internet."
Here in the studio, I'm honored to welcome Mr. Tadashi Shitaragi, member of the House of Represen-tatives.
Thanks for having me.
Sir, you've been tirelessly involved in regulations against certain depictions of fictional youth in manga and anime.
And I'm told that you have a high level of support from educators as well.
Ah ha ha ha!
As for the inter-net, sir,
what are your thoughts on net culture which is centered on the young?

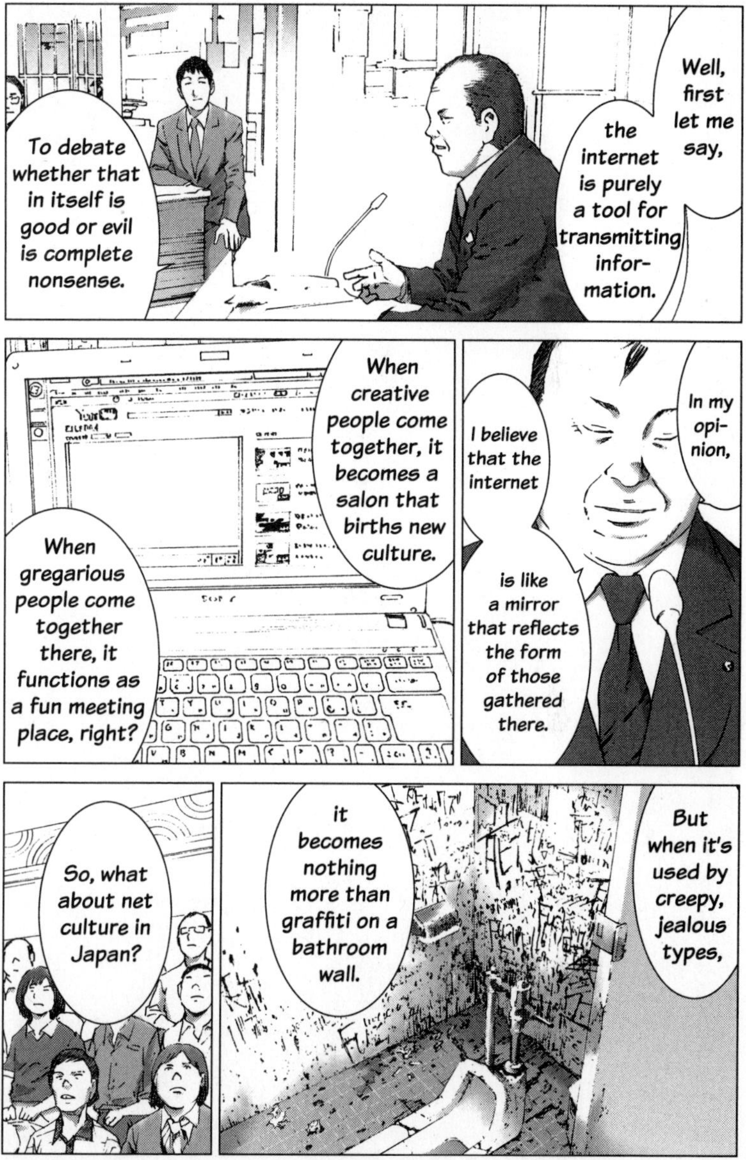
Well, first let me say,
the internet is purely a tool for transmitting infor-mation.
To debate whether that in itself is good or evil is complete nonsense.
In my opi-nion,
I believe that the internet
is like a mirror that reflects the form of those gathered there.
When creative people come together, it becomes a salon that births new culture.
When gregarious people come together there, it functions as a fun meeting place, right?
But when it's used by creepy, jealous types,
it becomes nothing more than graffiti on a bathroom wall.
So, what about net culture in Japan?

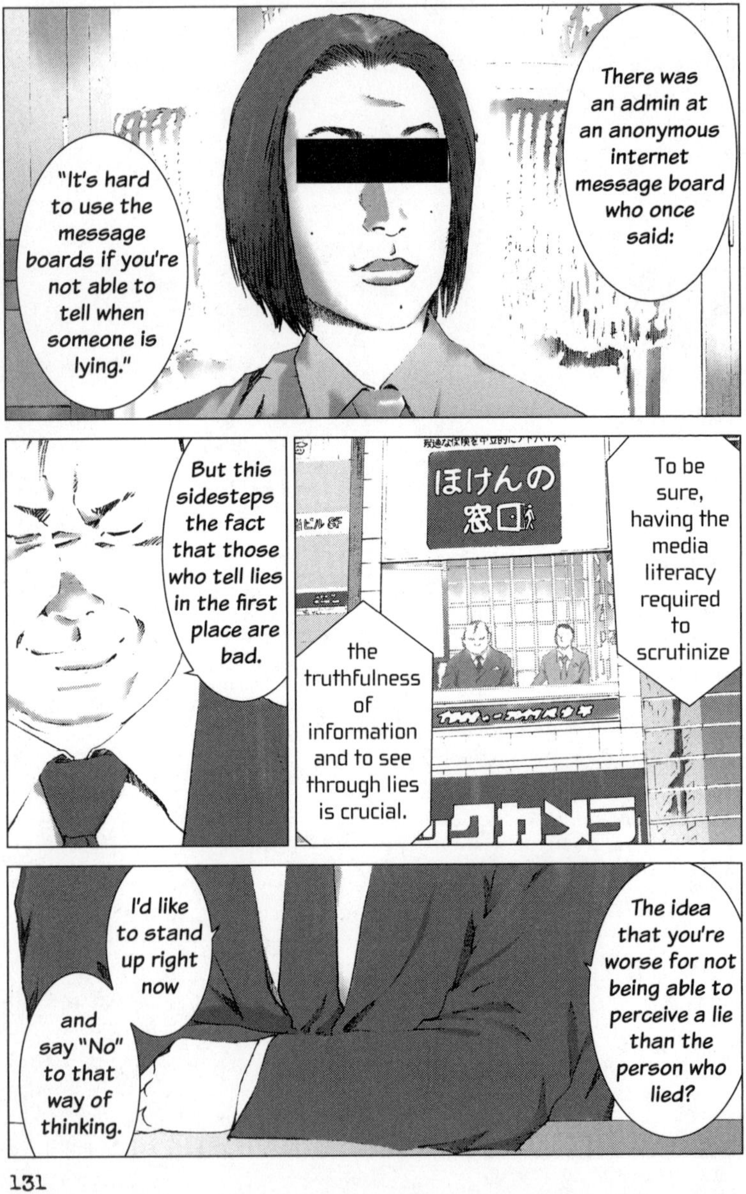
There was an admin at an anonymous internet message board who once said:
"It's hard to use the message boards if you're not able to tell when someone is lying."
ほけんの窓口
To be sure, having the media literacy required to scrutinize
the truthfulness of information and to see through lies is crucial.
But this sidesteps the fact that those who tell lies in the first place are bad.
The idea that you're worse for not being able to perceive a lie than the person who lied?
I'd like to stand up right now
and say "No" to that way of thinking.

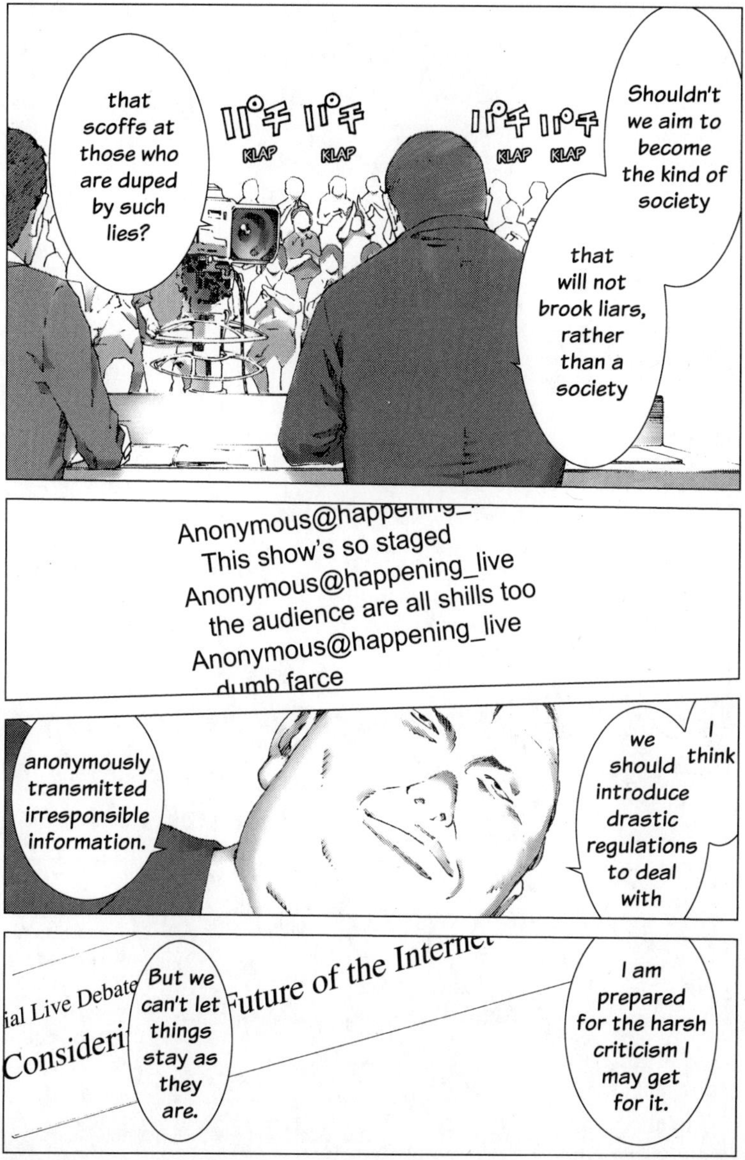
Shouldn't we aim to become the kind of society
that will not brook liars, rather than a society
パチ パチ
KLAP KLAP
パチ パチ
KLAP KLAP
that scoffs at those who are duped by such lies?
Anonymous@happening_
This show's so staged
Anonymous@happening_live
the audience are all shills too
Anonymous@happening_live
dumb farce
I think
we should introduce drastic regulations to deal with
anonymously transmitted irresponsible information.
I am prepared for the harsh criticism I may get for it.
But we can't let things stay as they are.
ial Live Debate
Consideri
Future of the Interne

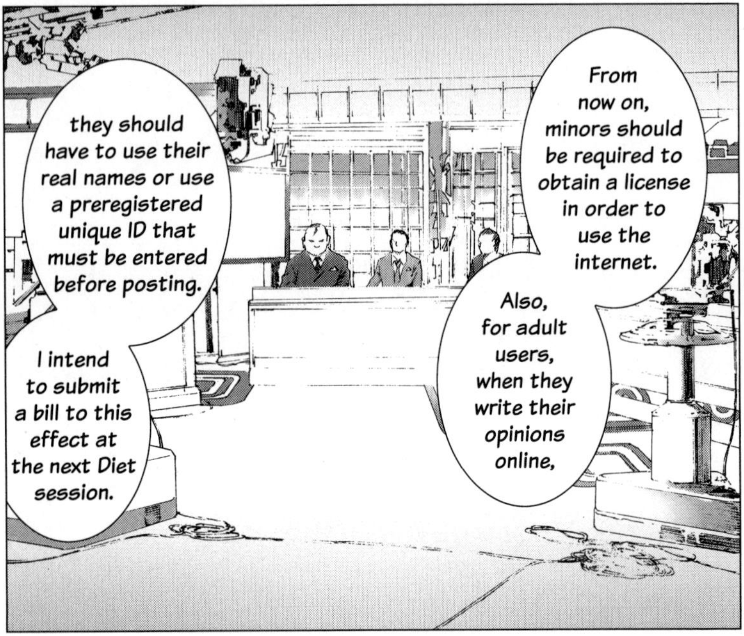
From now on, minors should be required to obtain a license in order to use the internet.
Also, for adult users, when they write their opinions online,
they should have to use their real names or use a preregistered unique ID that must be entered before posting.
I intend to submit a bill to this effect at the next Diet session.
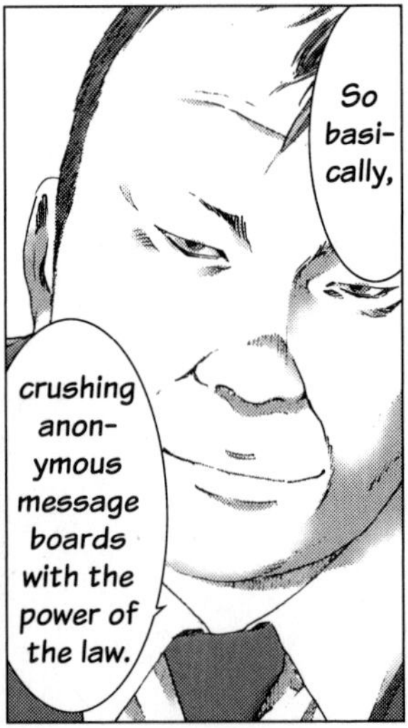
So basi-cally,
crushing anon-ymous message boards with the power of the law.
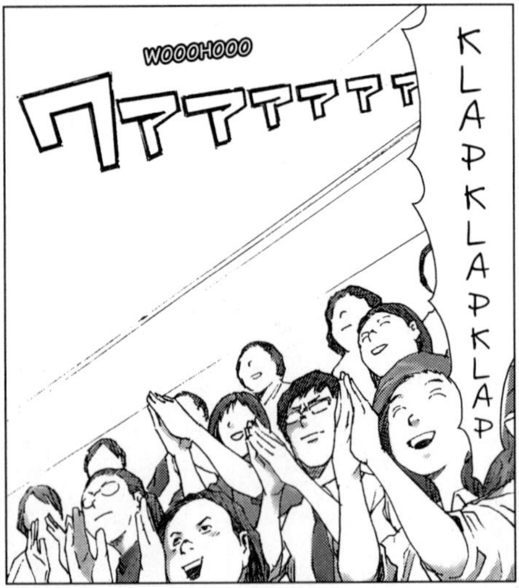
KLAPKLAPKLAP
WOOOHOOO
ワァァァァァァ

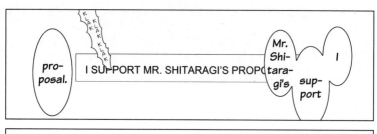

pro-posal.

I SUPPORT MR. SHITARAGI'S PROPO[SAL]

Mr. Shi-tara-gi's

I sup-port

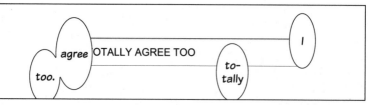

agree too.

[T]OTALLY AGREE TOO

I

to-tally

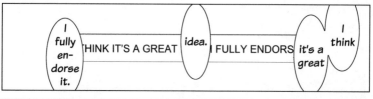

I fully en-dorse it.

[I] THINK IT'S A GREAT idea. I FULLY ENDORS[E]

it's a great

I think

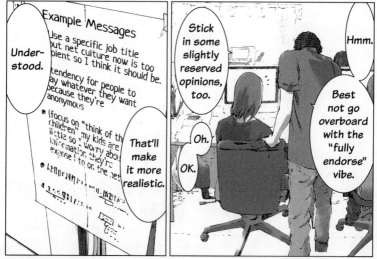

Example Messages

Use a specific job title but net culture now is too [vi]olent so I think it should be.

Under-stood.

[a] tendency for people to [s]ay whatever they want because they're anonymous.

● (focus on "think of the children"; my kids are little so I worry about [in]formation they're expose[d] to on the net

That'll make it more realistic.

Stick in some slightly reserved opinions, too.

Hmm.

Oh.

OK.

Best not go overboard with the "fully endorse" vibe.

134

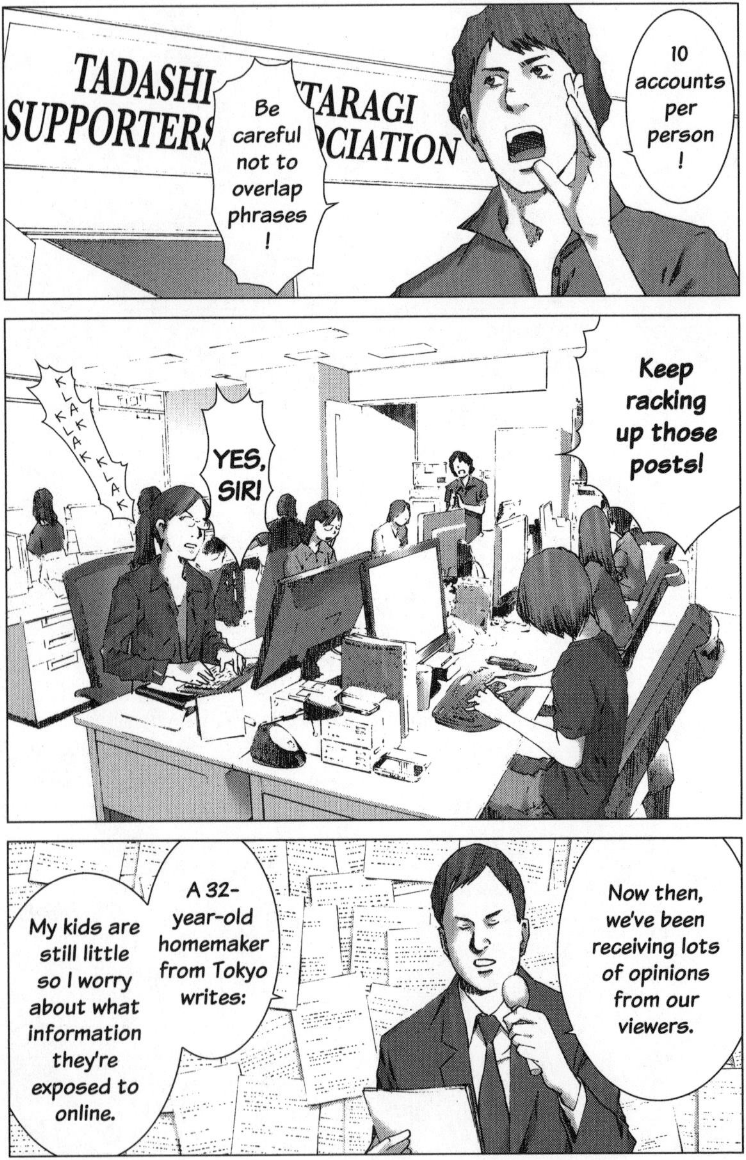
10 accounts per person!
Be careful not to overlap phrases!
TADASHI TARAGI
SUPPORTERS OCIATION
Keep racking up those posts!
YES, SIR!
KLAK KLAK KLAK KLAK
Now then, we've been receiving lots of opinions from our viewers.
A 32-year-old homemaker from Tokyo writes:
My kids are still little so I worry about what information they're exposed to online.

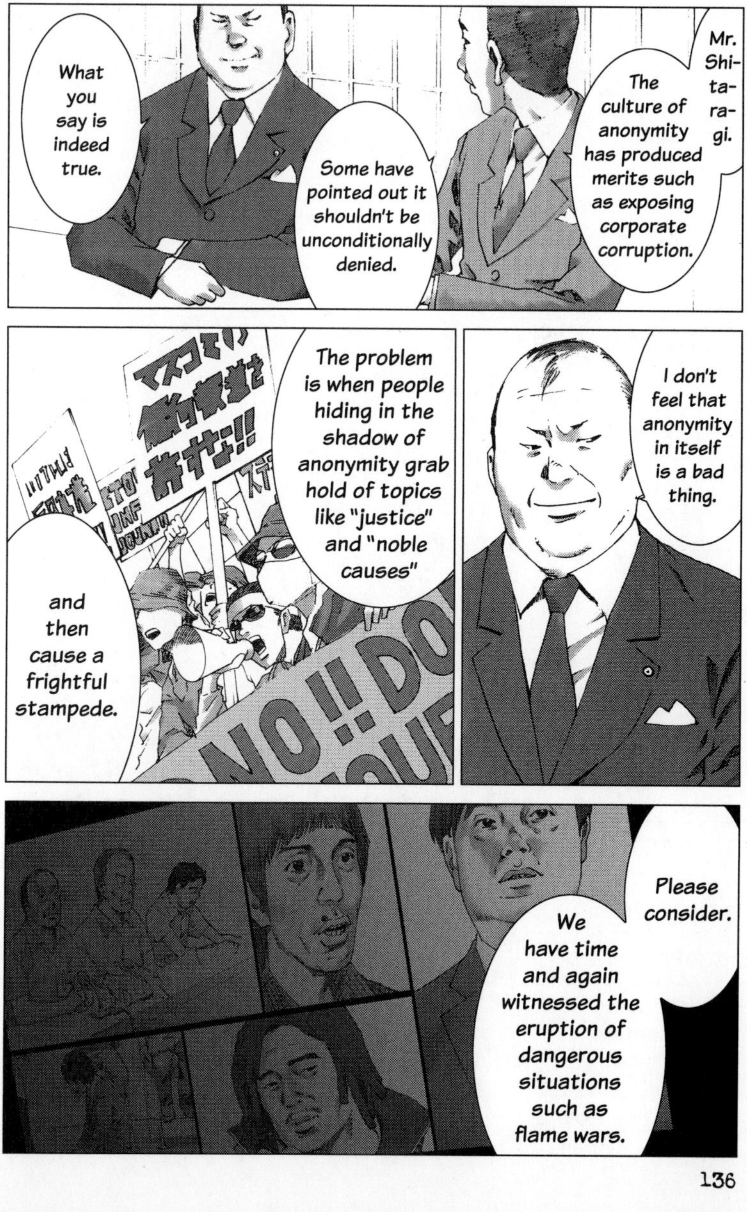
Mr. Shi-ta-ra-gi.
The culture of anonymity has produced merits such as exposing corporate corruption.
Some have pointed out it shouldn't be unconditionally denied.
What you say is indeed true.
I don't feel that anonymity in itself is a bad thing.
The problem is when people hiding in the shadow of anonymity grab hold of topics like "justice" and "noble causes"
and then cause a frightful stampede.
Please consider.
We have time and again witnessed the eruption of dangerous situations such as flame wars.

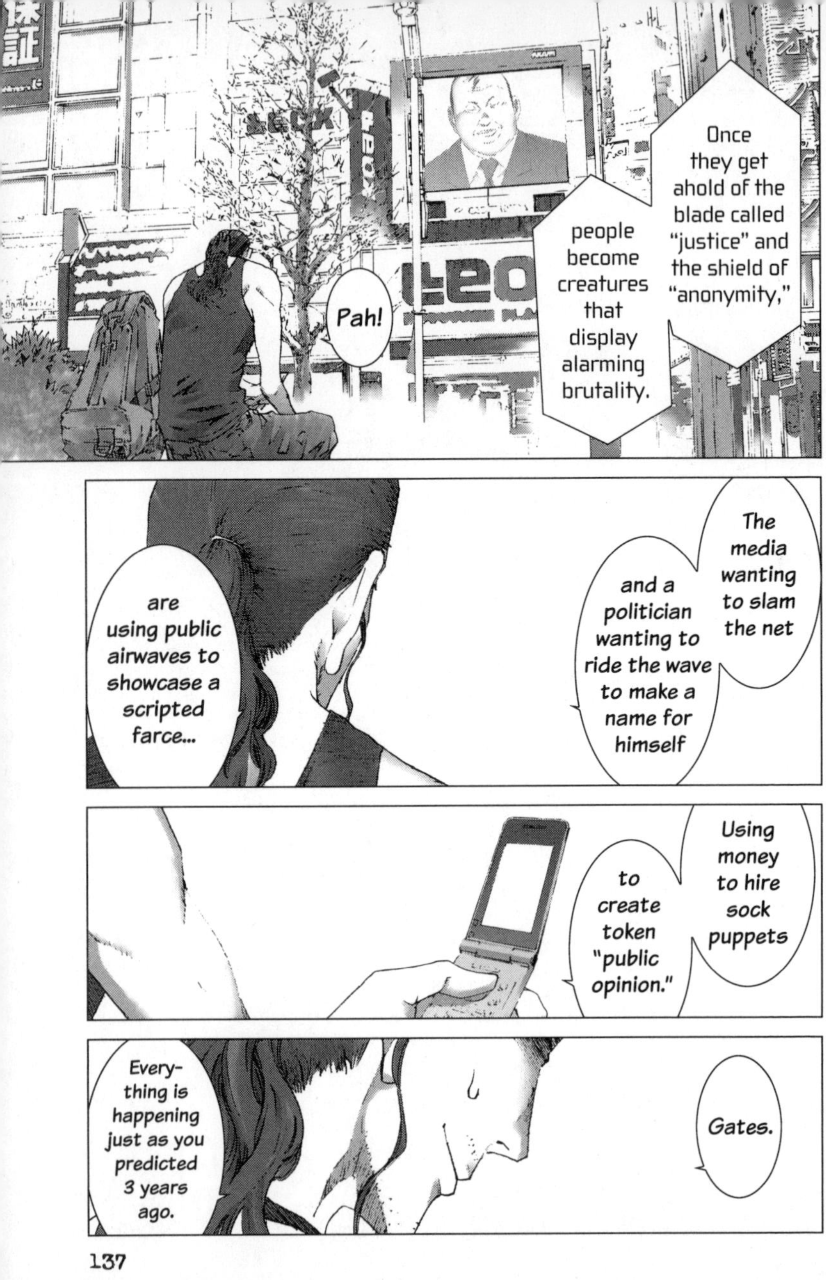
Once they get ahold of the blade called "justice" and the shield of "anonymity,"
people become creatures that display alarming brutality.
Pah!
The media wanting to slam the net
and a politician wanting to ride the wave to make a name for himself
are using public airwaves to showcase a scripted farce...
Using money to hire sock puppets
to create token "public opinion."
Gates.
Every-thing is happening just as you predicted 3 years ago.

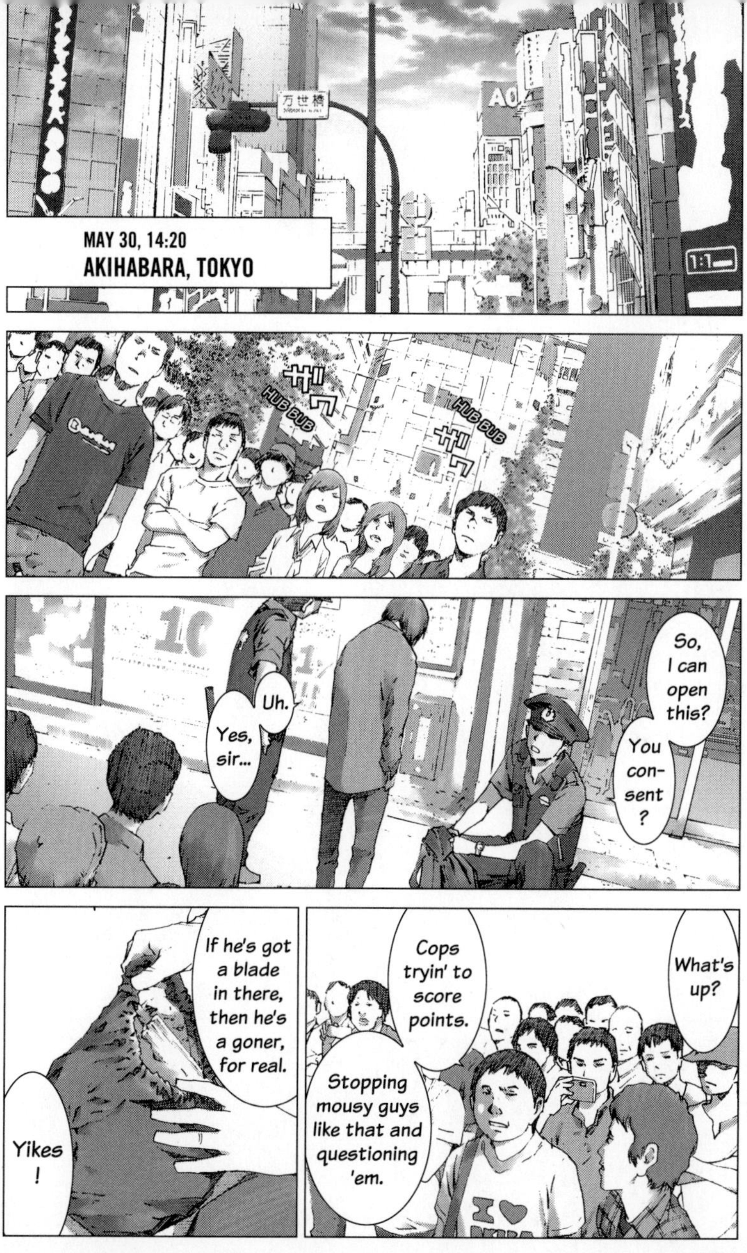
万世橋
MAY 30, 14:20
AKIHABARA, TOKYO
HUB BUB
HUB BUB
So, I can open this?
You consent?
Uh.
Yes, sir...
What's up?
Cops tryin' to score points.
Stopping mousy guys like that and questioning 'em.
If he's got a blade in there, then he's a goner, for real.
Yikes!

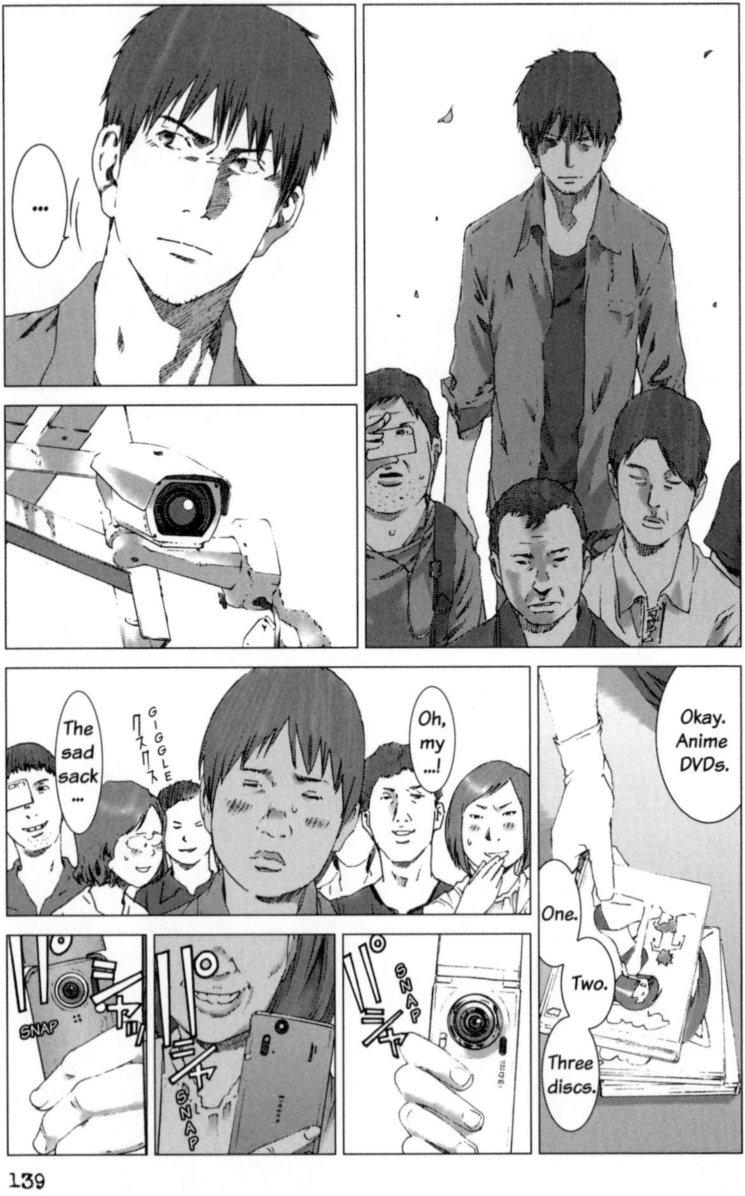
...
Okay. Anime DVDs.
One.
Two.
Three discs.
Oh, my ...!
クスクス
GIGGLE
The sad sack ...
SNAP
SNAP
SNAP

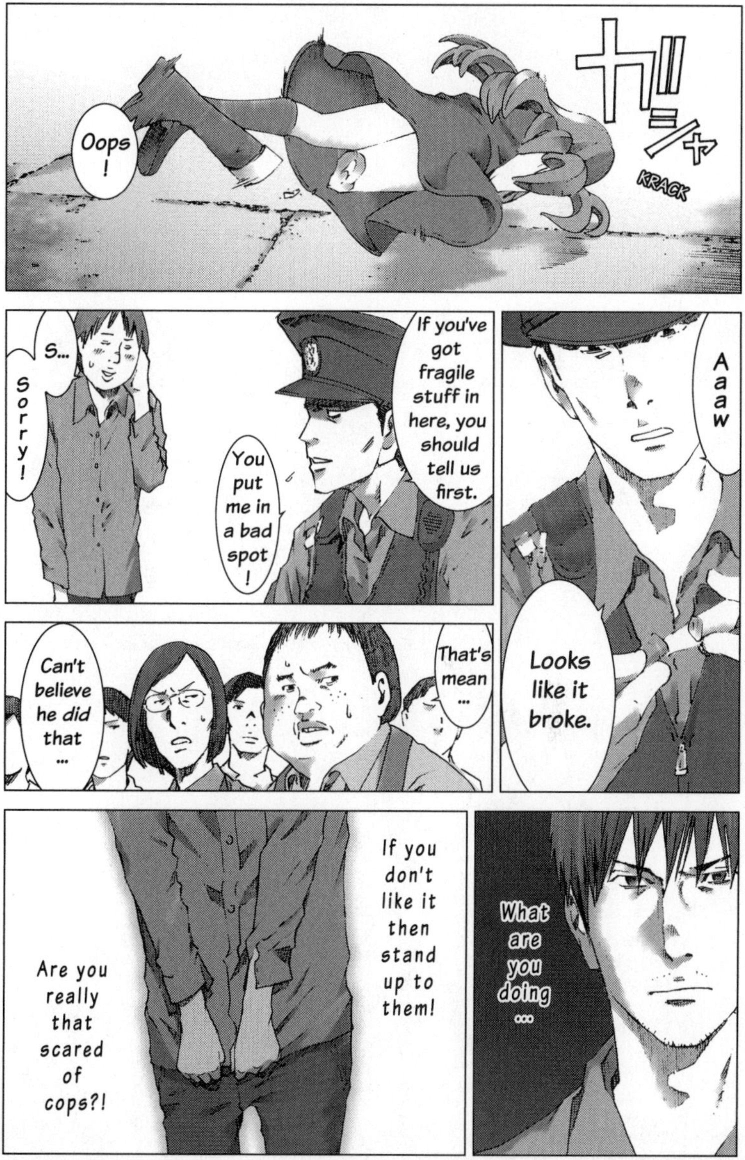
ガシャ
KRACK
Oops!
Aaaw
Looks like it broke.
If you've got fragile stuff in here, you should tell us first.
You put me in a bad spot!
S...
Sorry!
That's mean...
Can't believe he *did* that...
What are you doing...
If you don't like it then stand up to them!
Are you really that scared of cops?!

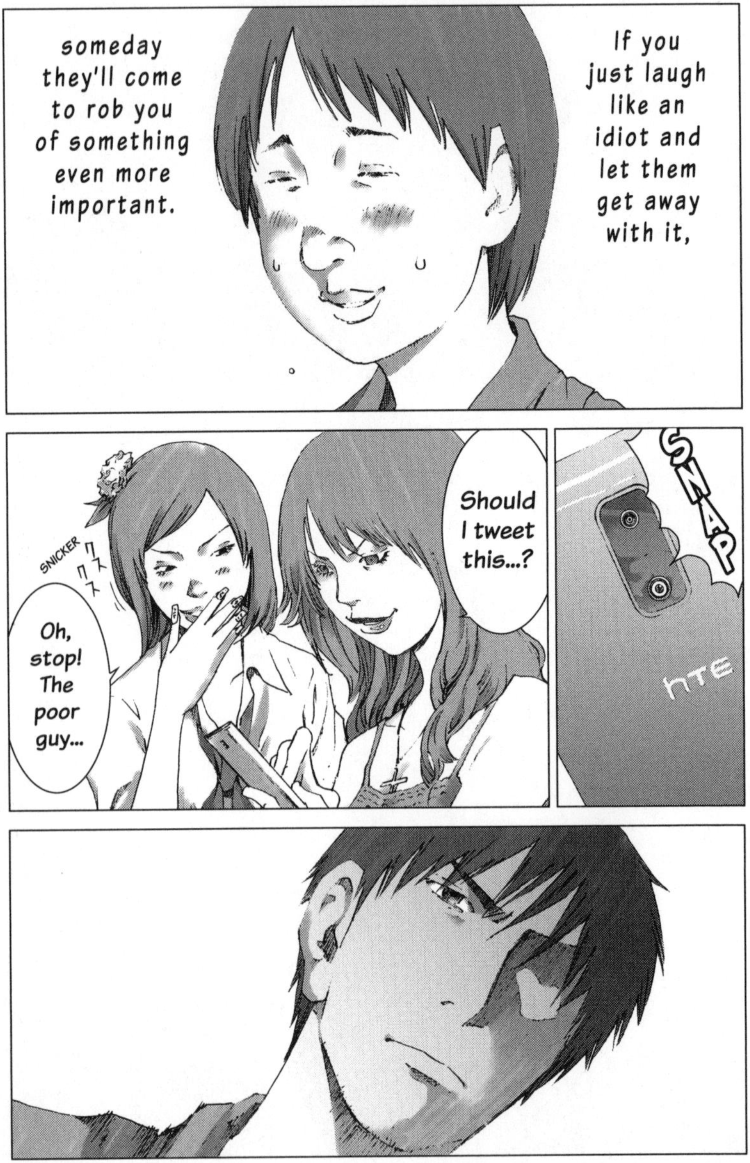
If you just laugh like an idiot and let them get away with it,
someday they'll come to rob you of something even more important.
SNAP
hTE
Should I tweet this...?
SNICKER
クスクス
Oh, stop! The poor guy...

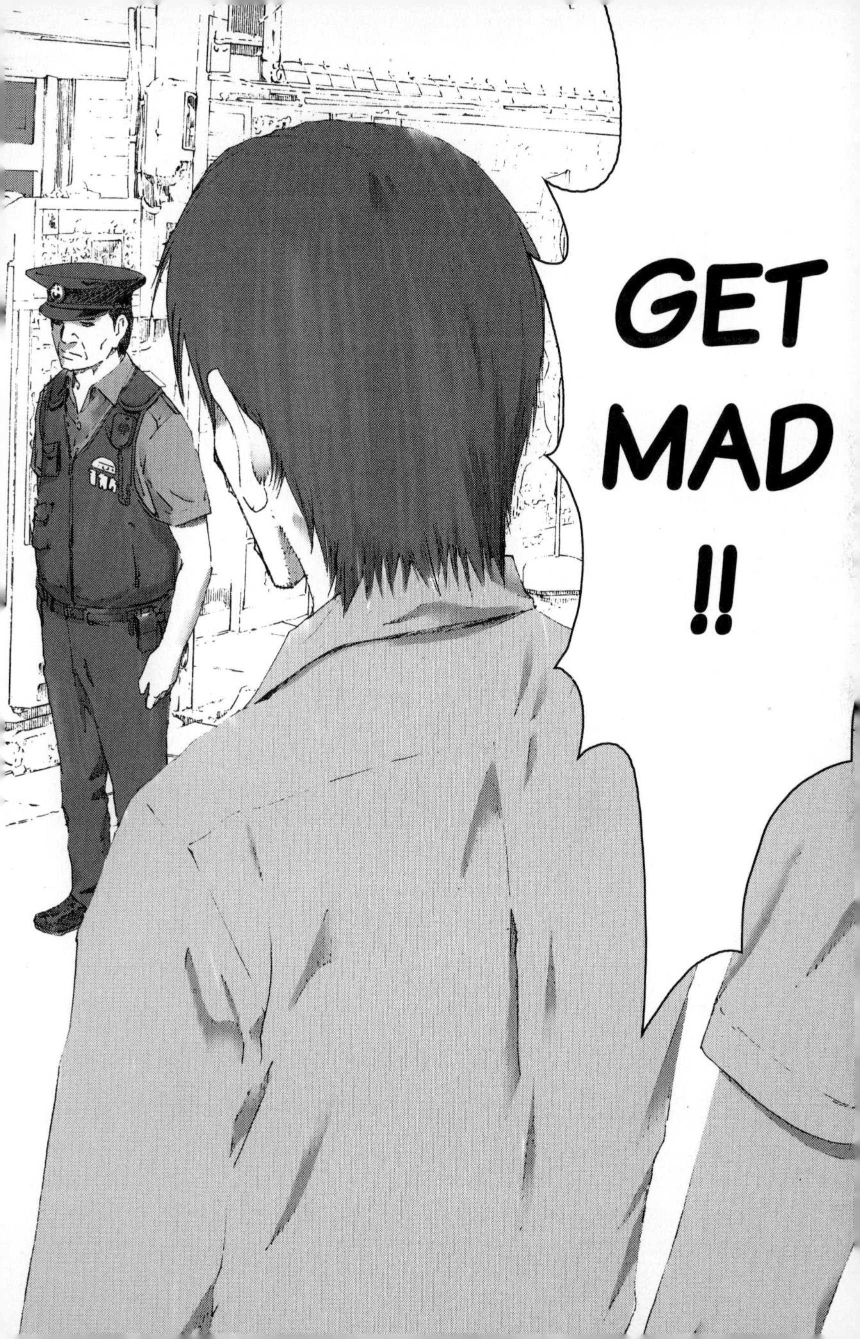
GET MAD !!

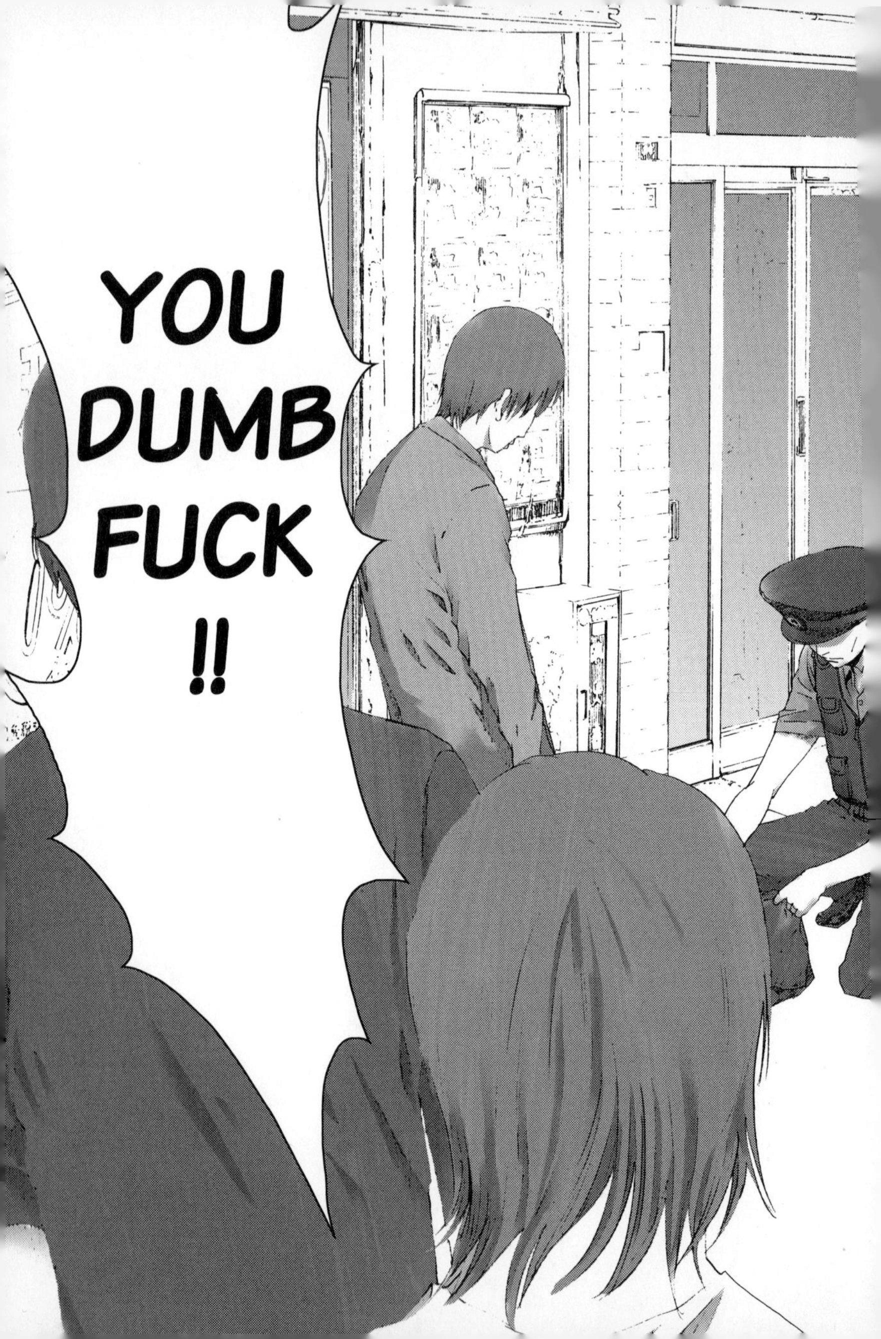
YOU DUMB FUCK !!

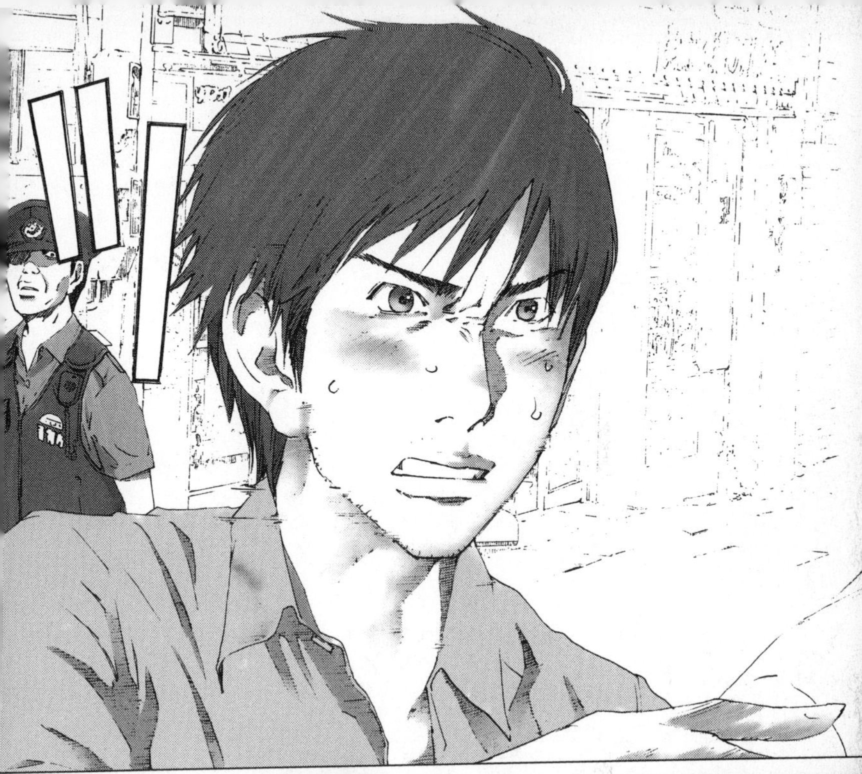
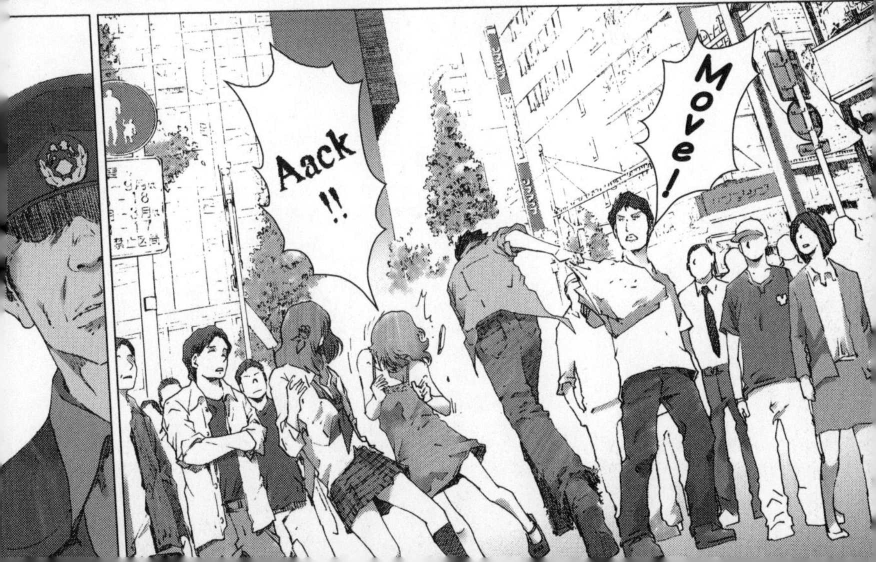
Move!
Aack !!

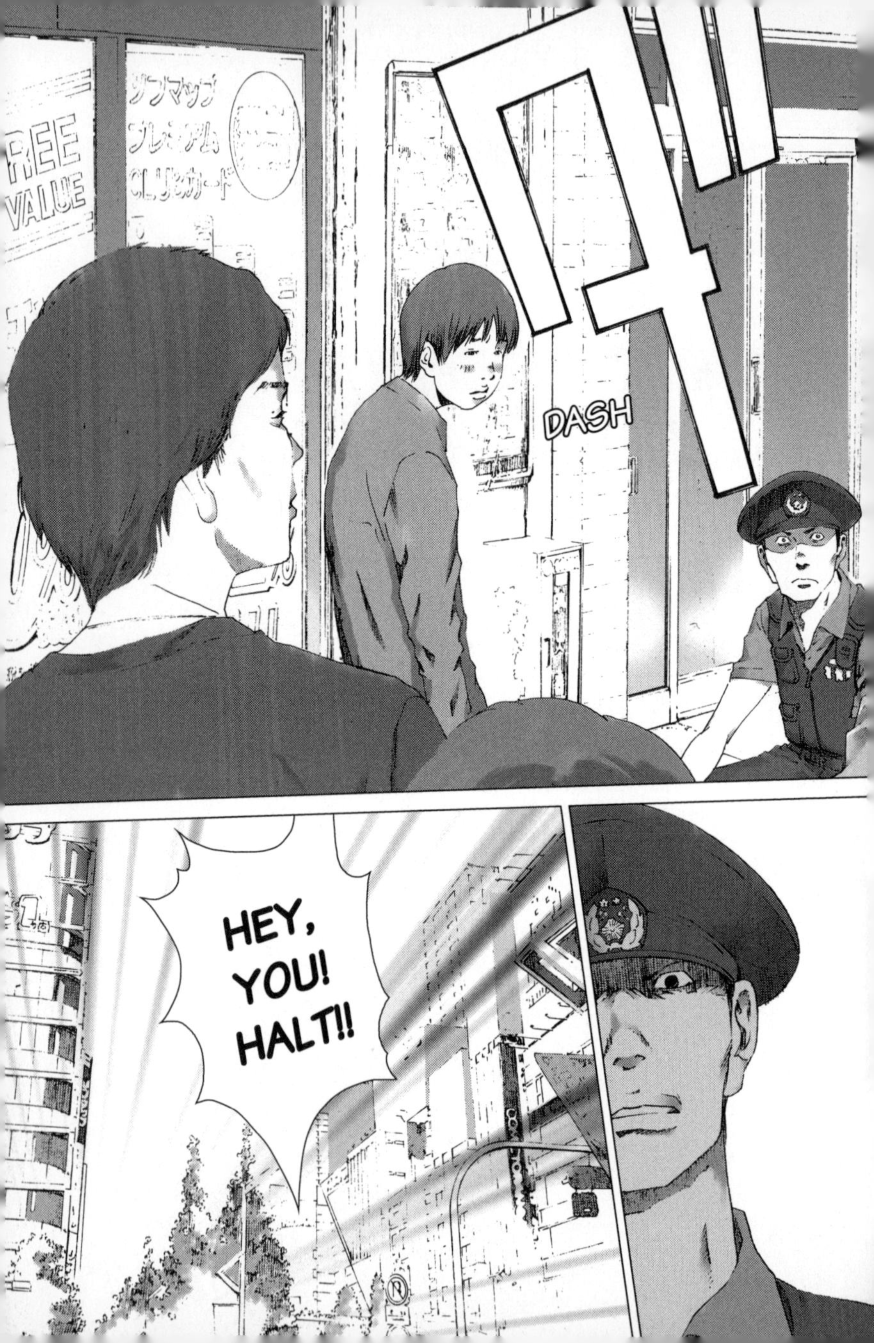
REE
VALUE
DASH
HEY, YOU! HALT!!

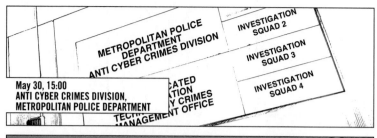

METROPOLITAN POLICE DEPARTMENT
ANTI CYBER CRIMES DIVISION
INVESTIGATION SQUAD 2
INVESTIGATION SQUAD 3
INVESTIGATION SQUAD 4
May 30, 15:00
ANTI CYBER CRIMES DIVISION,
METROPOLITAN POLICE DEPARTMENT
This is a 3D CG rendering of Paperboy based on
images from surveillance footage.
As I thought, without the eyes,
it's still not conclusive.
In all the surveillance footage we've gotten so far,
the eyes are the one thing that's never shown.
Lieu-tenant!
Eye-witness intel from Mansei-bashi Pre-cinct!

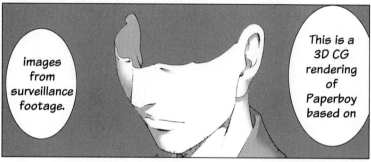

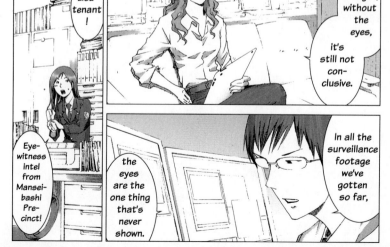

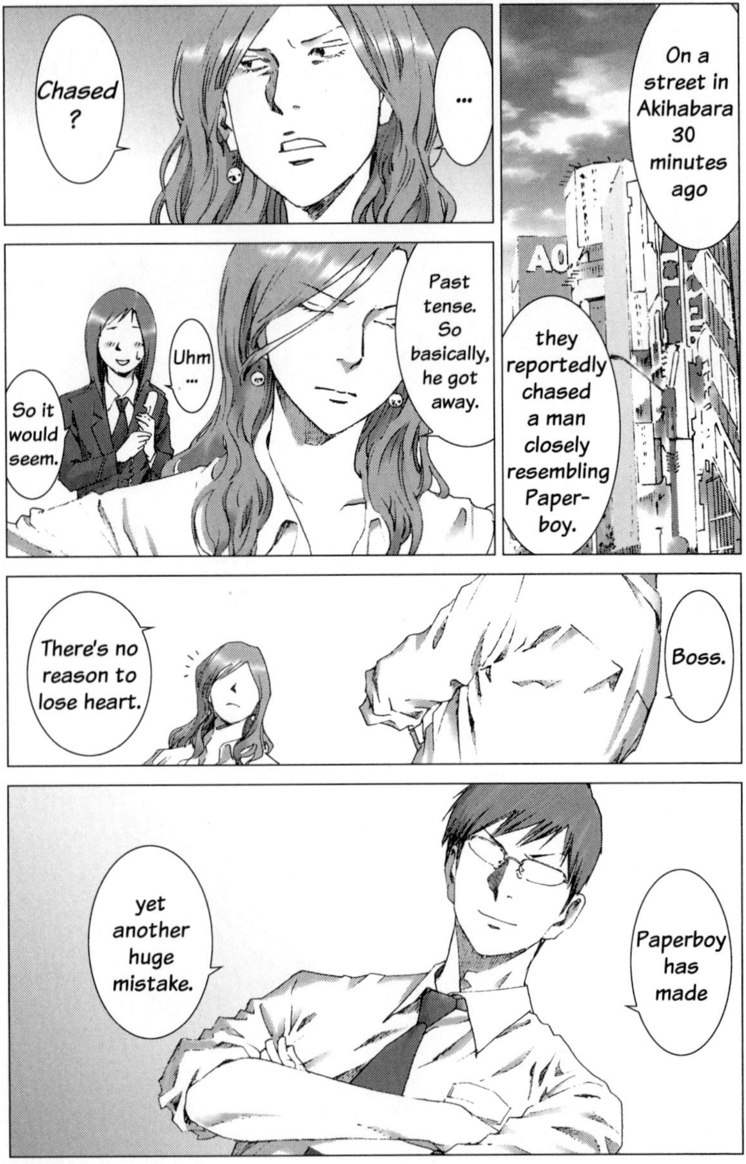

On a street in Akihabara 30 minutes ago
they reportedly chased a man closely resembling Paper-boy.
...
Chased?
Past tense. So basically, he got away.
Uhm ...
So it would seem.
Boss.
There's no reason to lose heart.
Paperboy has made
yet another huge mistake.

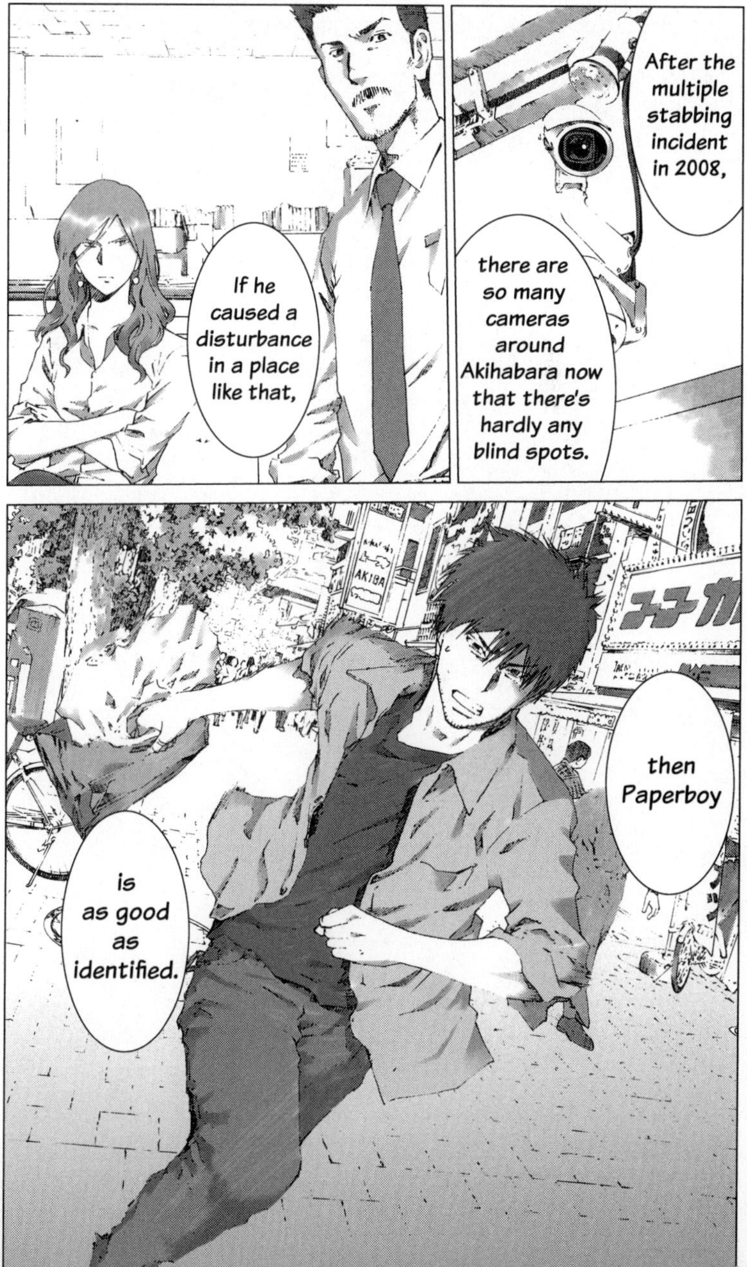
After the multiple stabbing incident in 2008,
there are so many cameras around Akihabara now that there's hardly any blind spots.
If he caused a disturbance in a place like that,
AKIBA
then Paperboy
is as good as identified.

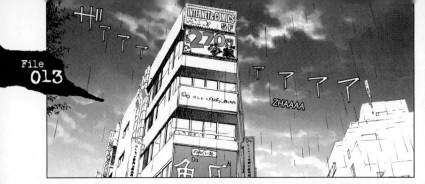

File
013

INTERNET & COMICS 5F
270円
ZHAAAA

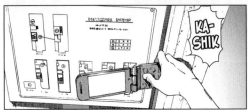

KA-
SHIK

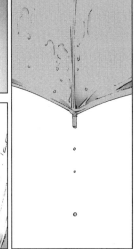

EMERGENCY EXIT

Please do not block this door!!

ka-shik

ka-shik

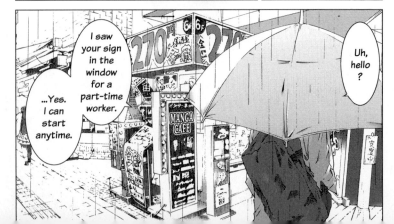

MANGA CAFE
270円 6F

I saw your sign in the window for a part-time worker.

...Yes. I can start anytime.

Uh, hello?

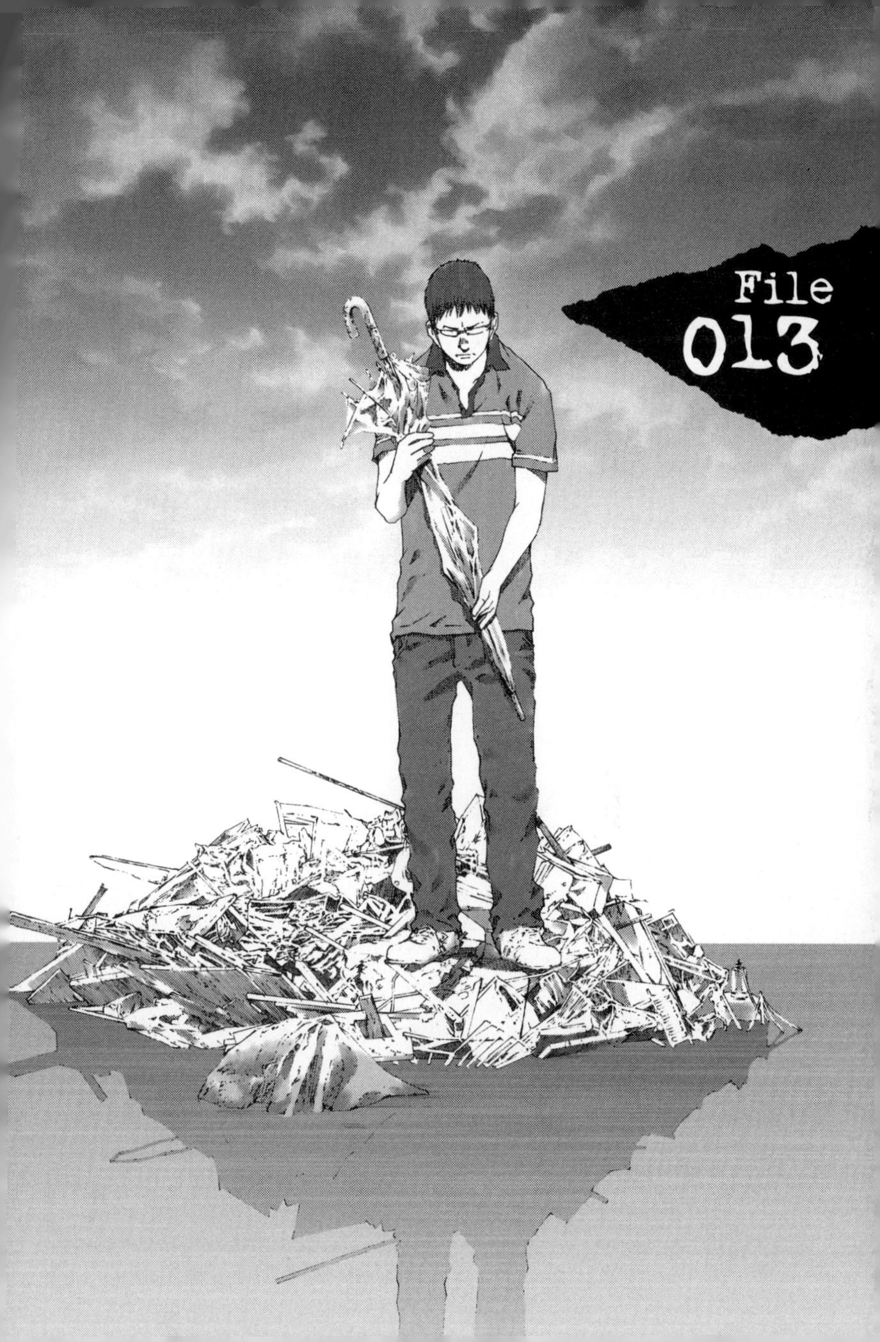
File
013

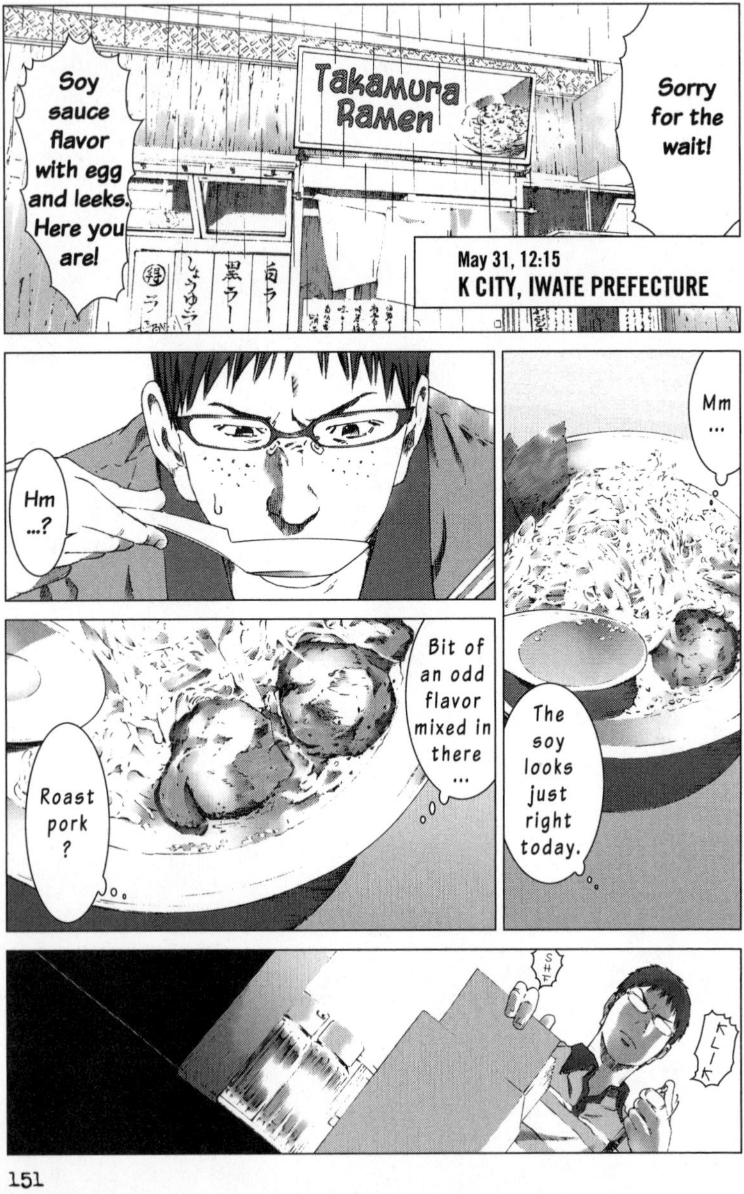
Sorry for the wait!
Takamura Ramen
Soy sauce flavor with egg and leeks. Here you are!
May 31, 12:15
K CITY, IWATE PREFECTURE
Mm ...
The soy looks just right today.
Hm ...?
Bit of an odd flavor mixed in there ...
Roast pork ?
SHF
KLIK

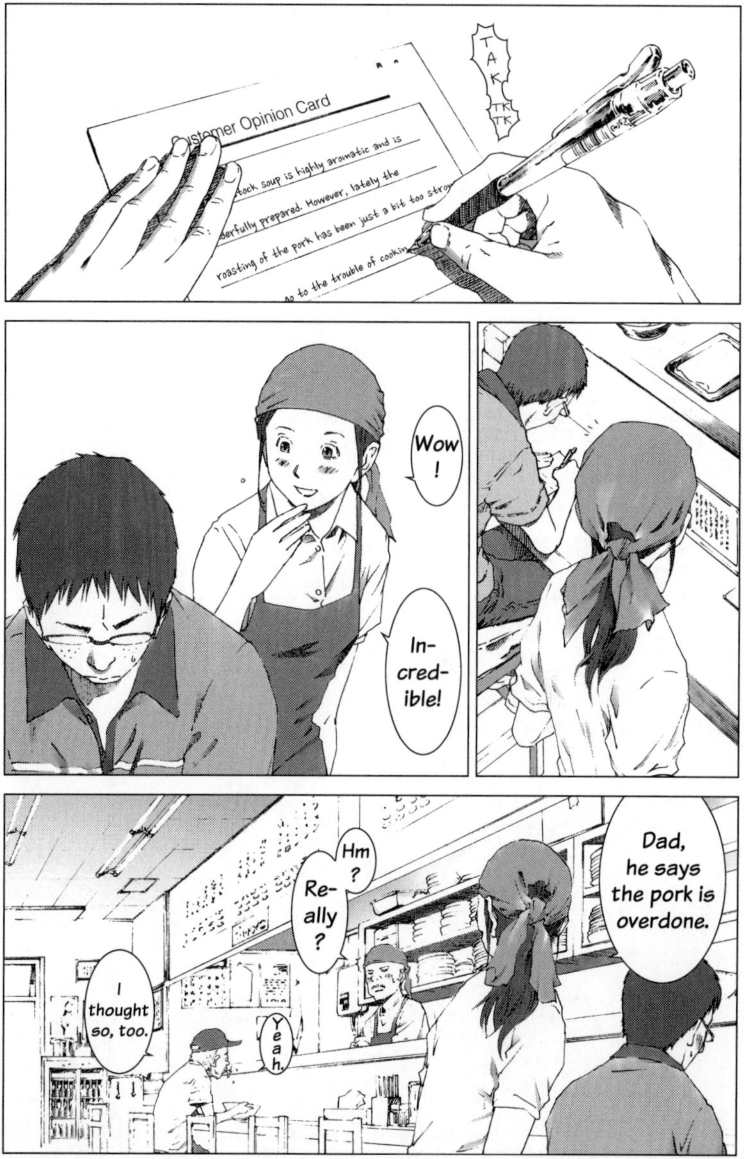

TAK TK TK
Customer Opinion Card
tock soup is highly aromatic and is
derfully prepared. However, lately the
roasting of the pork has been just a bit too stro
o to the trouble of cookin
Wow!
In-credible!
Dad, he says the pork is overdone.
Hm?
Re-ally?
Yeah.
I thought so, too.

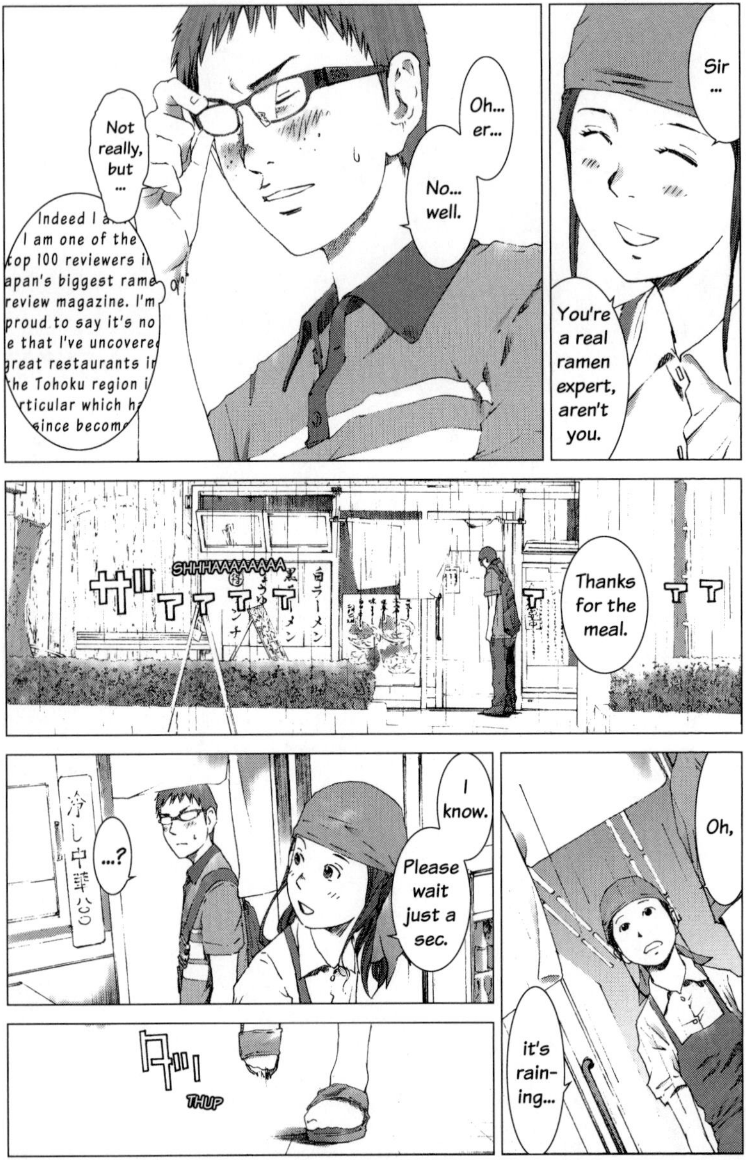
Sir ...
You're a real ramen expert, aren't you.
Oh... er...
No... well.
Not really, but ...
Indeed I a
I am one of the
top 100 reviewers i
apan's biggest rame
review magazine. I'm
proud to say it's no
e that I've uncovere
great restaurants i
the Tohoku region i
rticular which ha
since become
Thanks for the meal.
SHHHAAAAAAAA
Oh,
it's rain- ing...
I know.
Please wait just a sec.
...?
THUP

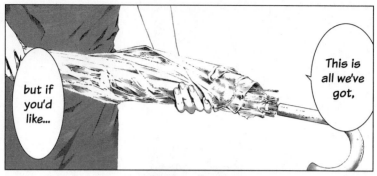

This is all we've got,

but if you'd like...

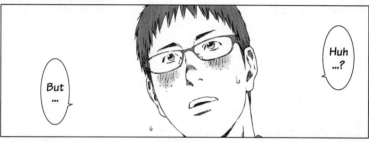

Huh ...?

But ...

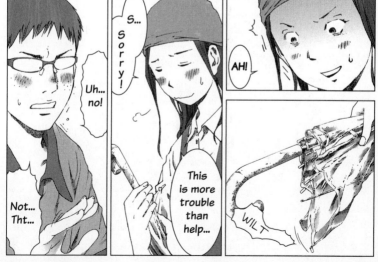

S... Sorry!

Uh... no!

Not... Tht...

This is more trouble than help...

AH!

WILT

154

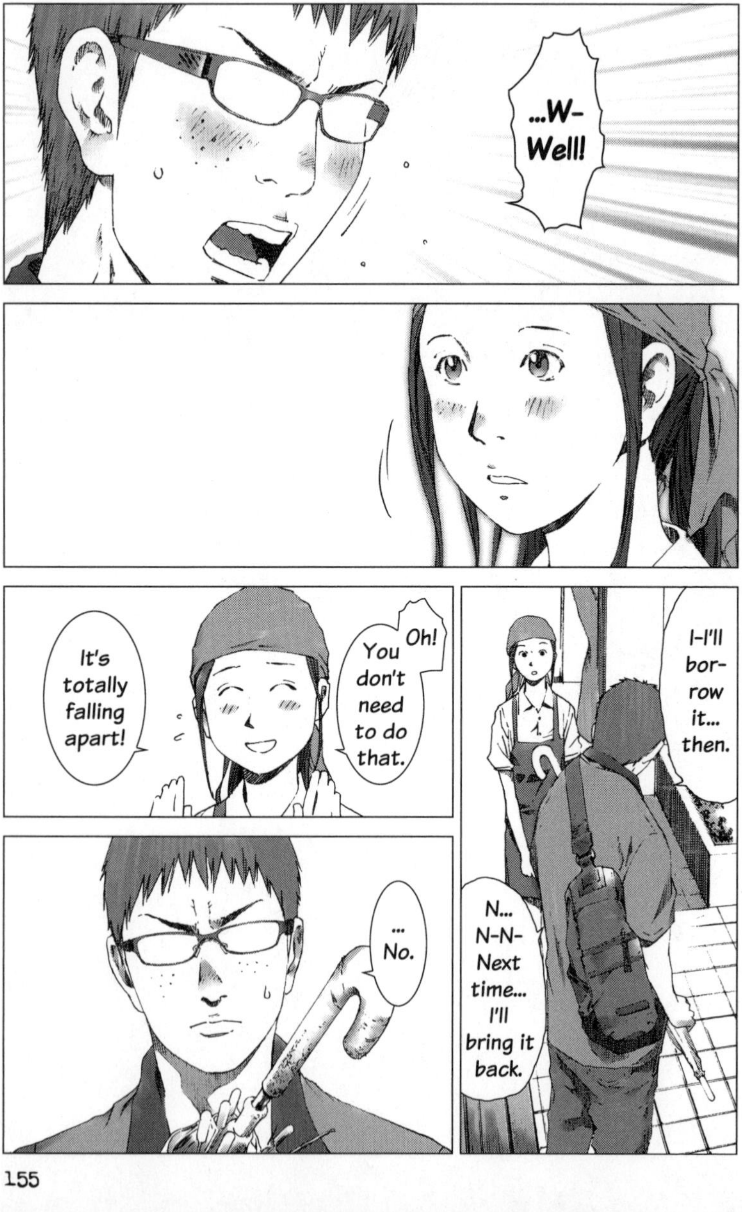
...W-
Well!
I-I'll borrow it... then.
N... N-N-Next time... I'll bring it back.
Oh!
You don't need to do that.
It's totally falling apart!
... No.

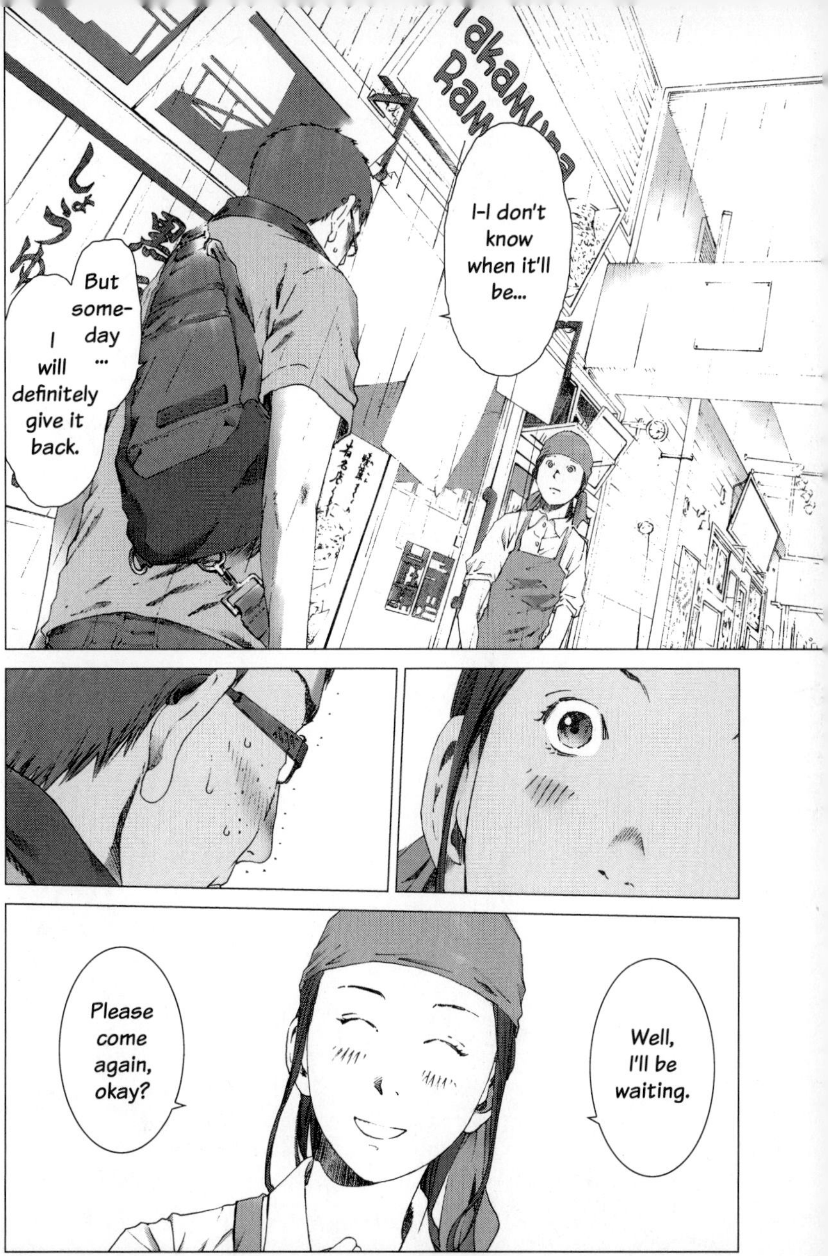
I-I don't know when it'll be...
But someday... I will definitely give it back.
Well, I'll be waiting.
Please come again, okay?

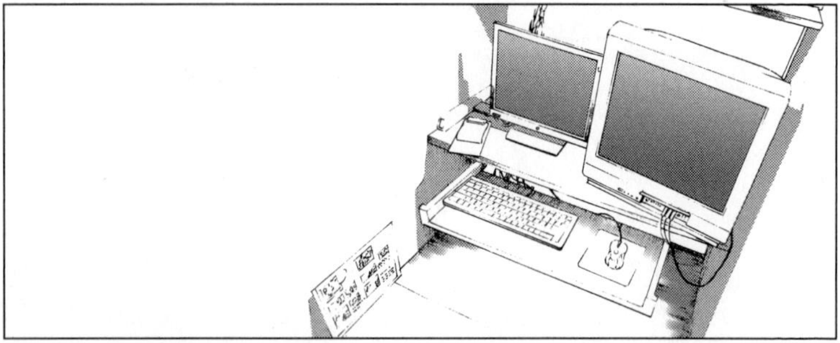

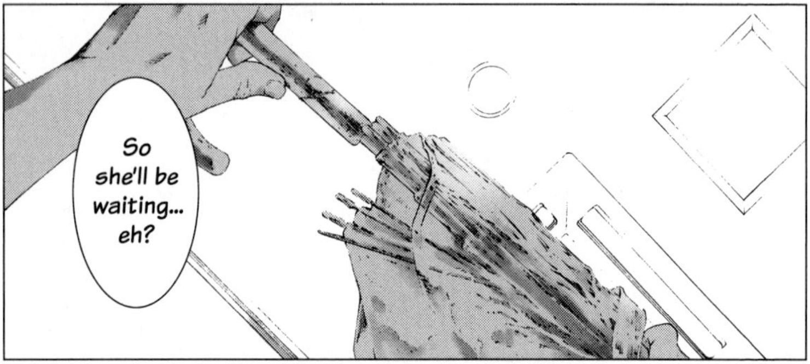
So she'll be waiting... eh?

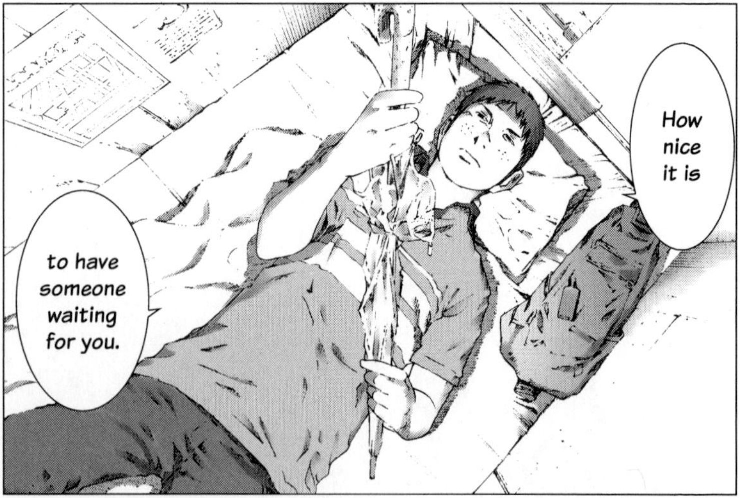
How nice it is
to have someone waiting for you.

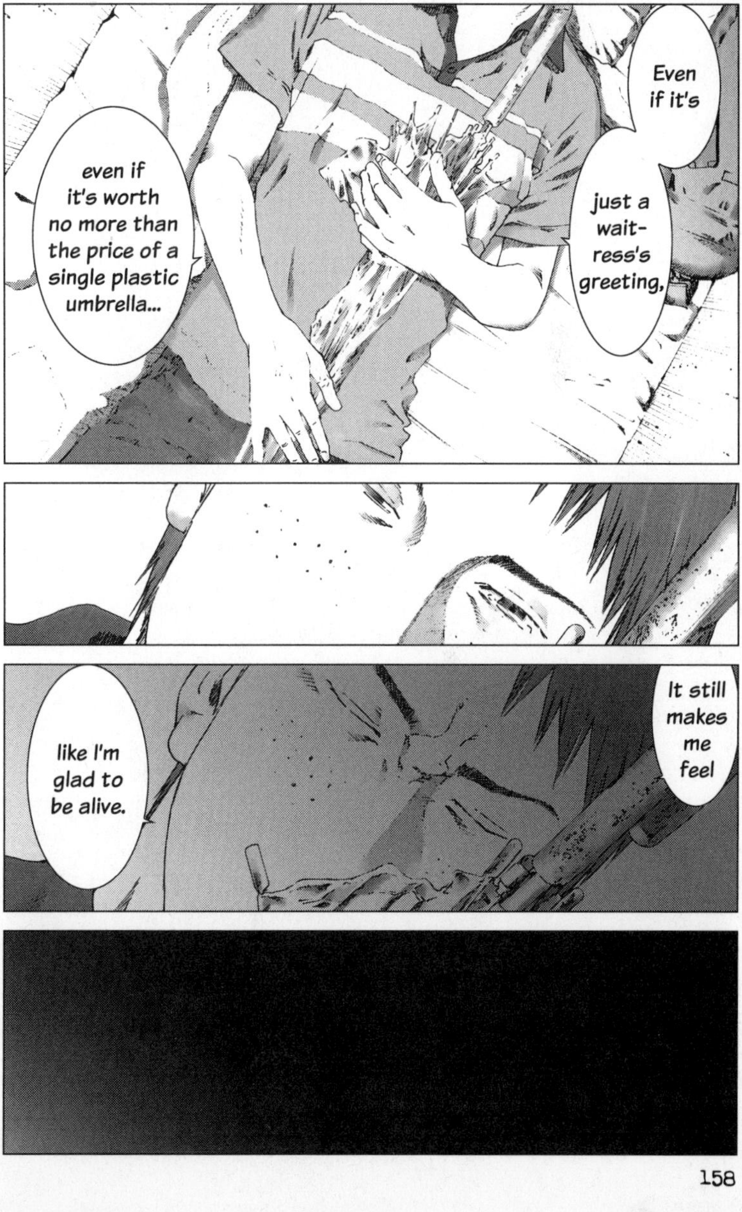
Even if it's
just a wait-ress's greeting,
even if it's worth no more than the price of a single plastic umbrella...
It still makes me feel
like I'm glad to be alive.

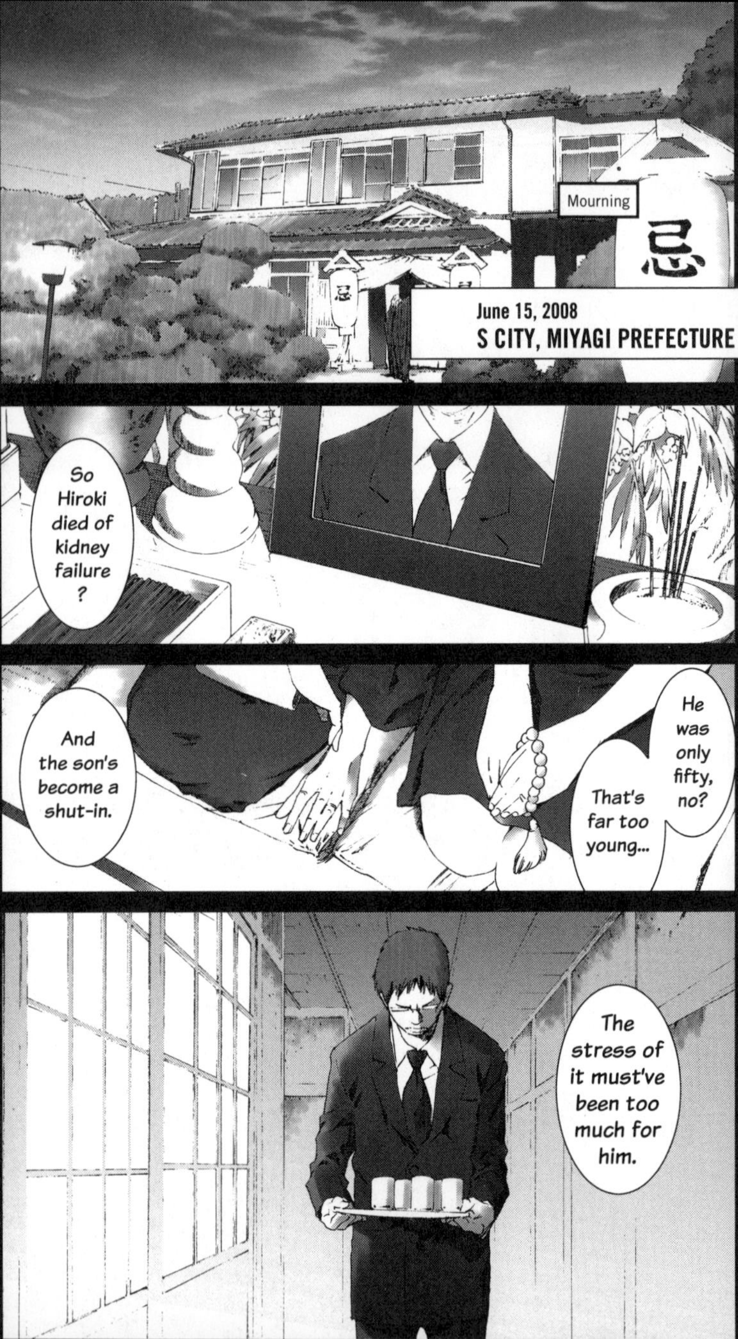
Mourning
忌
June 15, 2008
S CITY, MIYAGI PREFECTURE
So Hiroki died of kidney failure?
He was only fifty, no?
That's far too young...
And the son's become a shut-in.
The stress of it must've been too much for him.

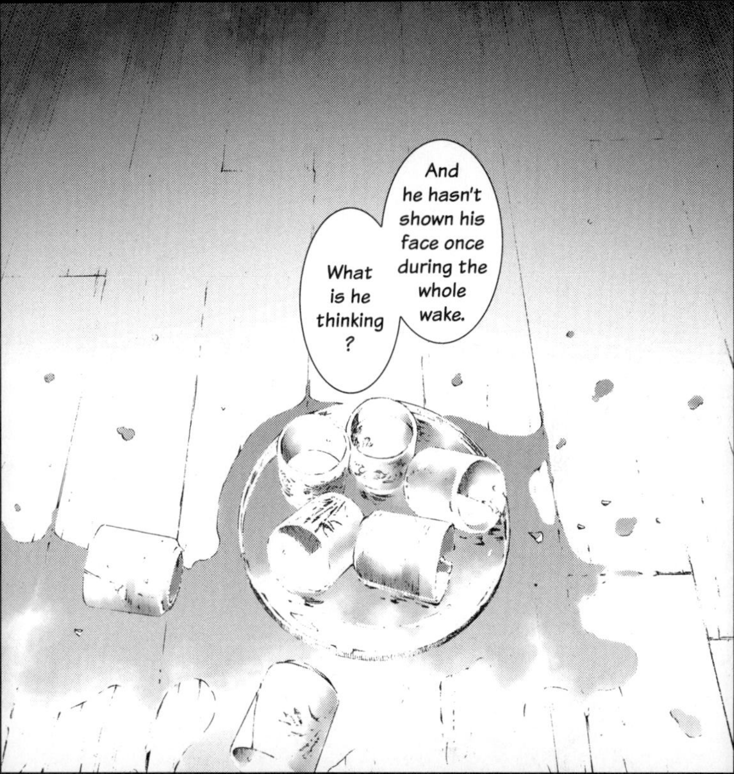
And he hasn't shown his face once during the whole wake.
What is he thinking?

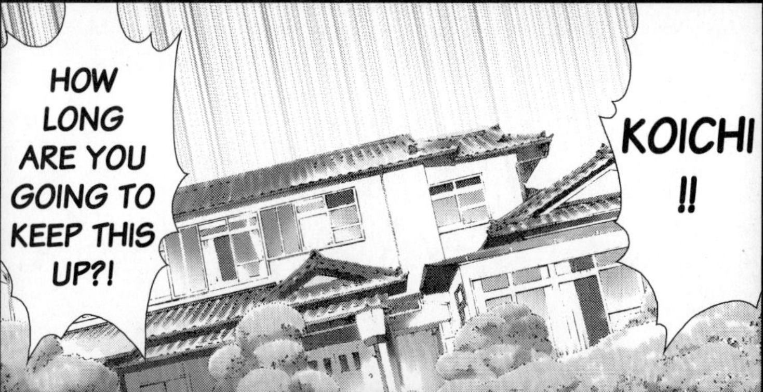
KOICHI!!
HOW LONG ARE YOU GOING TO KEEP THIS UP?!

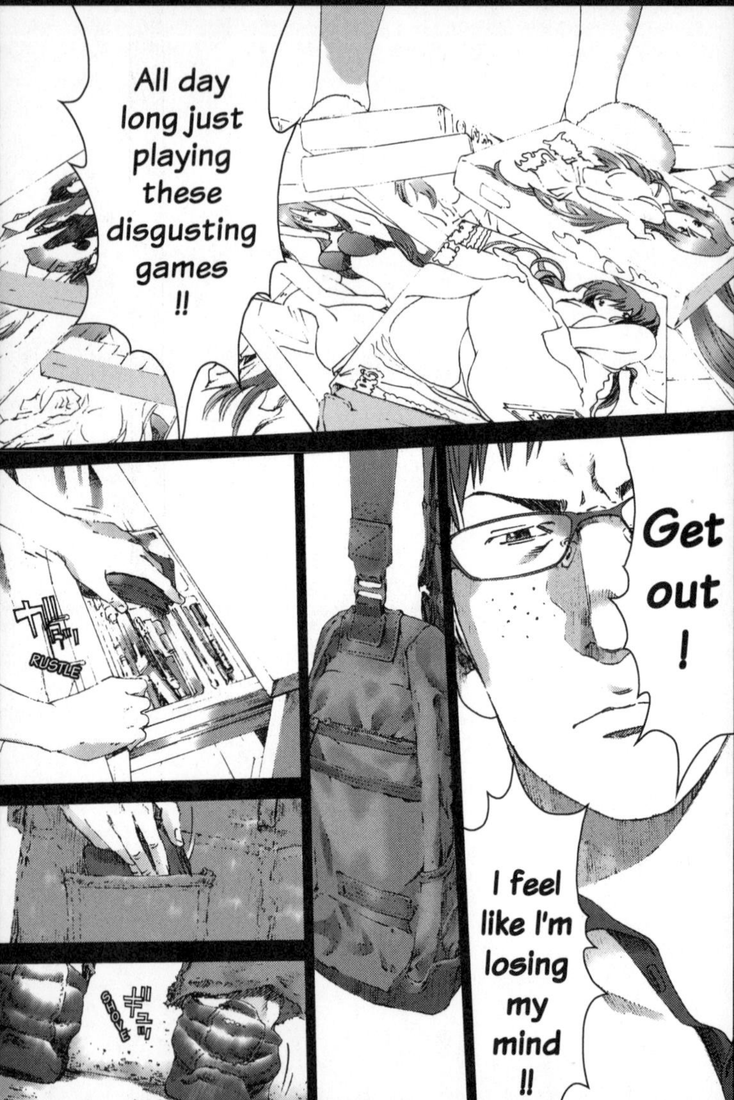
All day long just playing these disgusting games!!
Get out!
I feel like I'm losing my mind!!
RUSTLE
SHOVE

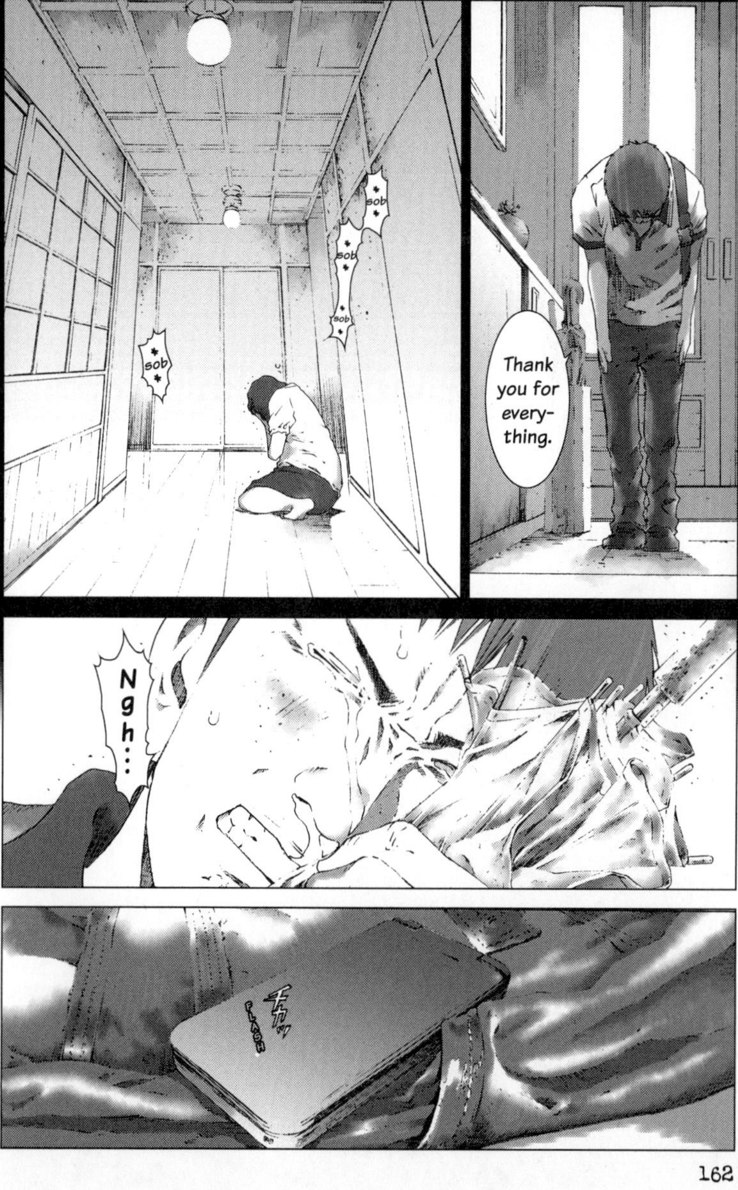
Thank you for every-thing.
sob
sob
sob
sob
Ngh...
FLASH

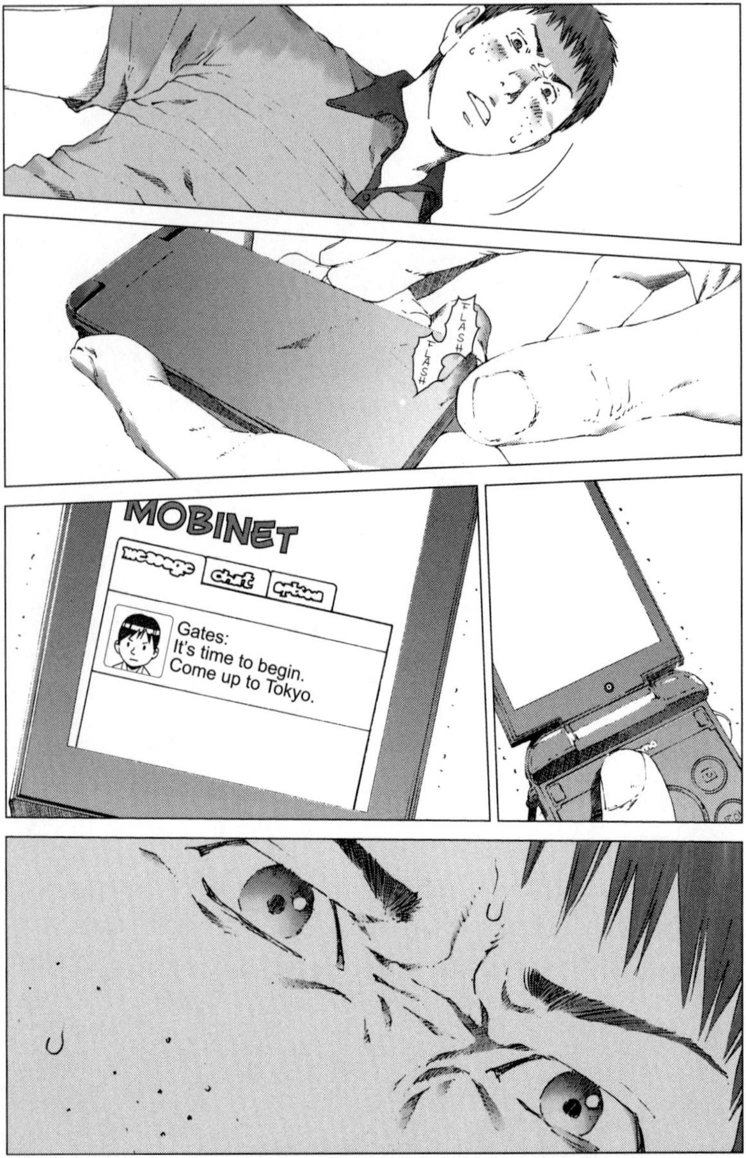
FLASH
FLASH
MOBINET
Gates:
It's time to begin.
Come up to Tokyo.

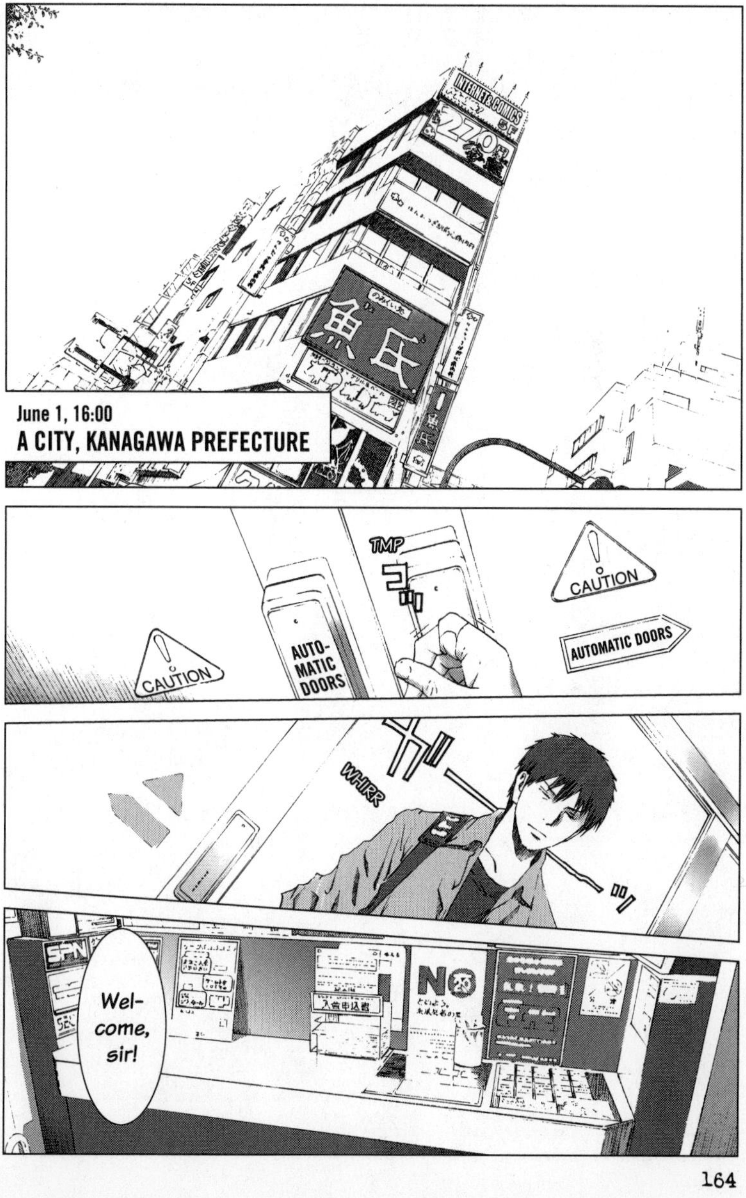
INTERNET&COMICS
June 1, 16:00
A CITY, KANAGAWA PREFECTURE
CAUTION
AUTOMATIC DOORS
TMP
AUTO-MATIC DOORS
CAUTION
WHIRR
SPN
Wel-come, sir!
NO

Internet booth. One hour, please.
Do you have a member card, sir?
No... It's my first time here.
Ah, please write your name and address here.
ねるそん・かとー・
(名)
お名前 フリガナ (姓)
Nelsin Kato-Ricart
区町村
区市郡
都道府県
ご住所 フリガナ (〒)
ご意見・ご
Heh...

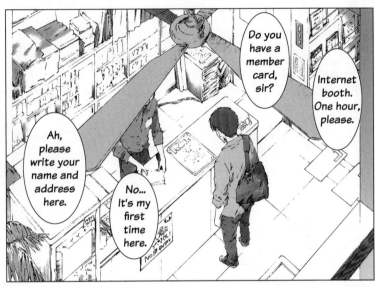

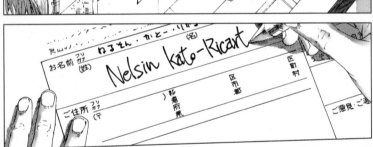

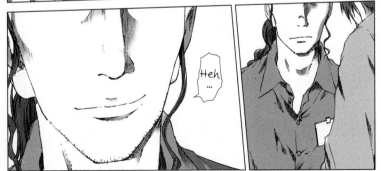

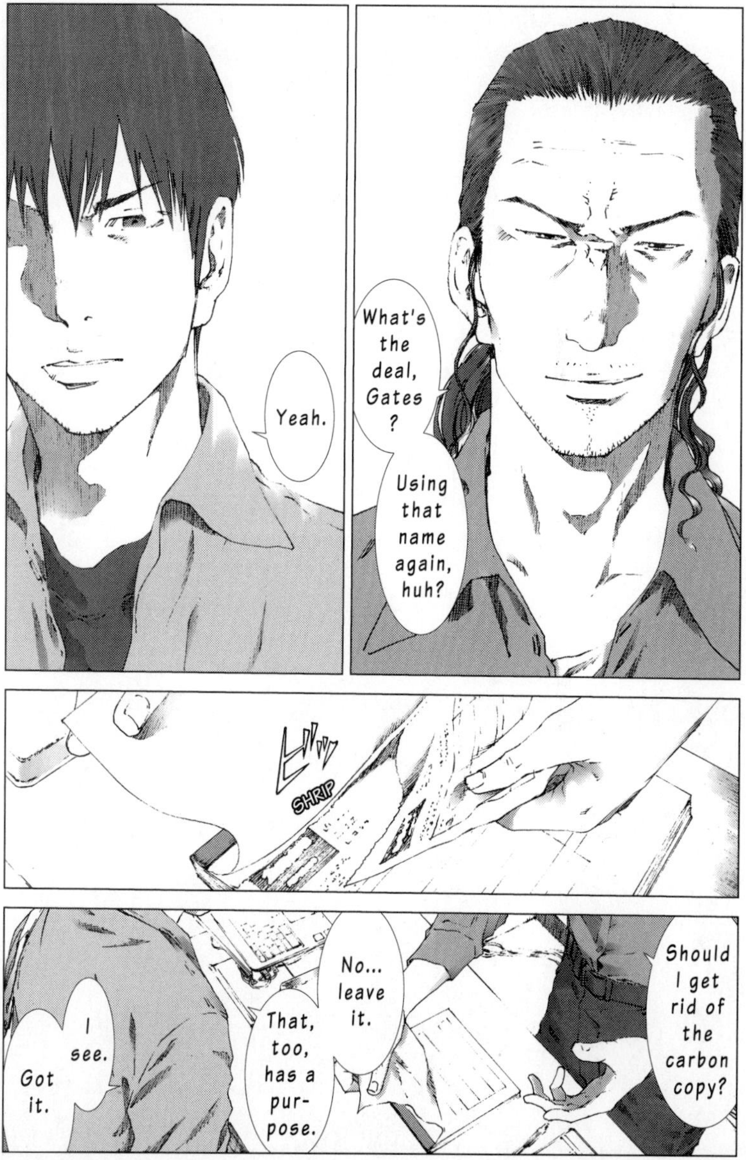
What's the deal, Gates?
Using that name again, huh?
Yeah.
SHRIP
Should I get rid of the carbon copy?
No... leave it.
That, too, has a purpose.
I see.
Got it.

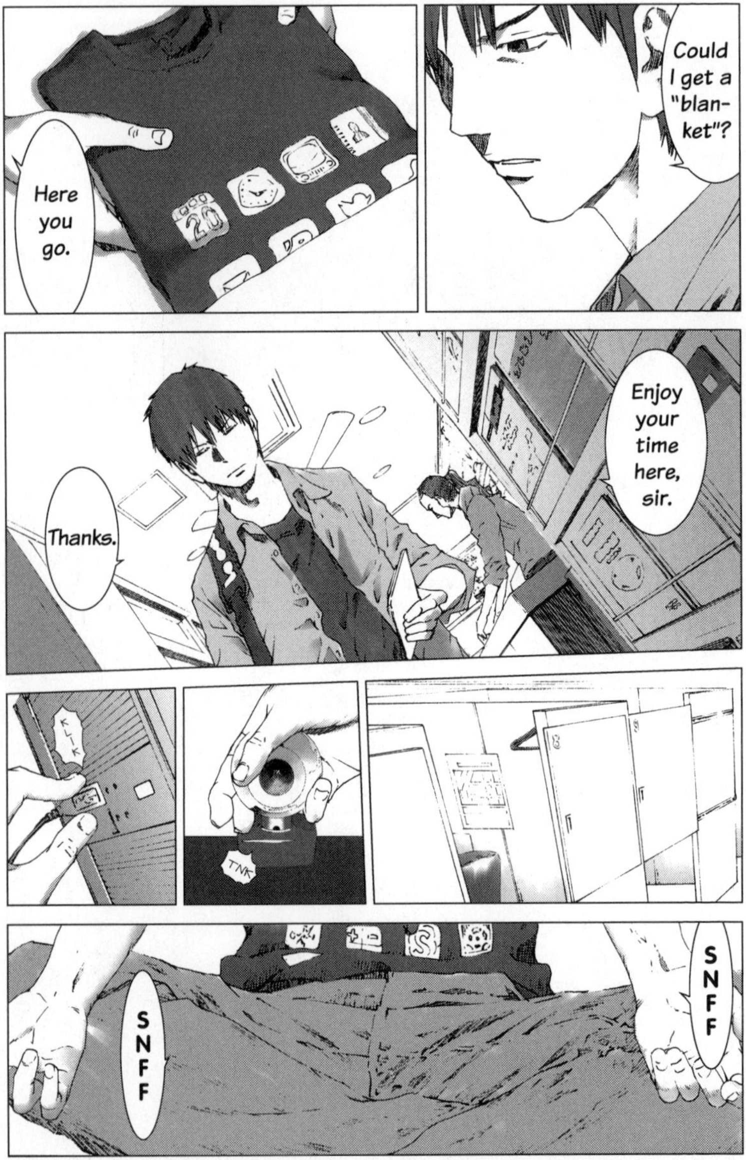
Could I get a "blanket"?
Here you go.
Enjoy your time here, sir.
Thanks.
TNK
KLIK
SNFF
SNFF

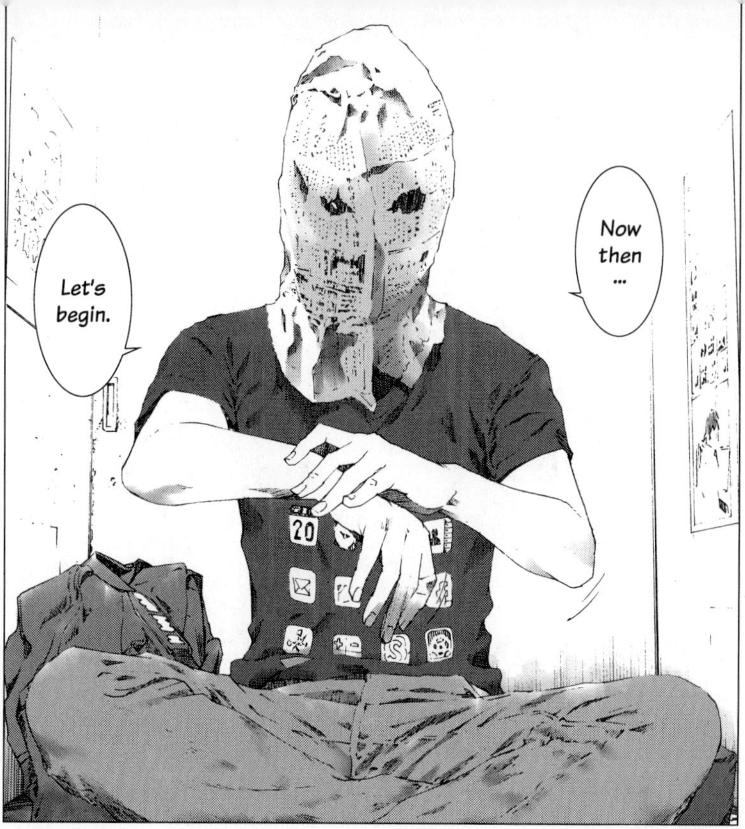
Now then ...
Let's begin.
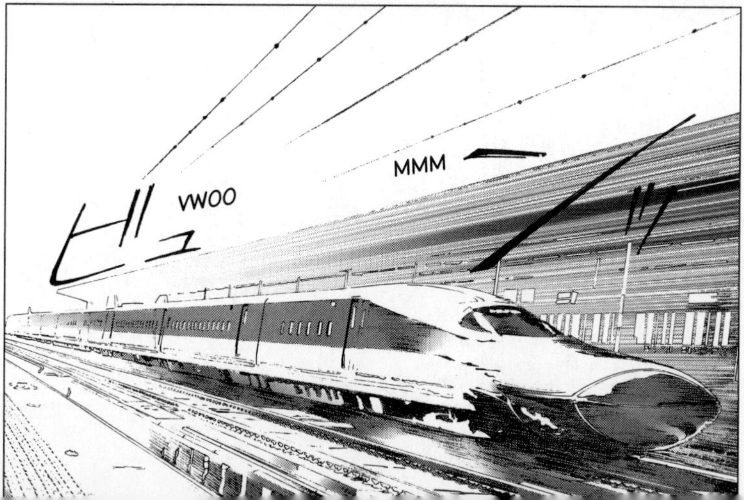
VWOO
MMM

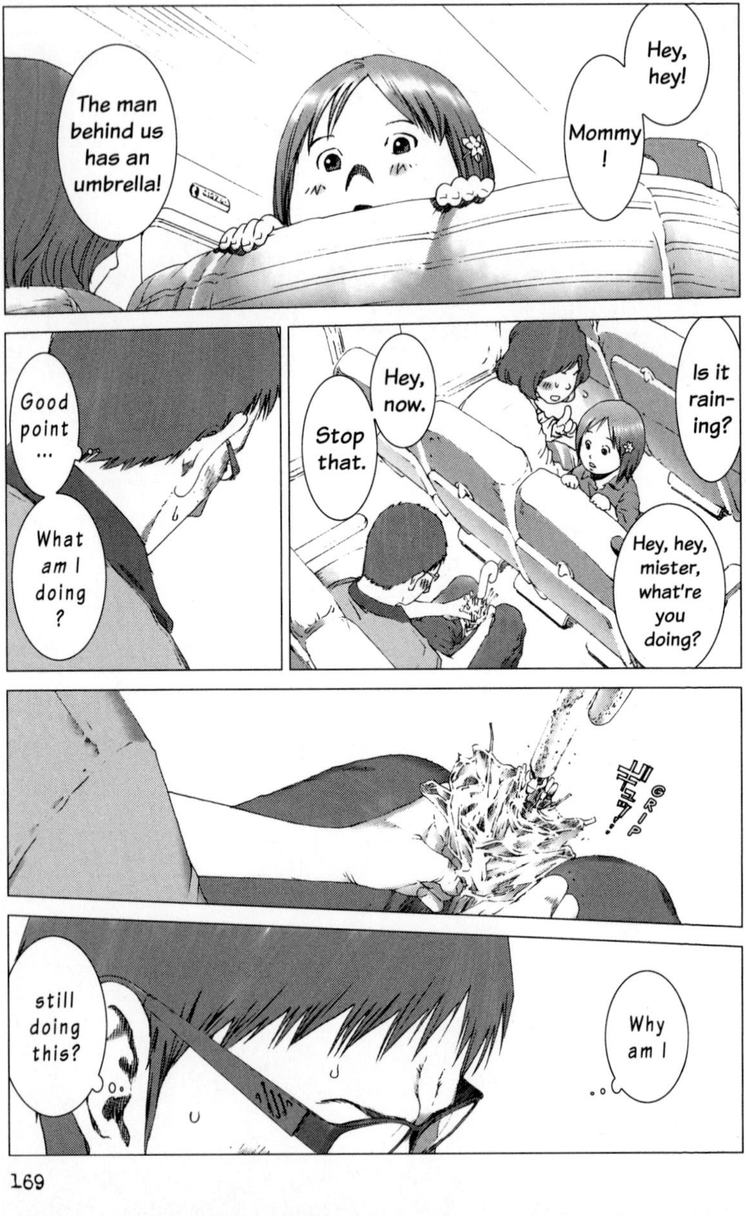

Hey, hey!
Mommy!
The man behind us has an umbrella!
Is it raining?
Hey, hey, mister, what're you doing?
Hey, now.
Stop that.
Good point...
What am I doing?
GRIP
Why am I
still doing this?

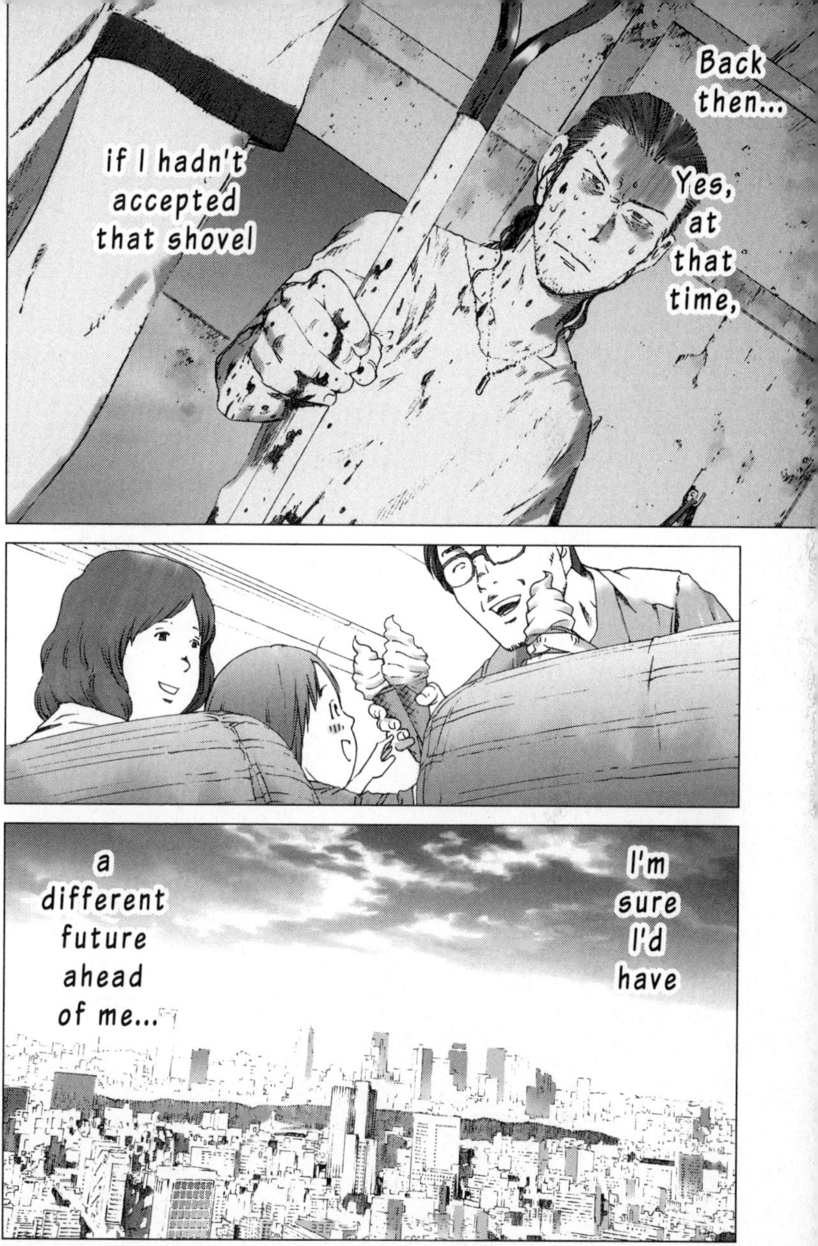
Back then...
Yes, at that time,
if I hadn't accepted that shovel
I'm sure I'd have
a different future ahead of me...

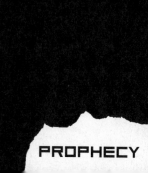

PROPHECY

File 014

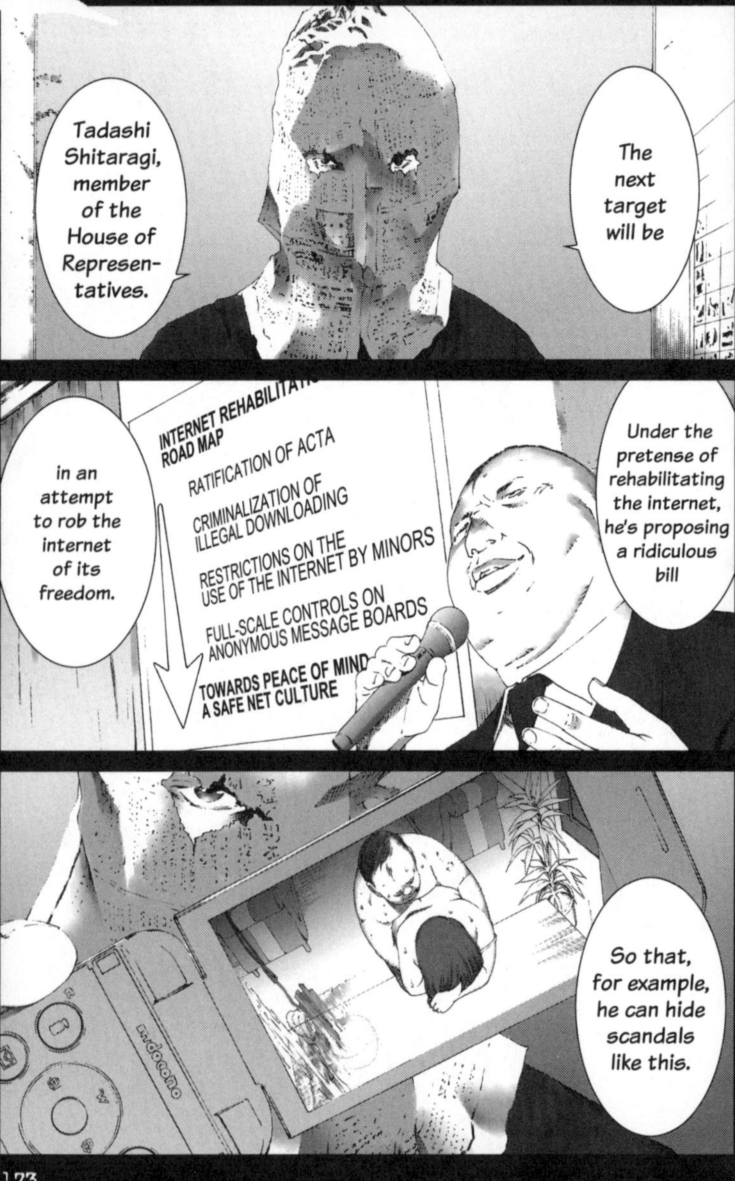
The next target will be
Tadashi Shitaragi, member of the House of Representatives.
Under the pretense of rehabilitating the internet, he's proposing a ridiculous bill
INTERNET REHABILITATI
ROAD MAP
RATIFICATION OF ACTA
CRIMINALIZATION OF ILLEGAL DOWNLOADING
RESTRICTIONS ON THE USE OF THE INTERNET BY MINORS
FULL-SCALE CONTROLS ON ANONYMOUS MESSAGE BOARDS
TOWARDS PEACE OF MIND A SAFE NET CULTURE
in an attempt to rob the internet of its freedom.
So that, for example, he can hide scandals like this.

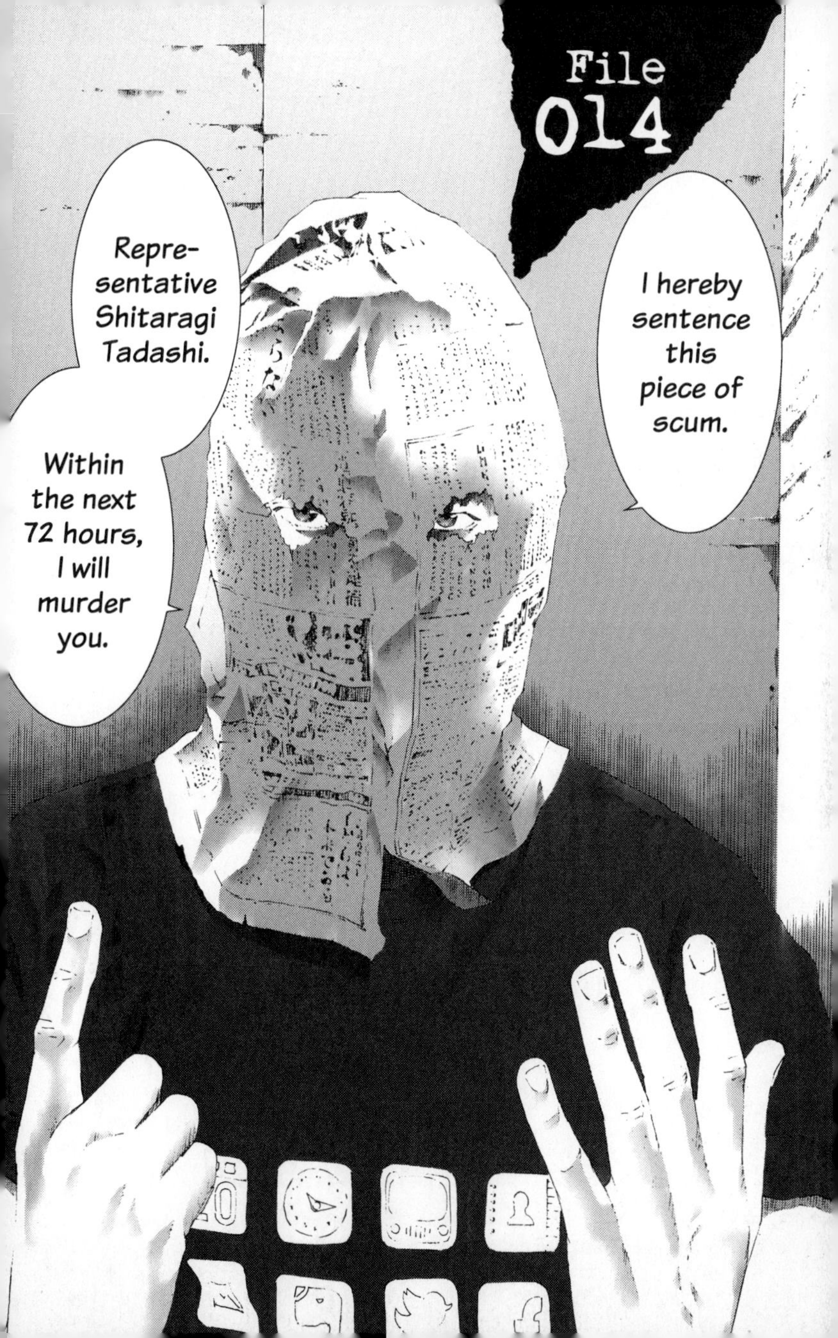
File 014
I hereby sentence this piece of scum.
Repre-sentative Shitaragi Tadashi.
Within the next 72 hours, I will murder you.

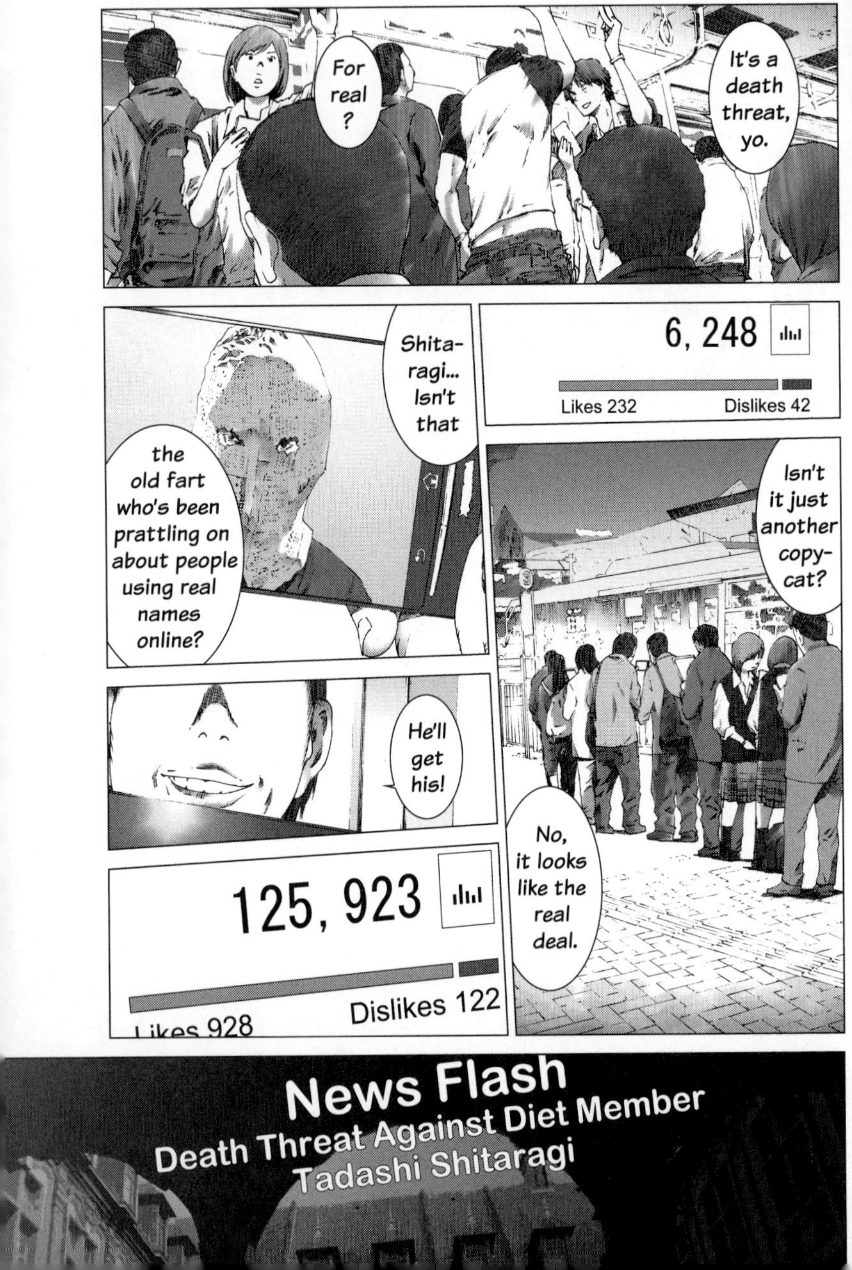
It's a death threat, yo.
For real?
6, 248
Likes 232
Dislikes 42
Isn't it just another copy-cat?
No, it looks like the real deal.
Shita-ragi... Isn't that
the old fart who's been prattling on about people using real names online?
He'll get his!
125, 923
Likes 928
Dislikes 122
News Flash
Death Threat Against Diet Member Tadashi Shitaragi

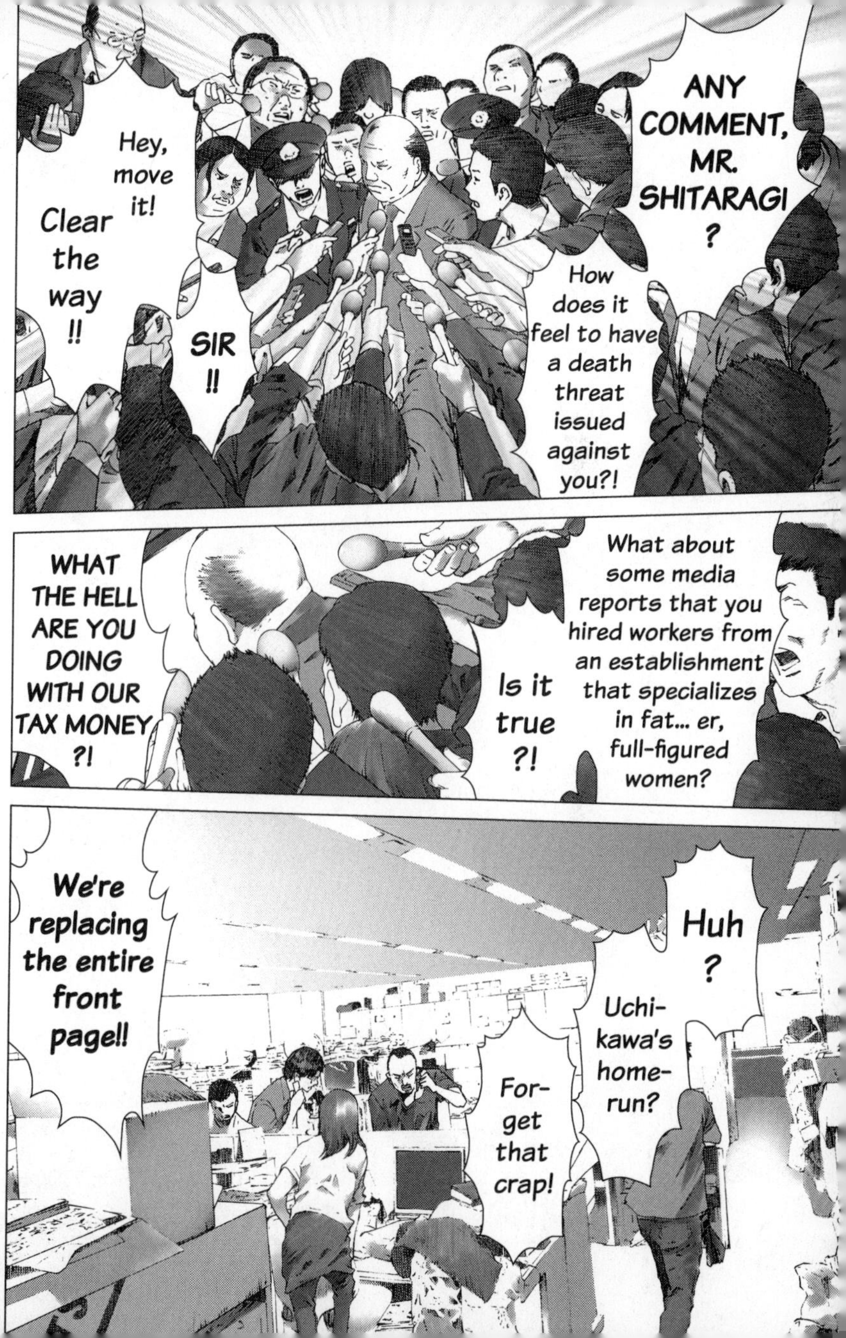
ANY COMMENT, MR. SHITARAGI?
How does it feel to have a death threat issued against you?!
SIR!!
Hey, move it!
Clear the way!!
What about some media reports that you hired workers from an establishment that specializes in fat... er, full-figured women?
Is it true?!
WHAT THE HELL ARE YOU DOING WITH OUR TAX MONEY?!
Huh?
Uchi-kawa's home-run?
For-get that crap!
We're replacing the entire front page!!

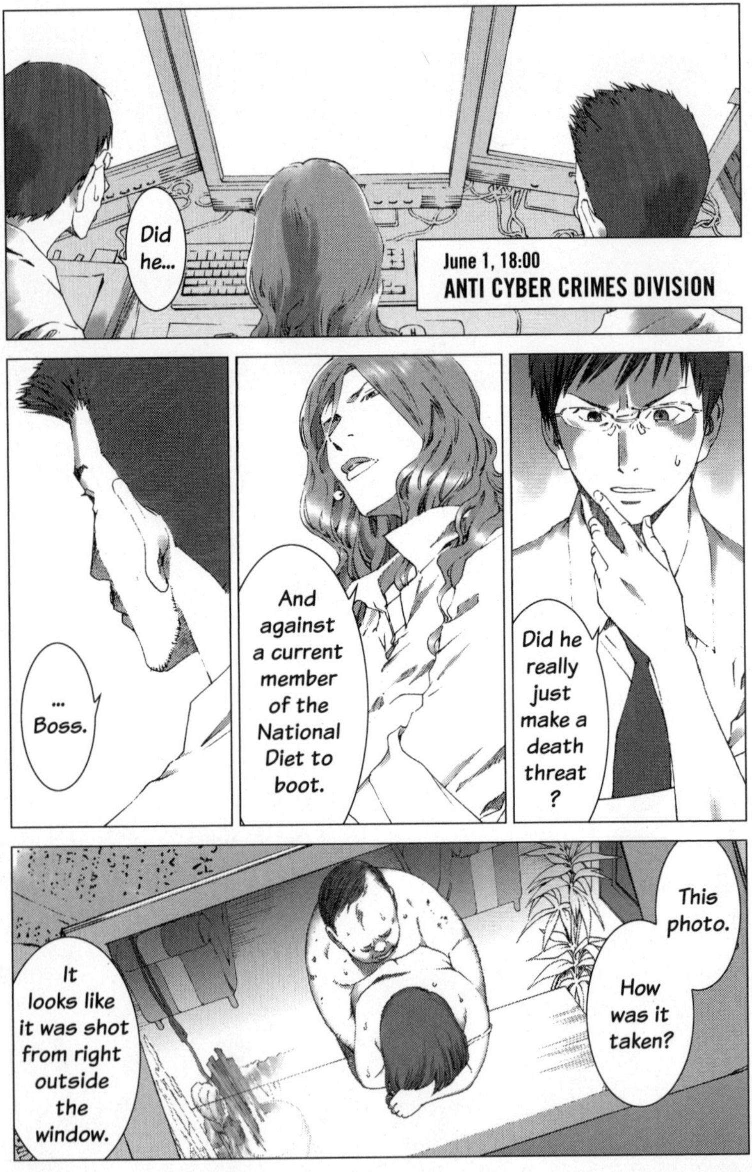
June 1, 18:00
ANTI CYBER CRIMES DIVISION
Did he...
Did he really just make a death threat?
And against a current member of the National Diet to boot.
... Boss.
This photo.
How was it taken?
It looks like it was shot from right outside the window.

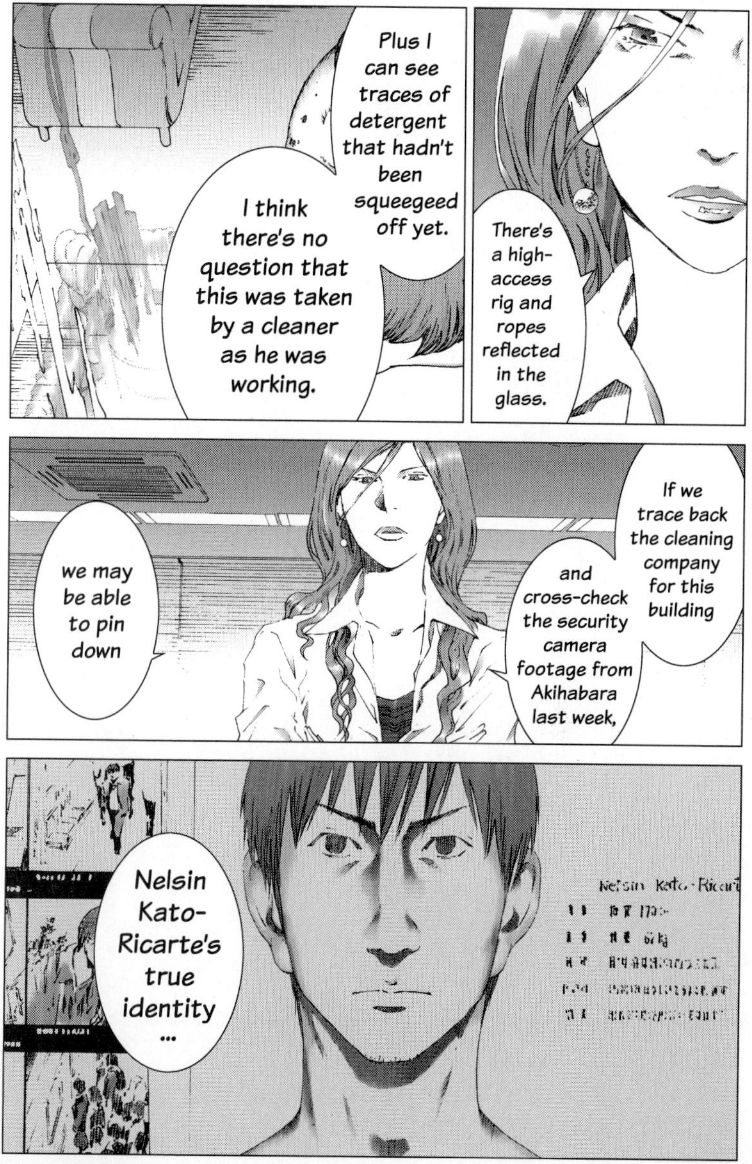
There's a high-access rig and ropes reflected in the glass.
Plus I can see traces of detergent that hadn't been squeegeed off yet.
I think there's no question that this was taken by a cleaner as he was working.
If we trace back the cleaning company for this building
and cross-check the security camera footage from Akihabara last week,
we may be able to pin down
Nelsin Kato-Ricarte's true identity ...
Nelsin Kato-Ricart

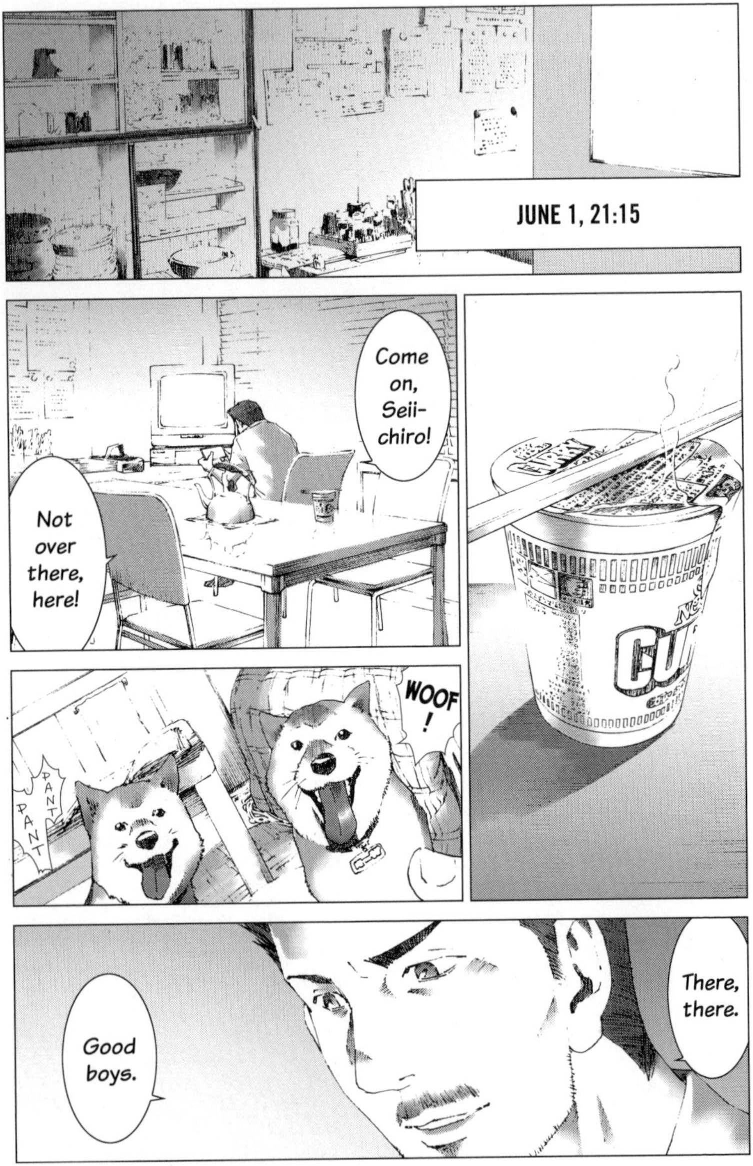
JUNE 1, 21:15
Come on, Seii-chiro!
Not over there, here!
WOOF!
PANT PANT
There, there.
Good boys.

Oka-moto.
What are you doing?
Ah!
Boss!
KLATTER
You have pet dogs?
Uh ... Yeah.
RIP
In fact,
Ichi-kawa told me about this.
It's this thing that helps care for pets.
I can use it to check on the room they're in
BEEP
FOOD
and I can even feed them, too.
GRAASH

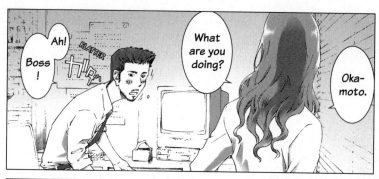

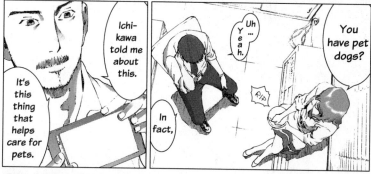

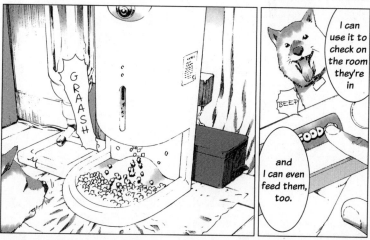

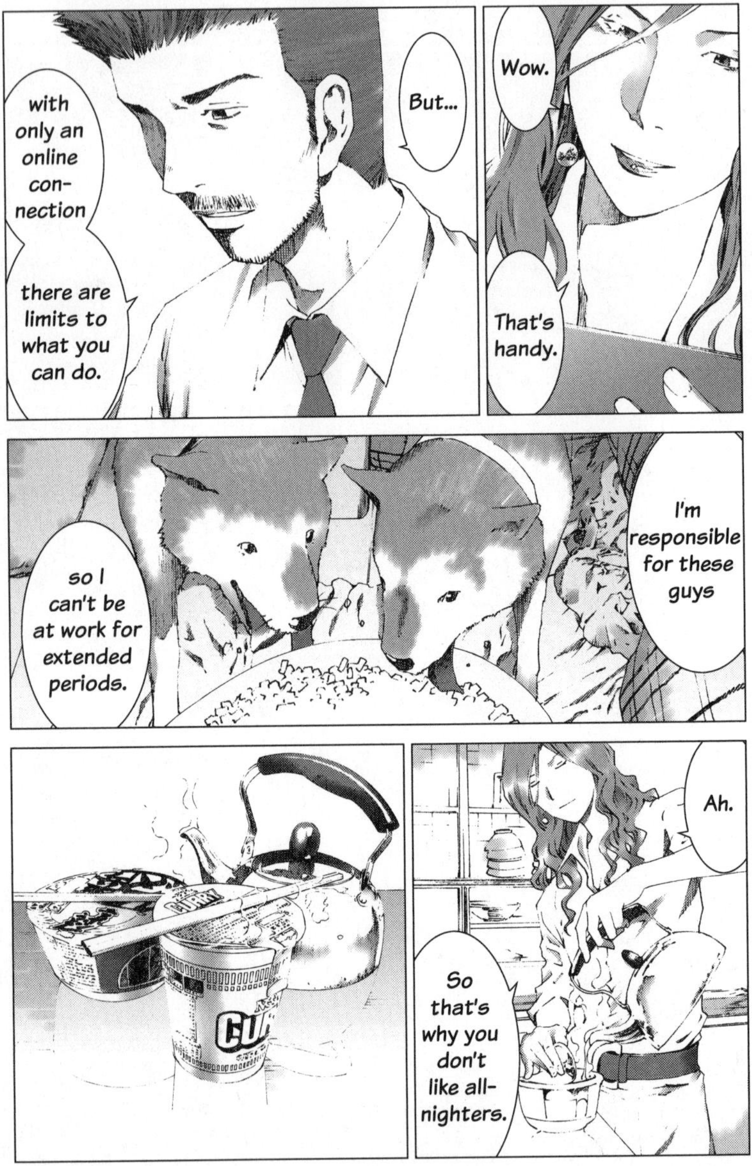
Wow.
That's handy.
But...
with only an online con-nection
there are limits to what you can do.
I'm responsible for these guys
so I can't be at work for extended periods.
Ah.
So that's why you don't like all-nighters.
CURRY

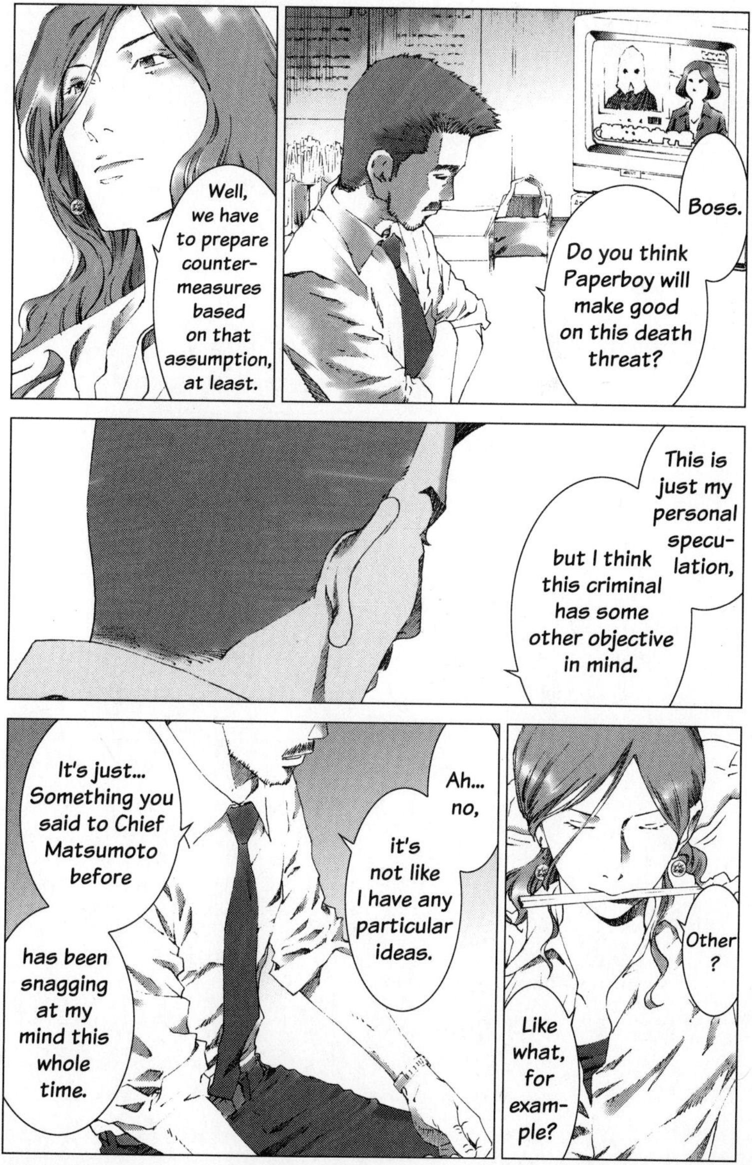

Boss.
Do you think Paperboy will make good on this death threat?
Well, we have to prepare counter-measures based on that assumption, at least.
This is just my personal specu-lation,
but I think this criminal has some other objective in mind.
Other?
Like what, for example?
Ah... no,
it's not like I have any particular ideas.
It's just... Something you said to Chief Matsumoto before
has been snagging at my mind this whole time.

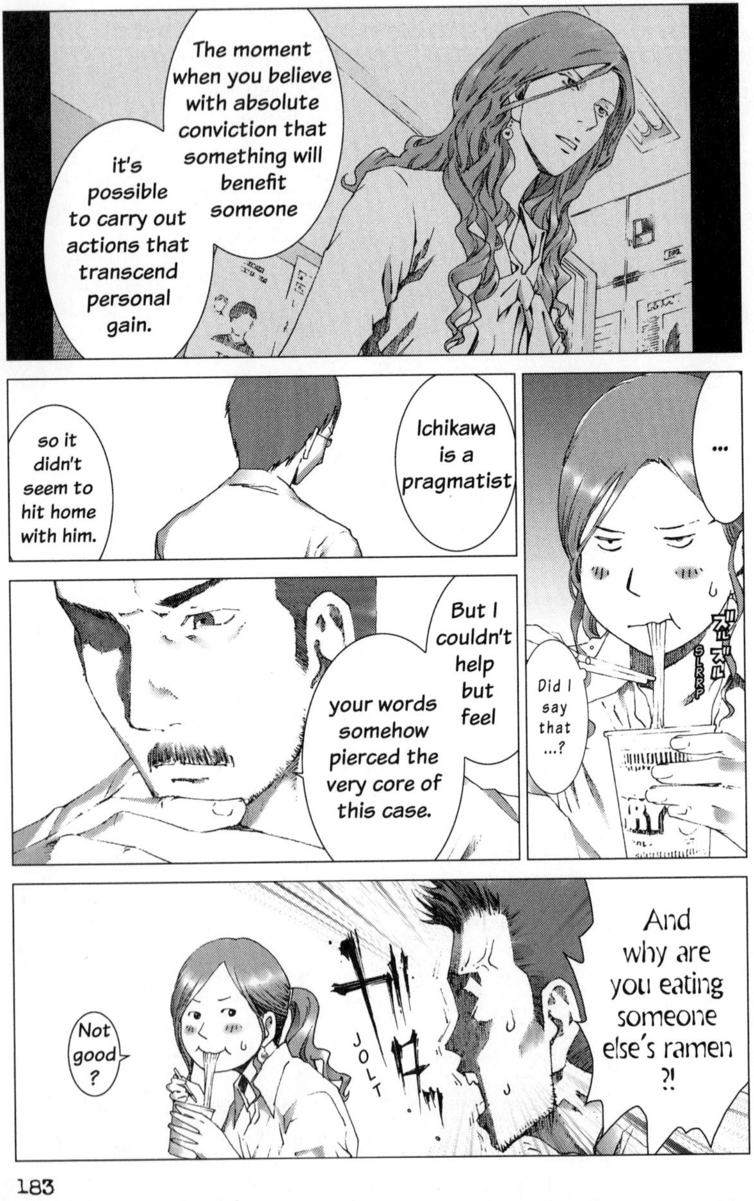
The moment when you believe with absolute conviction that something will benefit someone
it's possible to carry out actions that transcend personal gain.
...
SLRRP
Did I say that ...?
Ichikawa is a pragmatist
so it didn't seem to hit home with him.
But I couldn't help but feel
your words somehow pierced the very core of this case.
And why are you eating someone else's ramen ?!
JOLT
Not good ?

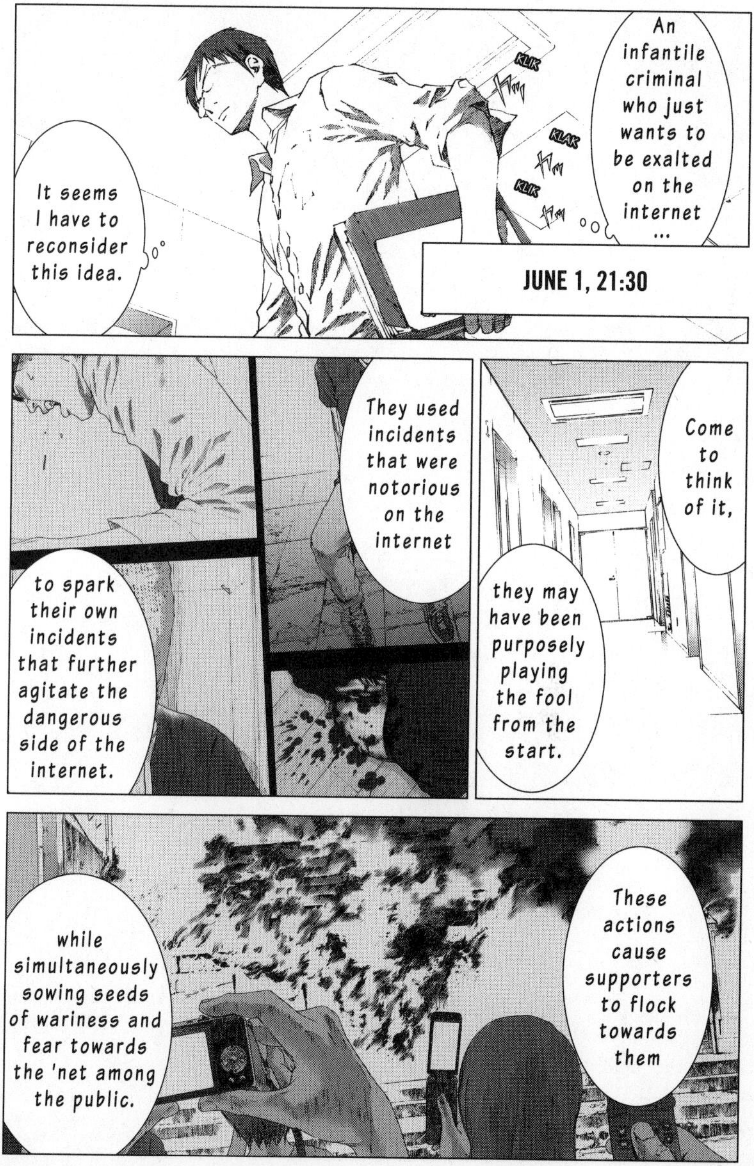
An infantile criminal who just wants to be exalted on the internet ...
KLIK
KLAK
KLIK
JUNE 1, 21:30
It seems I have to reconsider this idea.
Come to think of it,
they may have been purposely playing the fool from the start.
They used incidents that were notorious on the internet
to spark their own incidents that further agitate the dangerous side of the internet.
These actions cause supporters to flock towards them
while simultaneously sowing seeds of wariness and fear towards the 'net among the public.

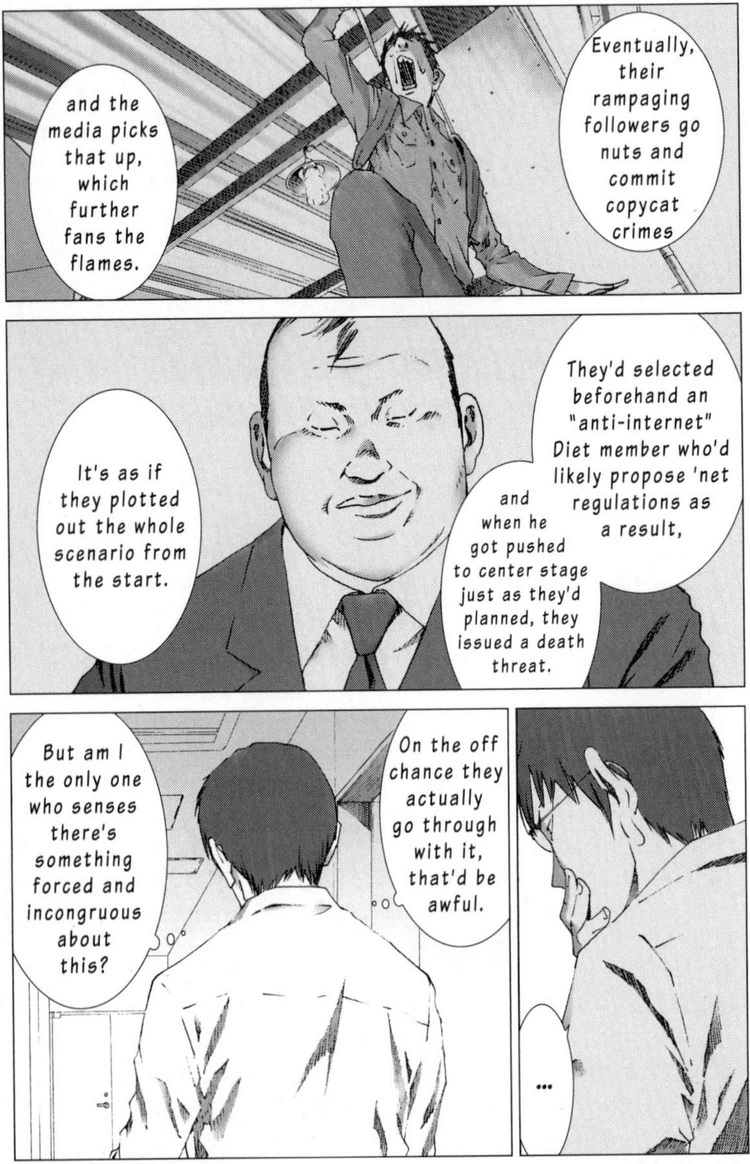
Eventually, their rampaging followers go nuts and commit copycat crimes
and the media picks that up, which further fans the flames.
They'd selected beforehand an "anti-internet" Diet member who'd likely propose 'net regulations as a result,
and when he got pushed to center stage just as they'd planned, they issued a death threat.
It's as if they plotted out the whole scenario from the start.
...
On the off chance they actually go through with it, that'd be awful.
But am I the only one who senses there's something forced and incongruous about this?

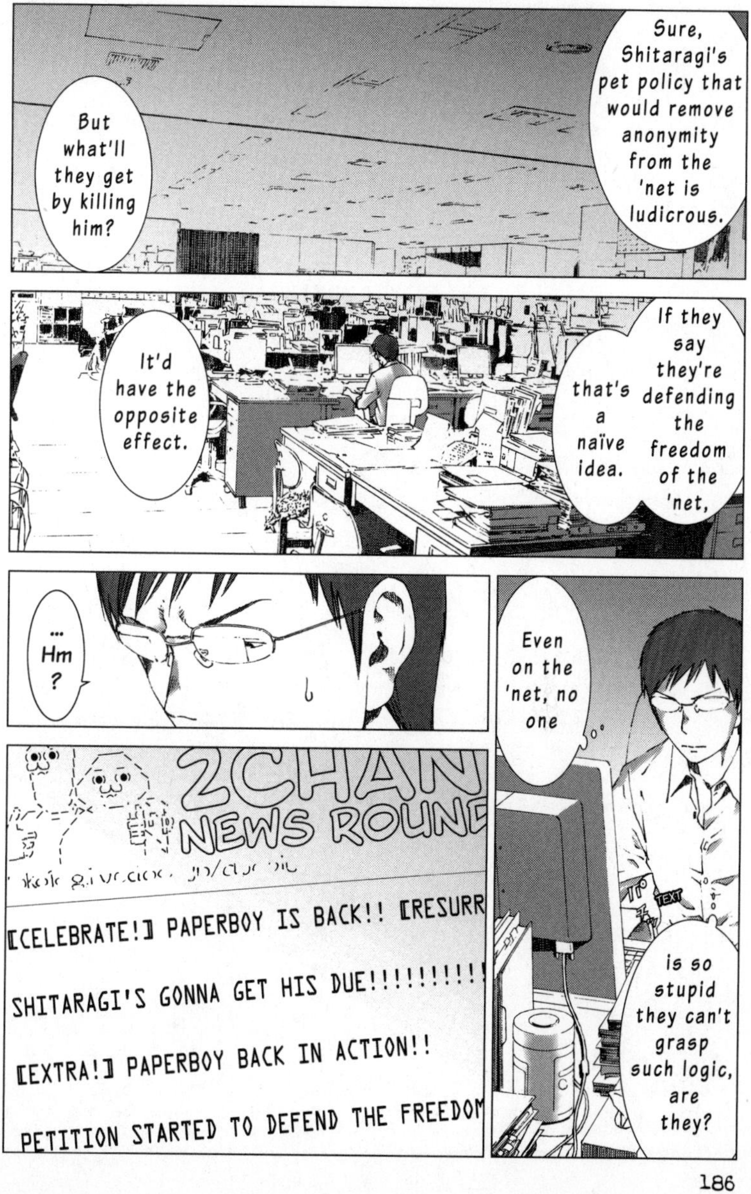

Sure, Shitaragi's pet policy that would remove anonymity from the 'net is ludicrous.
But what'll they get by killing him?
If they say they're defending the freedom of the 'net,
that's a naïve idea.
It'd have the opposite effect.
Even on the 'net, no one
is so stupid they can't grasp such logic, are they?
TEXT
... Hm?
2CHAN
NEWS ROUN
【CELEBRATE!】 PAPERBOY IS BACK!! 【RESURR
SHITARAGI'S GONNA GET HIS DUE!!!!!!!!!
【EXTRA!】 PAPERBOY BACK IN ACTION!!
PETITION STARTED TO DEFEND THE FREEDOM

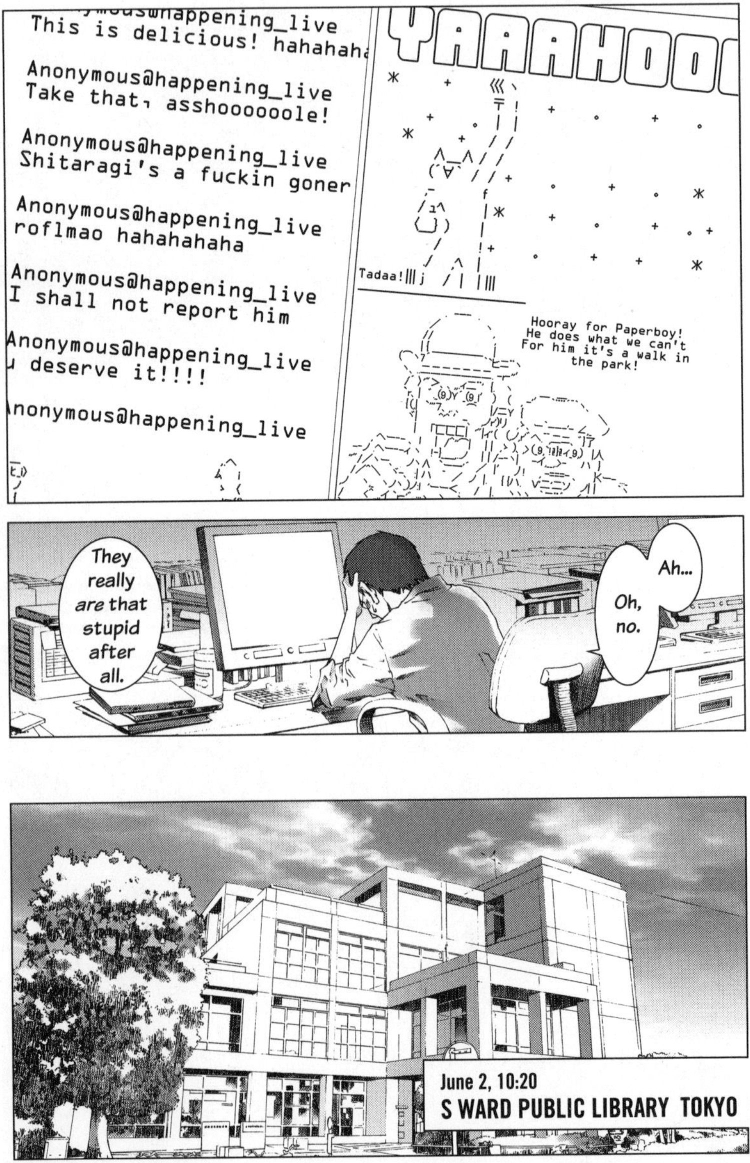
YAAAHOO
Tadaa!
Hooray for Paperboy! He does what we can't For him it's a walk in the park!
This is delicious! hahahaha
Anonymous@happening_live
Take that, asshoooooole!
Anonymous@happening_live
Shitaragi's a fuckin goner
Anonymous@happening_live
roflmao hahahahaha
Anonymous@happening_live
I shall not report him
Anonymous@happening_live
u deserve it!!!!
nonymous@happening_live
Ah... Oh, no.
They really *are* that stupid after all.
June 2, 10:20
S WARD PUBLIC LIBRARY TOKYO

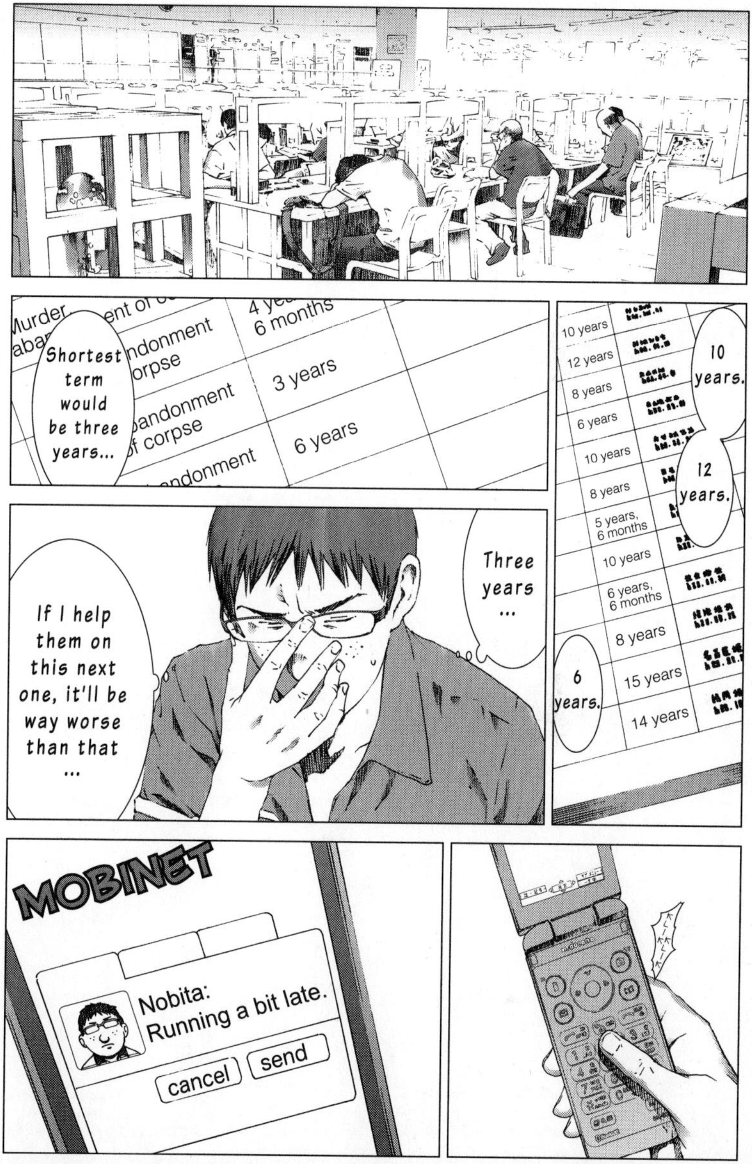
10 years
12 years
8 years
6 years
10 years
8 years
5 years, 6 months
10 years
6 years, 6 months
8 years
15 years
14 years
10 years.
12 years.
6 years.
Murder
abandonment of corpse
4 years 6 months
abandonment of corpse
3 years
abandonment of corpse
6 years
abandonment
Shortest term would be three years...
Three years ...
If I help them on this next one, it'll be way worse than that ...
MOBINET
Nobita: Running a bit late.
cancel
send

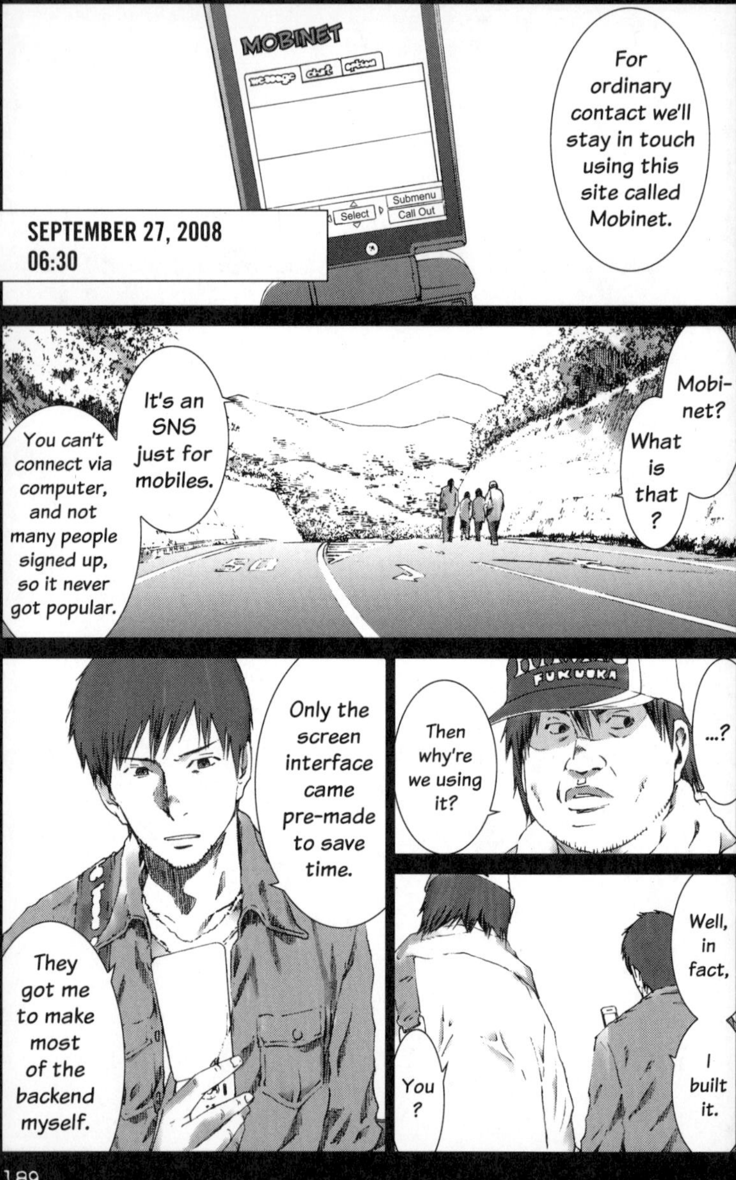

For ordinary contact we'll stay in touch using this site called Mobinet.
MOBINET
Submenu
Select
Call Out
SEPTEMBER 27, 2008
06:30
Mobi-net? What is that?
It's an SNS just for mobiles.
You can't connect via computer, and not many people signed up, so it never got popular.
FUKUOKA
...?
Then why're we using it?
Well, in fact, I built it.
You?
Only the screen interface came pre-made to save time.
They got me to make most of the backend myself.

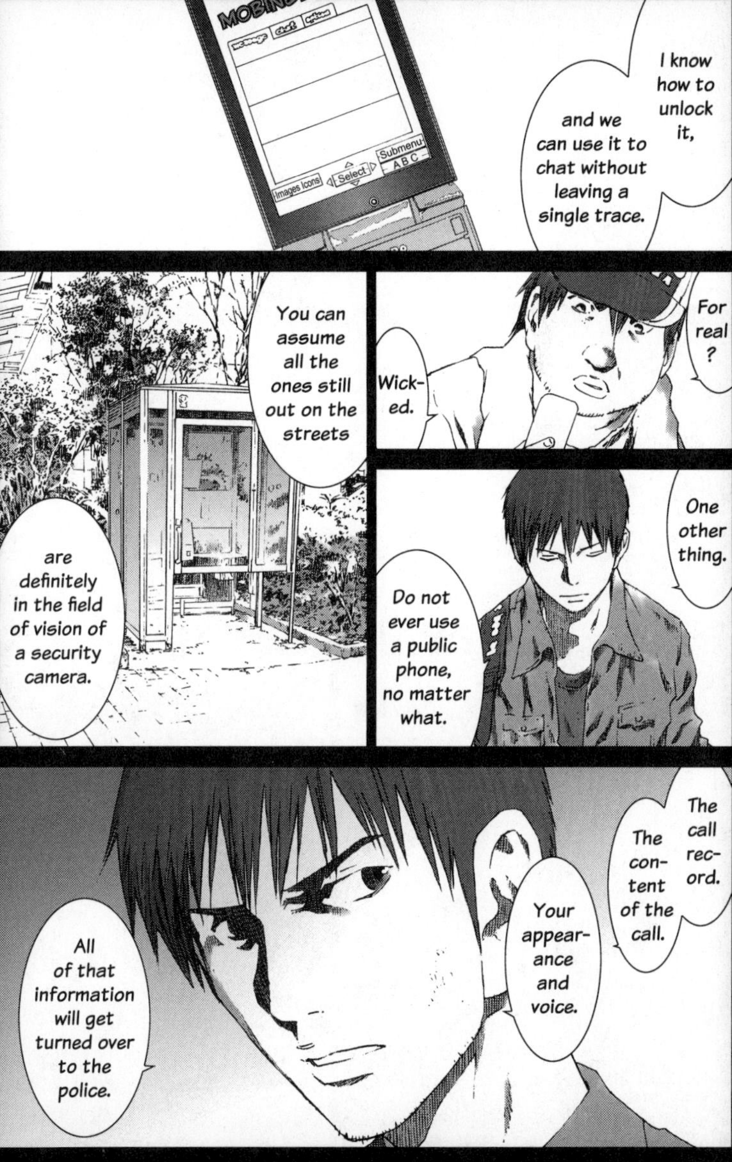
Submenu
A B C
Select
Images Icons
I know how to unlock it,
and we can use it to chat without leaving a single trace.
For real?
Wicked.
One other thing.
Do not ever use a public phone, no matter what.
You can assume all the ones still out on the streets
are definitely in the field of vision of a security camera.
The call record.
The content of the call.
Your appearance and voice.
All of that information will get turned over to the police.

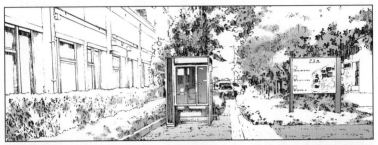

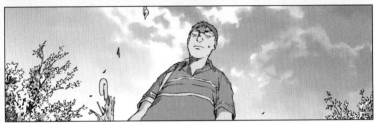

I wasn't really acting of my own free will.

I...

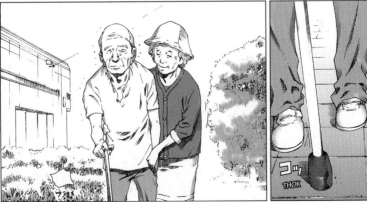

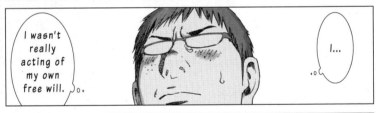

コッ
THOK

191

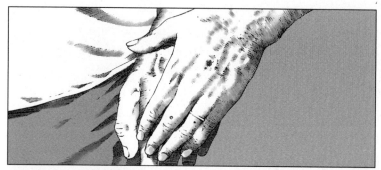

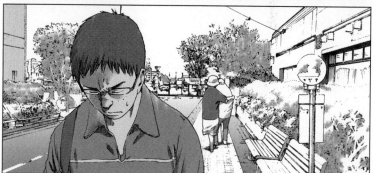

I don't know about the other three,

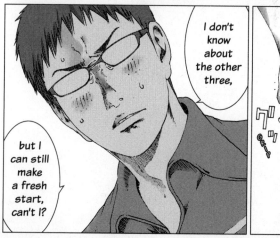

but I can still make a fresh start, can't I?

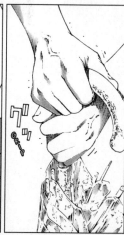

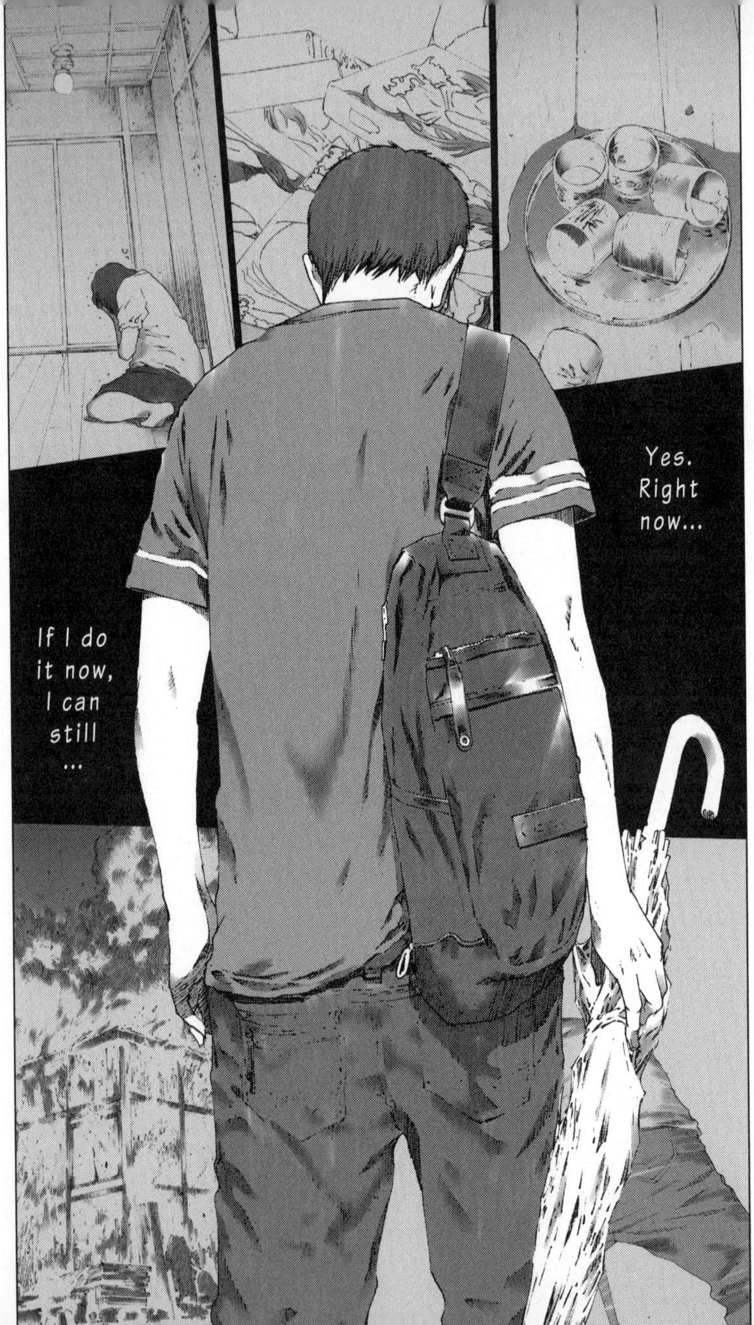
Yes. Right now...
If I do it now, I can still ...

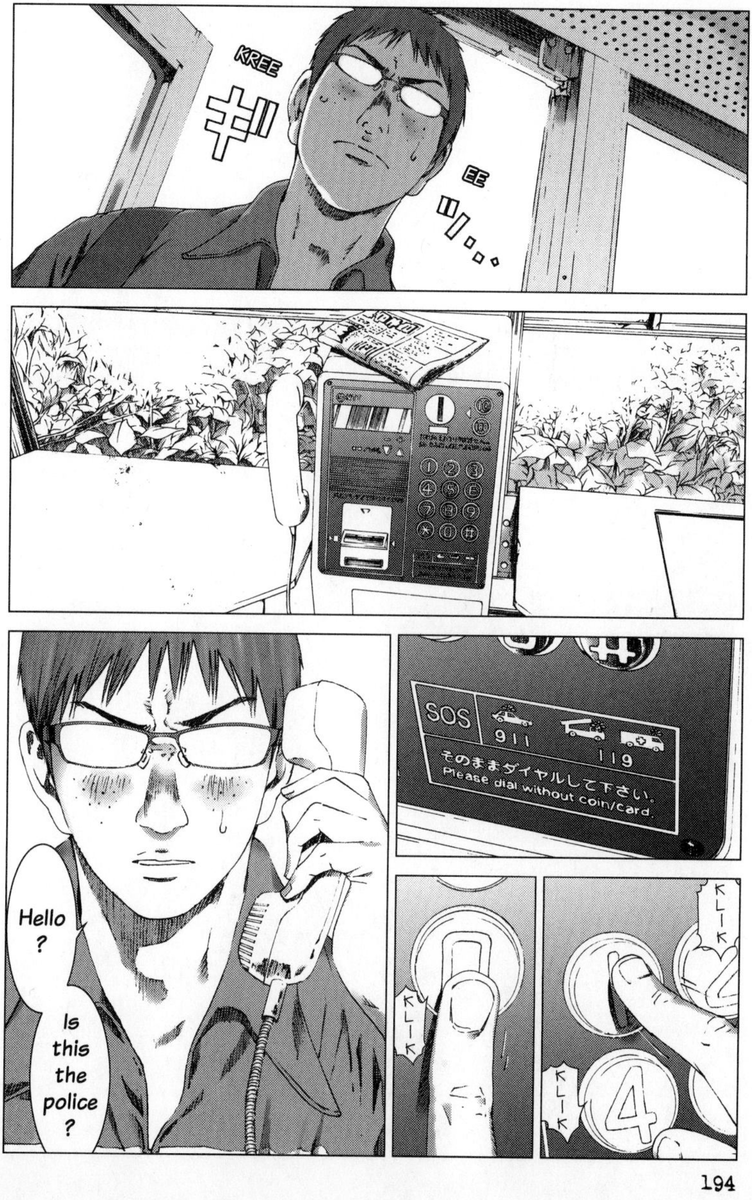
KREE
ギ
EE
ッ...
SOS
911
119
そのままダイヤルして下さい。
Please dial without coin/card.
KLIK
KLIK
KLIK
Hello?
Is this the police?

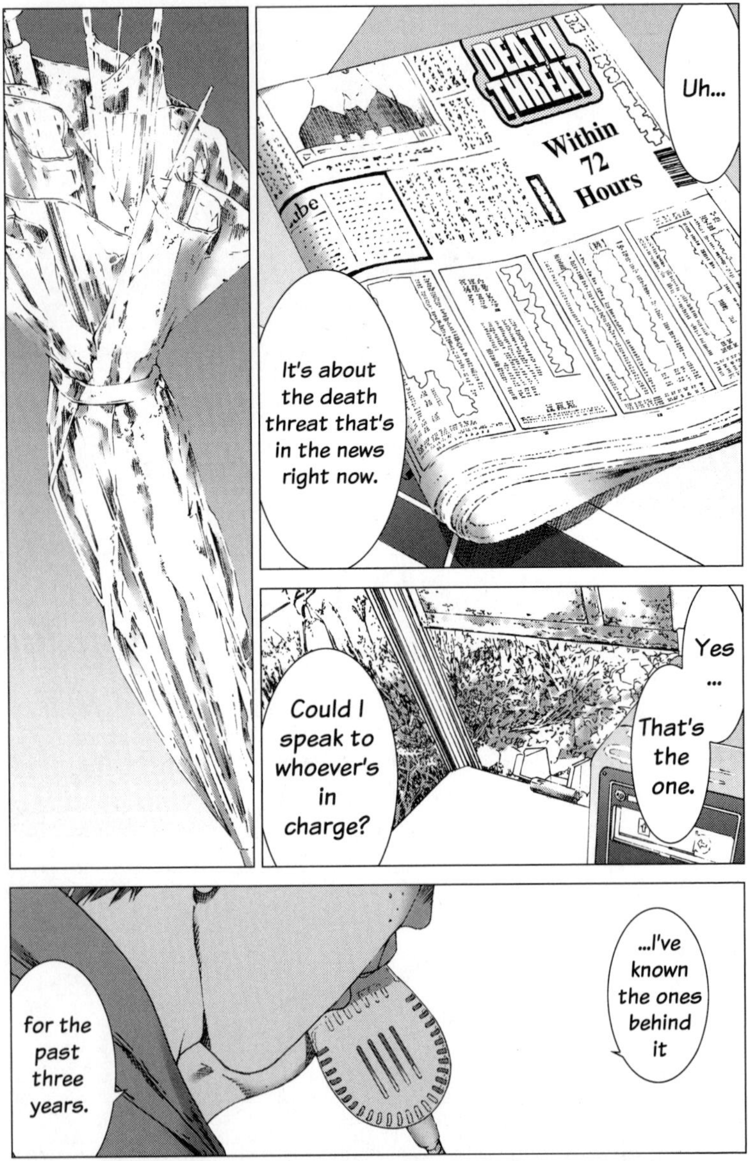
Uh...
DEATH THREAT
Within 72 Hours
It's about the death threat that's in the news right now.
Yes ...
That's the one.
Could I speak to whoever's in charge?
...I've known the ones behind it
for the past three years.

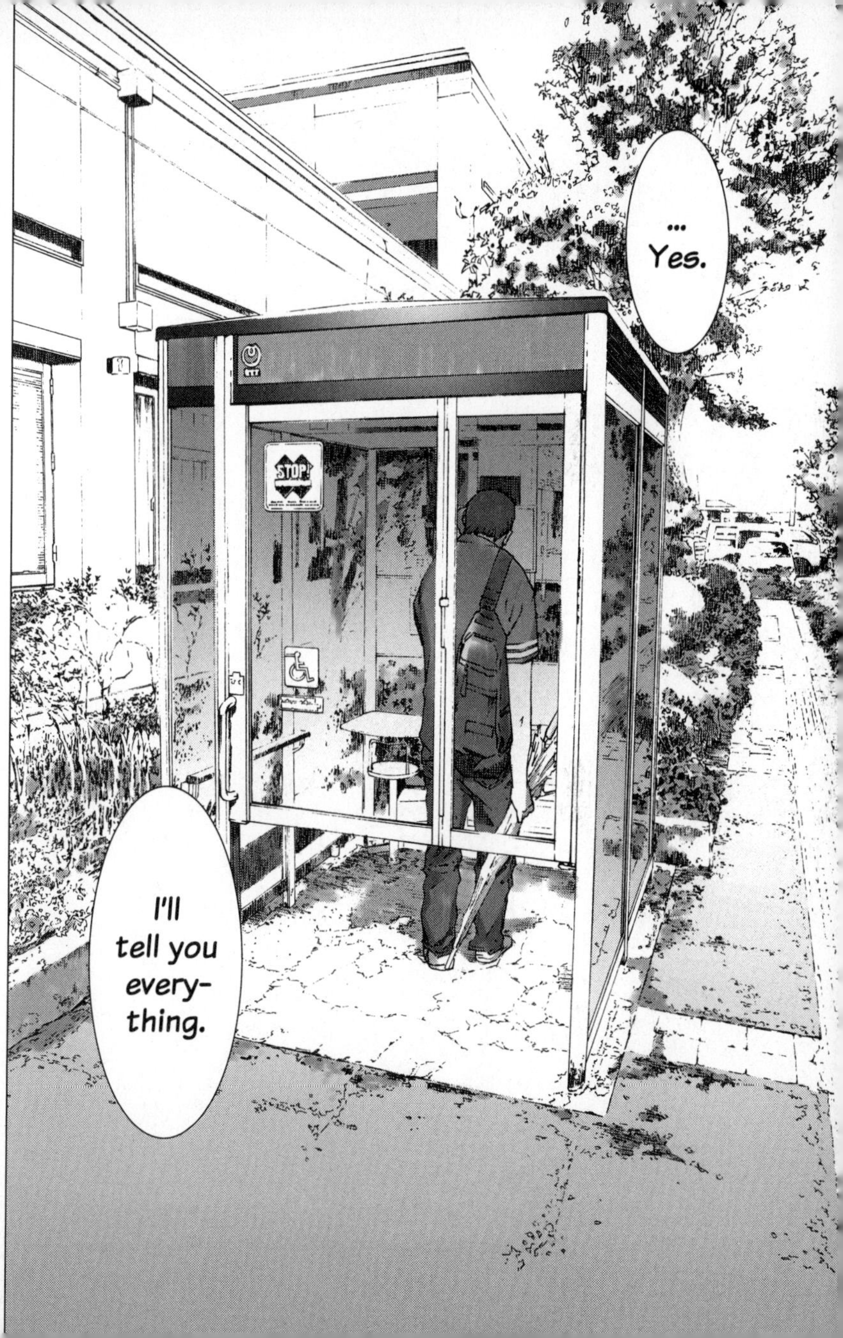
... Yes.
STOP!
I'll tell you everything.

PROPHECY
02 END

The terrorist Paperboy

S

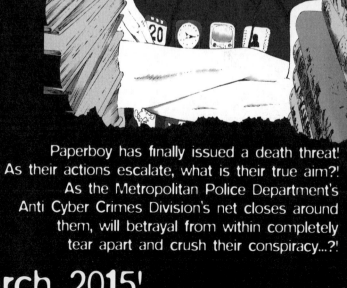

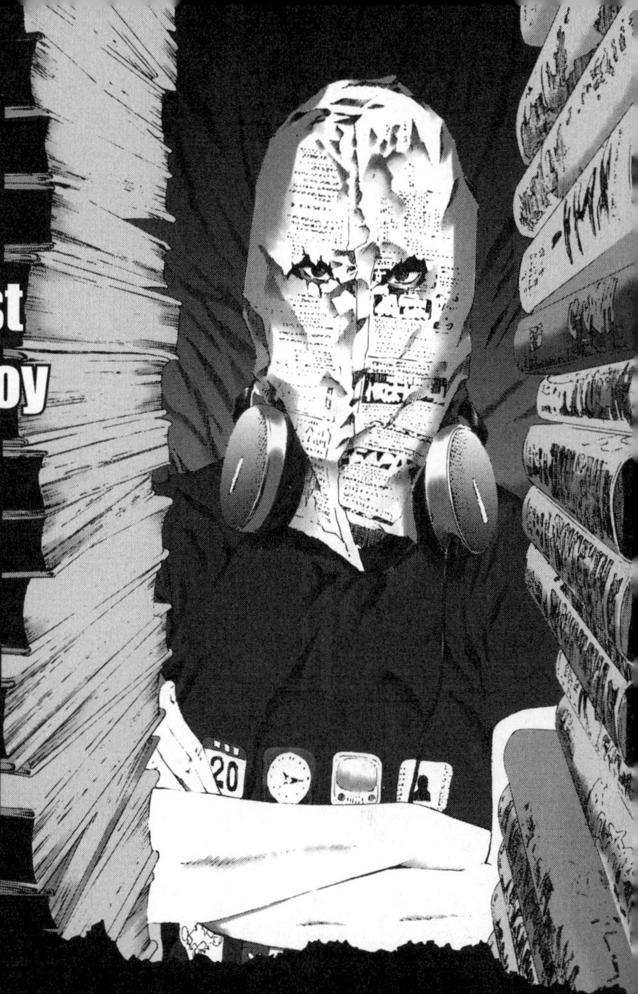

Paperboy has finally issued a death threat!
As their actions escalate, what is their true aim?!
As the Metropolitan Police Department's
Anti Cyber Crimes Division's net closes around
them, will betrayal from within completely
tear apart and crush their conspiracy...?!

March 2015!

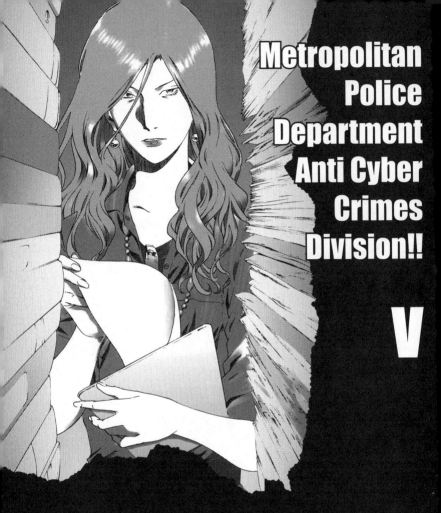

Metropolitan
Police
Department
Anti Cyber
Crimes
Division!!

V

PROPHECY

03 TETSUYA TSUTSUI

Final Volume

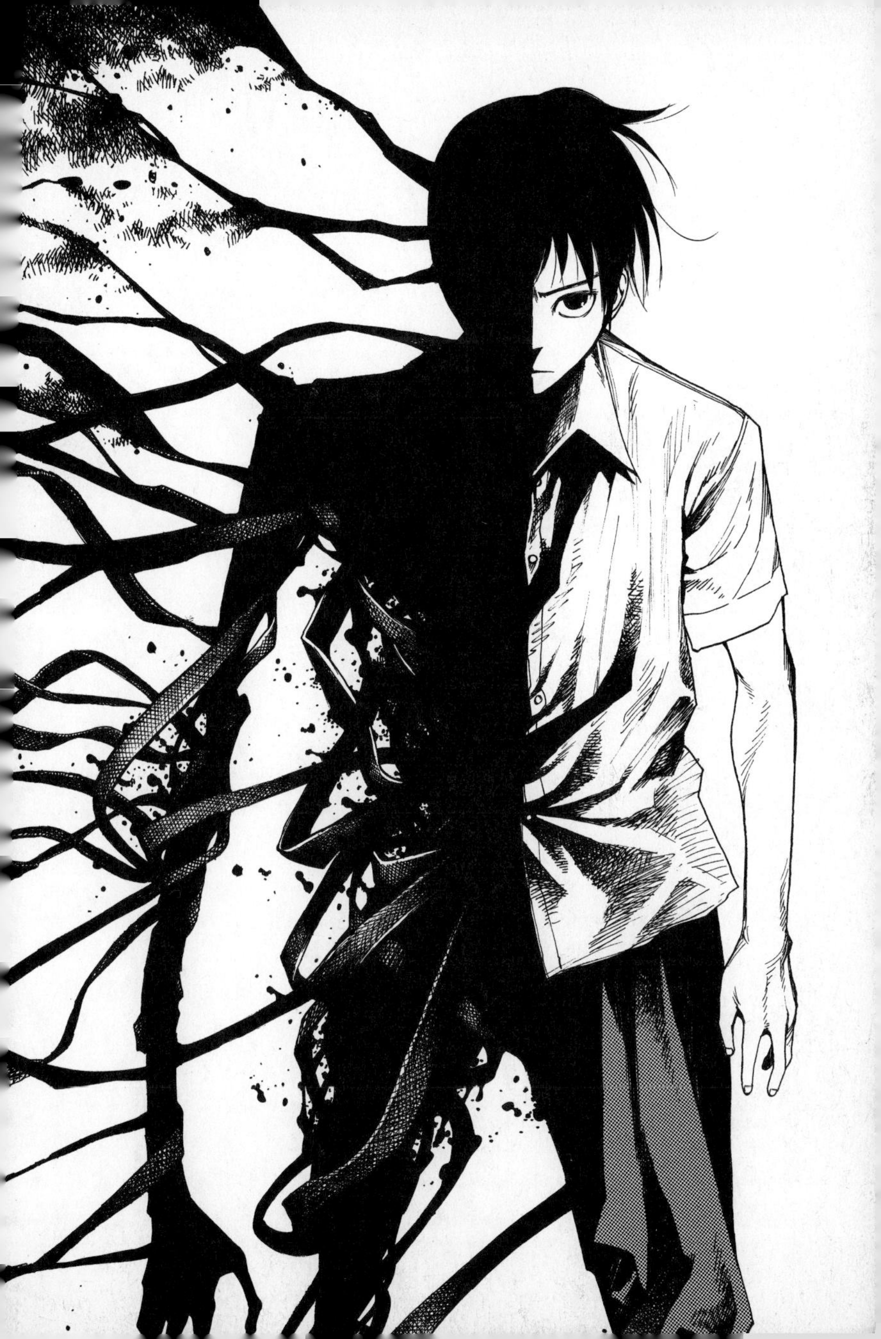

AJIN
DEMI-HUMAN

STORY: TSUINA MIURA
ART: GAMON SAKURAI

SAY YOU GET HIT BY A TRUCK AND DIE.
YOU COME BACK TO LIFE. GOOD OR BAD?

FOR HIGH SCHOOLER KEI—AND FOR AT LEAST FORTY-SIX OTHERS—
IMMORTALITY COMES AS THE NASTIEST SURPRISE EVER.

SADLY FOR KEI, BUT REFRESHINGLY FOR THE READER, SUCH A FEAT
DOESN'T MAKE HIM A SUPERHERO. IN THE EYES OF BOTH THE GENERAL
PUBLIC AND GOVERNMENTS, HE'S A RARE SPECIMEN WHO NEEDS TO BE
HUNTED DOWN AND HANDED OVER TO SCIENTISTS TO BE EXPERIMENTED
ON FOR LIFE—A DEMI-HUMAN WHO MUST DIE A THOUSAND DEATHS
FOR THE BENEFIT OF HUMANITY.

Prophecy, part 2

Translation: Kumar Sivasubramanian
Production: Grace Lu
          Nicole Dochych
          Anthony Quintessenza

Copyright © 2012 Tetsuya Tsutsui / Ki-oon
All rights reserved.
First published in France in 2013 by Ki-oon,
an imprint of AC Media Ltd.
English translation rights arranged through
Tuttle-Mori Agency, Inc.
English language version produced by Vertical, Inc.

Translation provided by Vertical, Inc., 2015
Published by Vertical Comics, an imprint of
Vertical, Inc., New York

This is a work of fiction.

ISBN: 978-1-939130-77-8

Manufactured in the United States of America

First Edition

Vertical, Inc.
451 Park Avenue South
7th Floor
New York, NY 10016
www.vertical-inc.com